AQA English Language A

A2

2nd Edition

Adam Leyburn
Mark Saunders

Series editor
Dan Clayton

Nelson Thornes

First published in 2008 by Nelson Thornes Ltd

This edition published in 2013 by:
Nelson Thornes Ltd
Delta Place
27 Bath Road
CHELTENHAM
GL53 7TH
United Kingdom

13 14 15 16 17 / 10 9 8 7 6 5 4 3 2 1

A catalogue record for this book is available from the British Library

ISBN 978 1 4085 2198 4

Cover photograph by Ocean/Corbis
Illustrations include artwork drawn by Harry Venning, David Russell Illustration and Pantek Arts Ltd

Page make-up by OKS Prepress, India

Printed and bound in Spain by GraphyCems

Acknowledgements

The authors and publishers wish to thank the following for permission to use copyright material.

Text: pp17 and 18, By permission of Oxford University Press, *Jane Austen's Letters* edited by Deirdre Le Faye (1997); p20, *The Oxford English Dictionary* 2nd edition edited by John Simpson and Edmund Weiner (1989) definition of 'chav'; p22, Tony Thorne for a table from his report, 'Classifying Campus Slang at King's College London'; p23, Penguin Group for an extract from David Crystal, *The Stories of English*, Allen Lane (2004). Copyright © David Crystal 2004; p24, *The Oxford English Dictionary* 2nd edition revisions (2007) definitions of 'darknet', 'microsite' and 'toolset'; p24, Oxford Dictionaries Online (2013) definitions of 'boccia' at URL http://oxforddictionaries.com/definition/english/boccia, 'goalball' at URL http://oxforddictionaries.com/definition/english/goalball, 'medal' http://oxforddictionaries.com/definition/english/medal and 'podium' at URL http://oxforddictionaries.com/definition/english/podium; p25, John Mullan for an extract from his article, 'English as a foreign language', *The Guardian*, 7 March 2003; pp32 and 33, Cambridge University Press for extracts from Jean Aitchison, 'The Language Web: The Power and Problem of Words', BBC Reith Lectures (1996). Copyright © Jean Aitchison; p37 Figs. 14 and 15, two diagrams from David Crystal, *The Encyclopedia of Language*, 1st edition, (1987); p38 Fig. 16, Language Map by Sundeep Matharu, Greenford High School, first published in *emagazine* 15 (February 2002) by kind permission of the English and Media Centre; p45, Deborah Cameron, *Myth of Mars and Venus* (2008) By permission of Oxford University Press; p46, American Psychological Association for Table 1 (adapted), pp583–586, from Hyde, J. S. (2005). 'The Gender Similarities Hypothesis', *American Psychologist*, 60(6), 581–592. doi:10.1037/0003-066X.60.6.581; p48, Newlife Foundation for Disabled Children for an extract from its website; p52 Table 11, Multilingual Matters for a table by Jenny Cheshire, 'Reading research findings' in *Dialect and Education: Some European Perspectives*, eds. Cheshire, Edward, Musterman and Weltens (1989) pp200–215; p54, Darrell Lum for an extract from *Oranges are Lucky* copyright Bamboo Ridge Press; p54, Pearson Education for an extract from Karen King-Aribisala *Kicking Tongues* 1998; p54, Linton Kwesi Johnson for an extract from 'Sonny's Lettah'; p55, Palgrave Macmillan for a data extract from Mark Sebba, 'Catford Girls Possee' in *Contact Languages: Pidgins and Creoles* (1997); p63 Fig. 25, 'The Circle of World English', p11, in Tom McArthur, 'English Languages?', *English Today*, Vol. 3 (1987) pp9–13; p64, 'Three Concentric Circles of Englishes' by Braj B Kachru, Professor Emeritus of Linguistics, University of Illinois; p68, Neal Oribio for his extract from 'Deaf Ear' in *Contact Languages: Pidgins and Creoles* by Mark Sebba, Palgrave Macmillan (1997); p68, Diabetes Association of Jamaica for the cartoon from Kowaiti Bay; p74 Extract 1, Home Office published: 9 June 2010 Policy: Securing borders and reducing immigration, Minister: The Rt Hon Theresa May MP Crown Copyright; p74 Extract 2, timesofmalta.com; p74 Extract 3, The Economist Newspaper Limited, London (18 December 2012); p77 Fig. 31, By kind permission of Lesley Milroy; p83, Constable & Robinson for Sir Walter Raleigh letter from J. E. Lewis (ed), *The Mammoth Book of Private Lives* 1999; p84, Marginalia Press for R. Hamilton and N. Soames (eds), *Intimate Letters*, 1994; pp84 and 85, Ben Brougham, http://www.electricdialogue.com/age-of-informality; pp89 and 90, John Honey, *Does Accent Matter?* Faber and Faber, 1989. 978-0571145096; pp107 and 108, Telegraph Media Group Limited 'How the Queen's English has grown more like ours', *The Daily Telegraph*, 4 December 2006; p109 and 110, Emma Clarke for her blog http://www.emmaclarke.com/blogs/2007/october/received-pronunciation; pp114–116, Copyright Guardian News & Media Ltd 2013; p118, Copyright Guardian News & Media Ltd 2000; pp119 and 120 © Telegraph Media Group Limited 2012; pp122 and 123, Souvenir Press Ltd for an extract from James Finn Garner, 'Little Red Riding Hood' in *Politically Correct Bedtime Stories* by James Finn Garner (1994); pp123–125, Philip Beadle 'Mind your language – and know what it means', *The Guardian*, 16 May 2006; pp150 and 151, J. J. Gumperz, 'Discourse Strategies' from P. Drew and J. Heritage (eds.) *Talk at Work* 1992 Cambridge University Press; p160, Gordon Brown's Labour Party Conference speech 2006 Public Domain; pp163 and 164, ITN Source for an extract from a news report with Jon Snow and Lucy Manning, Channel 4 News, 20 November 2006; pp183 and 184, Solo Syndication; pp185–187, Telegraph Media Group Limited for article 'Text-speak: language evolution or just laziness?' by Anne Merritt, Copyright Guardian News & Media Ltd 2013; p195, Pearson Education Ltd for an extract from Alan Gardiner, 'Political Correctness' in *A Level Study Guide: AS and A2 English Language* by Alan Gardiner, Longman (2000) p108; p196, *Made in America* by Bill Bryson, published by Black Swan. Reprinted by permission of The Random House Group Ltd; p199, 'Does My Head Look Big In This?' text copyright © Randa Abdel-Fattah, 2005 reproduced by permission of Scholastic Ltd. All rights reserved. Also reprinted by permission of Pan Macmillan Australia Pty Ltd. Copyright © Randa Abdel-Fattah, 2005; p200, Bernard MacLaverty, *A Time to Dance*, Jonathan Cape (1982) Reprinted by permission of The Random House Group Ltd.

Photos: p2 Fig. 1 (left), Eleanor Bentall/Corbis; p2 Fig. 1 (right), Robert Harding/Robert Harding World Imagery/Corbis; p5 Fig. 3, iStockphoto; p6 Fig. 4, Mary Evans Picture Library; p8 Fig. 5, Atlaspix/Alamy; p9 Fig. 6, Mary Evans Picture Library; p10, The British Library for extracts from Robert Cawdrey, 'Table Alphabeticall – Powdered Talk'. Copyright © British Library Board shelfmark 1568/3913; p11, Nathan Bailey, 'Dictionarium Brittanicum'. Copyright © British Library Board, www.bl.uk/learning; p4; p12 Fig. 7, Peter Horree/Alamy; p14 Fig. 8, Fotomas/TopFoto; p16 Fig. 9, Getty Images; p26, Copyright Guardian News & Media Ltd 2013; p27, The Geological Society of London's blog (blog.geolsoc.org.uk); p29, © David Malki ! Courtesy wondermark.com; p36 Fig. 13, Hulton Archive/Getty; p40 Fig. 17, Stock Connection Blue/Alamy; p52 Fig. 21, Kevin Dodge/Corbis; p56 Fig. 22, Getty Images; p75 Fig. 29, Rune Hellestad/Corbis; p80 Fig. 31, Bob Johns/Alamy; p83 Fig. 32, Portrait of Sir Walter Raleigh, 1598 (oil on panel), Segar, William (fl.1585-d.1633) (attr. to)/National Gallery of Ireland, Dublin, Ireland/The Bridgeman Art Library; p84 Fig. 33, Hulton Archive/Getty; p88 Fig. 34, Jeff Morgan 08/Alamy; p107 Fig. 2, PA Photos; p113 Fig. 3, The Royal Society; p115 Fig. 4, Photodisc/Getty; p131 Fig. 1, Mark Leech/Offside; p136 Fig. 4, ITV/Rex Features; p137 Fig. 5, Brian J. Ritchie/Hotsauce/Rex Features; p139 Fig. 7, Matthew Chattle/Alamy; p143 Fig. 10, PA Photos; p153 Fig. 13, Detail Nottingham/Alamy; p160 Fig. 16, Scott Barbour/Getty; p163 Fig. 17, Ken Mckay/Rex Features; p169 Fig. 18, Mike Booth/Alamy; p180 Fig. 2, London News Pictures/Rex Features; p185, Peter Titmuss/Alamy; p189, Getty Images; p203 Fig. 4, © Hodder & Stoughton.

Every effort has been made to trace the copyright holders but if any have been inadvertently overlooked the publisher will be pleased to make the necessary arrangements at the first opportunity.

Contents

Introduction

Nelson Thornes has worked hard to ensure this book and the accompanying online resources offer you excellent support for your A Level course. You can feel assured that they match the specification for this subject and provide you with what you need for this course.

These print and online resources together **unlock blended learning**; this means that the links between the activities in the book and the activities online blend together to maximise your understanding of a topic and help you achieve your potential.

These online resources are available on  which can be accessed via the internet at **http://live.kerboodle.com**, anytime, anywhere. If your school or college subscribes to this service you will be provided with your own personal login details. Once logged in, access your course and locate the required activity.

For more information and help visit **http://www.kerboodle.com**.

Icons in this book indicate where there is material online related to that topic. The following icons are used.

Learning activity

These resources include a variety of interactive and non-interactive activities to support your learning.

Progress tracking

These resources include a variety of tests that you can use to check your knowledge on particular topics (Test yourself) and a range of resources that enable you to analyse and understand examination questions (On your marks…).

Research support

These resources include WebQuests, in which you are assigned a task and provided with a range of web links to use as source material for research.

Study skills

These resources support you and help develop a skill that is key for your course, for example planning essays.

Analysis tool

These resources feature text extracts that can be highlighted and annotated by the user according to specific objectives.

How to use this book

The structure of this book mirrors the specification: it is split into two units (Unit 3 Language explorations and Unit 4 Language investigations and interventions), which are then broken down further into Sections A and B. Each section begins with an introduction to the topics that will be covered and concludes with exam (Unit 3) or coursework (Unit 4) preparation and suggestions for further reading. This is followed by feedback on the Coursework and Classroom activities, as well as the Data response exercises. At the back of the book, you will find answers to the Topic revision exercises and a glossary of key terms.

The features in this book include the following.

Learning objectives

At the beginning of each section you will find a list of learning objectives that contain targets linked to the requirements of the specification.

Key terms

Terms that you will need to be able to define and understand.

Research points

Linguistic research that has been carried out in the area you are studying.

Thinking points

Questions that check your understanding of the research point.

Activities

Starter activities, Language around you, Classroom and Extension activities all appear throughout. Coursework activities appear throughout Unit 4.

Feedback on the Classroom activities and Coursework activities is provided at the end of each section.

Links

Links to other areas in the textbook that are relevant to what you are reading.

Data response exercises

Questions based on given data. Feedback on the Data response exercises is provided at the end of each section.

Looking ahead

Points relating to how English language skills can be applied in the future outside the classroom, with particular reference to research, finding sources, essay and report writing, problem solving, analysis and critical thinking.

Think about it

Questions that offer the chance to reflect on the theories that have been introduced.

Further reading

Suggestions for other texts that will help you in your study and preparation for assessment.

Topic revision exercises/Topic summaries

Brief revision exercises to test your knowledge of each topic in Unit 3. Key points that summarise topics in Unit 4. Answers to the Topic revision exercises are provided at the back of the book.

Study tip

Hints to help you with your study and to prepare for your exam.

Practice questions

Questions in the style that you may encounter in your exam. Practice questions are reproduced by permission of the Assessment and Qualifications Alliance.

Nelson Thornes is responsible for the solution(s) given and they may not constitute the only possible solution(s).

Web links in the book

As Nelson Thornes is not responsible for third party content online, there may be some changes to this material that are beyond our control. In order for us to ensure that the links referred to in the book are as up-to-date and stable as possible, the websites are usually homepages with supporting instructions on how to reach the relevant pages if necessary.

Please let us know at **kerboodle@nelsonthornes.com** if you find a link that doesn't work and we will do our best to redirect the link, or to find an alternative site.

Introduction to this book

Your continuing study of English Language

English is a language with a long history and what looks like a healthy future, but there has always been a debate about what 'English' really means and to whom it belongs. What is 'proper' English? Is there really such a thing? Who decides? What is happening to English as it spreads around the world? What is technology doing to the language we use? Why do people feel so strongly about their own language and that of others? How does language use vary among different groups of people? Do men and women speak different languages? In your second year of study of A Level English Language, you'll be looking at these questions and many others.

In continuing your A Level in English Language you are building on the skills you developed in your AS year and extending them to help you learn more about – and engage in – the big debates like those above. You'll also be doing your own bit to add to what we know about language, by carrying out your own language investigation: a project that involves collecting your own data and analysing it.

From its origins in the 5th century AD, right up to the present time, the English language has grown and spread. Much of the history of the language mirrors the history of the nation: its different regional varieties reflect its patchwork of Norman, Anglo-Saxon and Norse influences, while its range of 'loan words' from other languages (not so much loaned as nicked!) is a result of centuries of colonial expansion. And much of the language exported to other parts of the world, like India, Africa and the USA, is now coming back to us in noticeably different forms, all adding to the range and variety of the language.

Even the words that have stayed at home have changed as time has passed. A 'villain' hasn't always been a dodgy character in an East End boozer: he might have been your average farm labourer some 600 years ago. Likewise, the word 'hussy' used to be a fairly neutral, shortened version of housewife, not the rather negative term it has since become. So, the meanings of words shift as social values change, or as certain ideas become more entrenched.

And what of new words? There seems to be an insatiable need to create new words to describe the ways we live our lives: new words for technological advances (satnav, phishing and emoticon), new acronyms and blends of existing words for different lifestyles and social groups (tweens, hipsters and chavettes – if you're confused about what any of these terms mean, you'll find out at the end of this introduction), new phrases and euphemisms for business people to confuse and bamboozle us with (blue sky thinking, misspeaking, downsizing). The pace of language change is now more rapid than ever before. The growth of the internet means that a word dreamt up in one part of the world can almost instantly be picked up by other English speakers on the other side of the world. It might seem hard to remember a time before LOL, hashtag and nom nom, but it wasn't that long ago.

One of the elements you bring to this course is your own use of the English language. As an English user you are your own resource. That doesn't mean that you'll necessarily be used to analysing your own language or that of your peer group, family, ethnic group, region or gender, but you'll have your own way of saying things, your ways of expressing the multiple strands of your own identity, and you will be able to bring these into your study of English Language.

As you will have already discovered in the AS year, English has its own technical terms like many other areas of life, and one job you will have is to learn some of them. You've already mastered many of them and should now be familiar with the linguistic frameworks you need to analyse and explore different spoken, written or blended texts. You'll be building on these in your second year of study: revisiting grammatical terms that help you label and define language around you; consolidating your understanding of areas such as spoken and blended modes and stretching your range of analysis to include much older texts and data you've collected yourself.

One major difference between your AS year and this A2 year is that you will be undertaking a major piece of coursework called a language investigation, which is probably the closest you'll get to degree-level work without actually doing it. You will already be familiar with the AS Unit 2 Investigating representations coursework in which you will have selected, collected and analysed a range of texts or text extracts in order to explore how individuals, social groups, institutions, issues and events have been represented, but this is a bigger proposition. In your investigation you will be expected to formulate your own investigation into spoken language and collect your own data as part of this. This book will support you in this work by giving expert advice on how to approach this major piece of work.

As well as studying other people's use of English, and their attitudes towards language use, you will once again have the opportunity to produce your own writing, making your own contribution to a debate about language.

How is English Language A assessed?

In your AS Level work you will have encountered both exams and coursework. This continues at A Level where, again, the year will contain one exam and one coursework module: 40 per cent of the course is assessed through coursework with 60 per cent by an exam that you will take at the end of the course. This gives you a similar variety of different tasks to undertake as you encountered last year and will allow you to work in different ways, developing your understanding of how English is used – and sometimes abused.

As with the AS course, there are four assessment objectives (AOs) on which your actual marks will be based. These AOs refer to the different skills that are needed in each module. Broadly, they cover four main areas: writing about language itself; writing about the effects of language; understanding other people's ideas about language; and using language yourself.

It is not vital at this stage that you know in detail which AOs apply to which tasks, but it would be a good idea to spend some time getting to know them. You will find detailed explanations of the AOs in each section of the book and we have also tried to show you how they relate specifically to assessing the different parts of the course.

What does each unit cover?

The units are split into sections and then into topics, which are ordered in a way that should help you build up your knowledge in a logical progression.

In Unit 3 Language explorations, you will study language change and language variation.

For language change you will be looking at the ways in which the language has changed since 1600, part of the period known as Early Modern English, up to the present day. You will be tracing the development of English here and around the world and looking at many of the reasons for language change.

For language variation, you will explore the ways in which language use varies according to geographical location (regional/national) and social group (age, gender, social class and ethnicity). You will also be looking at the reasons for such variation and attitudes to it.

You will then move on to explore debates about these topics and pick apart the arguments and opinions of others. Your textual analysis skills – developed in your AS course – will be employed again to make sense of how writers construct their arguments, and you will be asked to evaluate what others say about language.

In Unit 4 Language investigations and interventions, your coursework unit, you will set about investigating an area of spoken English as part of your own research project. You will need to choose an area of investigation, set your own aims or hypothesis, collect your own data, analyse it and evaluate how what you've discovered relates to what others might have already said about language use.

You will be guided through the stages, from coming up with an idea through to suggestions for data collection and on to evaluating your project's success.

The second part of this unit builds upon your AS coursework: you will make your own contribution to one of the debates about language by writing a piece that offers an opinion or angle on a language issue, for example how women and men talk, how texting affects spelling, or attitudes towards regional varieties of English.

Where could it take you?

We hope that you find your study of English Language A Level interesting for its own sake, but the course will also open doors for you in employment and higher education. You may look to continue with English, focusing on one of a wide range of related courses offered by universities: sociolinguistics, for example, which looks at language and society, or applied linguistics, one part of which looks at how different languages work in different ways. The Language investigation unit in the A2 course, with its focus on original research, working with data and focus on independent thinking, is particularly good preparation for university-style dissertation projects. Other English and communications courses often include a significant element of language study too, so many of the elements of your AS and A2 courses will prove useful in these as well. Alternatively, the course could help you in many other areas, such as psychology, law, medicine, journalism, advertising and teaching.

Even if you decide to move totally beyond the subject, your course will have helped you to become a better language user, to express your thoughts more precisely and persuasively – skills valued in all areas of life.

The English Language A series

This book has been written to guide you through the essential content and assessment of your course. The online resources that accompany the book build on its content and will give you the opportunity to stretch yourself and to approach your study using different types of learning.

The writers of this book are experienced teachers. Their teaching experience means that they have an understanding of the best ways to explain the ideas you will encounter, and this knowledge has affected and influenced the design of the book.

Of course, we could not put everything into the book, and you will need to look beyond it to your teachers, fellow students and other sources. We have tried helping you in this by referring you to places where you can extend your study further. In wishing you the best for your course, we offer one last piece of advice: in studying English Language, some of the best resources are all around you. When you pick up a magazine, watch a film, send a text message or surf the internet, you are engaging with language on one of its many levels. Although previously you may have done these things without considering language issues, as a student of language you will understand how language underpins daily life.

Table 1

Term	Meaning
Blue sky thinking	Visionary new thinking about an issue, often without realistic planning (e.g. Heathrow Terminal 5).
Chavette	A female chav (chav + ette): a rather manufactured term used to describe a female variant of the chav social group.
Downsizing	Making a business smaller by sacking staff. But making it sound nice … like you're slimming down rather than throwing people out of work.
Emoticon	Emotion + icon: a word used to describe a graphical representation of a facial expression, often employed in online communication. The most well-known emoticon is probably the smiley :-)
Hashtag	The # symbol, now widely used on Twitter and beyond to signify either a theme to an online discussion or an ironic label suggesting a jokey way of relating to what has been tweeted (e.g. 'Just had to visit toilet for 3rd time in 20 minutes #ChickenMadrasMornings').
Hipster	A term used to describe a self-consciously fashionable individual who seeks out new forms of music, dress and facial hair to be several steps ahead of the mainstream. Often used pejoratively to label elitist and smug people who claim to listen to bands you've never heard before and that probably don't even exist.
LOL	Laugh Out Loud
Misspeaking	A euphemistic way of saying that you've been lying: for example, 'I didn't say anything rude about your boyfriend. I was misspeaking.'
Nom nom	An expression used to signify the noise someone or something makes while eating (often accompanied online by a picture of a cute kitten eating something/someone).
Phishing	A deliberately misspelled version of 'fishing'. Phishing is a form of online scamming in which you receive emails or messages that 'fish' for key information such as your bank account number and sort code.
Satnav	Satellite + navigation
Tween	A young person who has not quite reached teenage years but is between childhood and teenagerdom.

Language explorations

Assessment objectives:

- AO1 Select and apply a range of linguistic methods to communicate relevant knowledge using appropriate terminology and coherent, accurate written expression.

- AO2 Demonstrate critical understanding of a range of concepts and issues related to the construction and analysis of meanings in spoken and written language, using knowledge of linguistic approaches.

- AO3 Analyse and evaluate the influence of contextual factors on the production and reception of spoken and written language, showing knowledge of the key constituents of language.

Studying change and variation in the English language is at the heart of the Language explorations unit. In the AS Level units, you have focused on language in its immediate usage, mainly encountering differences of subject, audience, purpose and context. At A2, the scope is widened to include an understanding of how and why language changes across time and varies in relation to differing geographical regions and social factors.

Section A Language change and variation

There are thousands of different faces to English. Perhaps you have heard a Liverpool footballer say how he is 'made up for all of youse fans' (Scouse: 'really pleased for you all'). Maybe you have some favourite catchphrases from American movies ('alright already') or Australian soaps ('I'm stoked') – and arrange to meet up with friends in txtspk, using SMS to 'c u 2moz m8 ;-)'. Or, if you've been to a wedding, you may have heard the priest utter stranger, older phrases like 'let no man put asunder', or 'thy will be done, for thine is the kingdom'. Each of these, and many more, are part of the English language as it evolves, and spreads around Britain and the world. Section A of this unit introduces you to some of these different kinds of English and helps you to recognise, understand and evaluate them. In Section A of the exam you will need to choose between answering a question focused on language change or on language variation. The questions take the form of **data**-based tasks presenting material that could be drawn from written sources, statistics, **transcripts**, or other research and text-based sources.

Section B Language discourses

Section B of the examination draws on your full range of understanding of the areas of language change and language variation. For this task, you will be given a pair of texts relevant to a discourse (debate) about language change or variation, and an essay question that prompts you to write about the issues the texts raise. Section B of this unit has examples of the sorts of debate you are expected to know about and guidelines on how to tackle the essay. You will need to select material from the whole of the unit to develop your response, and to draw on some of the things that you have learned about at AS – so don't put those notes in the recycling bin just yet!

For guidance on how to cover the AOs in the exam, see the Exam preparation topics at the end of Sections A and B.

Key terms

Data: literally 'facts and statistics used for reference or analysis' (*Concise OED*); in this book it often refers to the texts you are asked to analyse.

Transcript: an accurate written record of a conversation or monologue, including hesitations and pauses.

A | Language change and variation

Introduction

The English language is in a constant process of change and variation, and yet it retains enough of a core to maintain its identity as 'English'.

Change is one major dimension of the language – that of its evolution over time. This section begins by giving you a short guide to the concept of language change, the ways in which change occurs, and the influence of the Old English and Middle English periods of the language. It then discusses the major characteristics of the modern English language since 1600.

Variation can be seen as another dimension of the language entirely – that of how these changes are taken up and used by different people. The variation research and examples later in this section arise from linguists investigating the 'here and now' of language: how it is used in a particular place, or by a particular group of people.

Section A of the examination contains two questions, one focused on language change and the other on language variation. Each question has paired material in the form of a text or data extract (there are examples of these sorts of pairing in the Exam preparation topic for Section A). In the examination you must select and write your response to *one* task only. Bear in mind that the relationship between language change and language variation is a complex one and, although each task will direct you towards particular areas of study, many of the concepts that you discovered in language change will hold true for variation as well, and vice versa.

Fig. 1 *The English language is taught throughout the whole of Britain ... and across the world*

How does language change?

In this topic you will:

- learn about the specific mechanisms for language change

- put the 'modern' era of English into context

- explore the concepts of change and standardisation.

Starter activity

Scan through the different sections of a Sunday newspaper, looking for unusual words and phrases such as:

- the jargon of sport or new technology

- words borrowed from the fashion or food of other countries

- popular phrases and 'invented' words

- the language of politics

- old-fashioned or historical words and phrases.

Note what interested you, and the context each was used in. Share these with your class.

Key terms

Phonology: the study of the way speech sounds are used in language.

Semantics: the study of how meaning is constructed in language.

Pragmatics: a broad term often used to relate to the gap between what words used actually mean and what the intended meaning is.

Orthography: the way in which letter shapes are formed on a page and the characters used.

The history of change in the English language is a turbulent one – often a kind of tug-of-war between those who sought to change it and those who wanted the particular English that they recognised preserved. The language is in a permanent state of flux. At any given time, this process has affected the way that a particular word is pronounced (**phonology**); the way in which you put words together in a sentence (grammar); what a word means (**semantics** and **pragmatics**); how a word is written and spelled (graphology and **orthography**), and the way in which a word is used and constructed (lexis and morphology).

Influences on language

Change is caused by a variety of influences that are constantly affecting the language. The relationship between English and the things that shape it can be so closely intertwined that it is difficult to separate the cause from the resulting changes (like, for example, the politics and language of New Labour at the turn of the 21st century, with words like 'spin', 'Blairite', 'The Third Way' and 'Cool Britannia' entering mainstream use alongside the 1997 Labour government). Some of the main areas of influence could be grouped in the following ways:

Historical events: The English language has been profoundly affected by waves of war, disease, military, political and industrial change, 'acts of God' and natural disaster.

Generational transfer: The transmission of language within families and from one generation to another forms a major part of the underlying fabric of English, especially where this creates the conditions for linguistic interplay between different cultures and traditions.

Geographical and world language issues: Change and variation is often reinforced by regional identities, whether these occur at a local level, within the British Isles, or in the different forms of English used around the globe. This can be seen in contrasting ways: sometimes regional changes isolate and accentuate the uniqueness of their particular variety; whilst another trend in the language is the increasing globalisation and exchange of English language forms.

Social factors: Dominant social aspects, such as gender, social class, age, ethnicity, occupation and sexuality play a major role in shaping the course of change within the language.

Technological advancements: Often the most visible and rapid form of change within English, the seemingly endless invention of new technologies is accompanied by a conveyor belt of new lexis and language forms. Conversely, older technology and its related language may become obsolete and fall out of use.

Education and politics: The responsibility of education in shaping language use and change over time is considerable. Language can be highly politicised, and this can lead to shifts in the freedoms or constraints within which language operates. This often takes the form of particular movements, like the political correctness debate, which you will already have come across in Unit 2, Section A.

Key terms

Old English: the earliest form of the English language, formed during Germanic invasions of Britain and lasting until the Norman invasion.

Middle English: the English language after the Norman invasion, often seen as lasting until the printing of English texts began to appear.

Inflection: a word is said to be inflected when it has a suffix attached to change the meaning.

Closed class: prepositions, determiners, conjunctions and pronouns are said to be closed class words as they are very rarely altered or added to over time.

Prestige: the concept of status applied to a particular language variety or the person who uses it.

Latinate: describing a word or other aspect of language derived from the Latin language.

Etymology: the study of the history of words, and what the origins were for any particular word, in terms of a source language or particular context of use.

Classroom activity 1

Using a dictionary that indicates the **etymology** of words, look up shorter, more frequent words that you use in English, like 'ship', 'wood' or 'the'. Make notes about their origins. You will need to familiarise yourself with the abbreviations used for different languages, for example, it might use initials like 'ON' for 'Old Norse'.

Looking ahead

Old and Middle English are not a major part of your course – but they are major areas of English study. If you are particularly interested in these earlier forms of English, you will be able to find specific units on them in most university English and linguistics courses.

Old English

Although it is not the prime focus of your examination, it is helpful to have a working idea of the main features of the **Old English** and **Middle English** periods, and the lasting ways in which they have shaped the modern form of the language.

The foundation stones for the English language were laid during invasions beginning as early as the 3rd century and extending across the next 500 years, by Jute, Angle, Saxon and Frisian warlords from Germanic north-western Europe. These invaders have come to be known collectively as the Anglo-Saxons, and they settled in and ruled much of Britain, bringing their own language known as Englisc.

It is from the culmination of these Anglo-Saxon invasions, around the 8th century, that the first significant surviving written English texts have been found, and it is possible to begin to chart the development of the English language in some detail from this point. After this, a further wave of invasion, this time from the more northerly Vikings of Scandinavia, added to the English language in its infancy.

One of the most distinctive features of Old English was the existence of an **inflection** system, using suffixes to mark the different functions of words.

Grammatically, Old English syntax often made use of a SOV (subject – object – verb) structure, which had been largely altered to the more common SVO structure by the time of the Modern English period. Much of the grammatical structure of English was laid down during the Old English period, with many pronouns, determiners, and other **closed class** words remaining largely unaltered right through to their modern usage.

Middle English

Pinpointing an exact series of dates between these different eras of English is not possible. English began to change dramatically again, entering what has become known as the Middle English period from around the time that the Danish Viking invaders began to briefly rule England, in the early 11th century. Many variations that had appeared between the Anglo-Saxon and Viking pronunciations and grammatical systems began to level out and take a step closer towards the form you would recognise in modern English usage.

The next major influence on the English language, the Norman French invasion in 1066, split language use in England in two: the new ruling classes spoke the **prestige** form of French and the conquered people spoke English (or the Celtic languages mentioned earlier, in the unconquered northern and western regions of Britain). The expansion of the English vocabulary continued apace, with many borrowings from French and **Latinate** sources, particularly in areas of power or learning, including the law, government, the military, medicine and the Church.

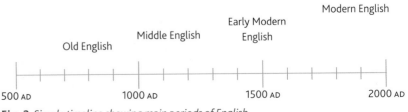

Fig. 2 *Simple timeline showing main periods of English*

Standardisation begins

Although there remained clear **dialect** differences between different regions of the country, a core of English usage had been adopted by the nation, and conditions had been generated that would herald the emergence of the modern English language. From the **Early Modern English** period onwards, there would be no further meddling from military invasions, and the direction of English would be characterised by the continued expansion of the language and the movement towards standardisation.

Research point

The Oxford English Corpus is a collection of written and spoken texts used to record and analyse word usage in the English language. It contains over 2 billion individual words and is expanding all the time. The ten most common nouns are given below.

1 time	2 person	3 year	4 way	5 day
6 thing	7 man	8 world	9 life	10 hand

These, and the vast majority of the first 100 nouns listed, are derived from the Germanic sources of the Old English period (with 'person' appearing from French, Latinate sources in the Middle English period).

Thinking points

1. What do the findings in the above Research point tell you about the influence of Anglo-Saxon English words?

2. What do you think are the most common words used overall in English? Compare your ideas with the corpus: http://oxforddictionaries.com/words/the-oec-facts-about-the-language.

Extension activity

Research the influence the different invader languages (Anglo-Saxon, Scandinavian, French, Latin) had on town and place names in the UK, and Celtic forms as well. Here are three examples to start you off:

- 'chester' or 'caster' – Latinate origin, meaning a fortification or camp
- 'ham' – Anglo-Saxon origin, meaning a settlement or farm
- 'strath' – from Celtic, Scots Gaelic, meaning a wide valley.

Work with a partner and use a UK road map to find out where the types of name you have found appear most commonly – and where they don't appear. For example, look in particular at the south-east of England, the north-east of England, Wales, and the north of Scotland, as well as other regions. Share the places you identified with another pair and discuss how they fit in with the story of Old and Middle English.

Topic revision exercise

1. List at least three of the main factors that influence language change. Give brief details for each.

2. What was the basic idea behind the way that the Old English inflection system worked?

3. How did French and Latinate language influence English during the Middle English period?

Fig. 3 *The works of Chaucer provide an extensive example of Middle English text*

Key terms

Dialect: the language variety of a geographical region or social background.

Early Modern English: the origin of the modern form of English we recognise today. It can be understood to extend from the emergence of the first printed English texts through to the expansion of the British Empire.

Study tip

Although you will need to be prepared to analyse texts from 1600 onwards, it is possible to trace some of the distinctive features of Early Modern English and Modern English discourse back to their Old and Middle English ancestors. Take care to base your points on the texts you are given and only make reference to features you can find evidence for.

Further reading

Although you will not be given any text earlier than 1600 in your exam (Early Modern English), it can be very interesting to read some Old and Middle English texts. Try searching on the internet for 'etexts' and 'facsimiles' of *Beowulf* and Chaucer to find some for yourself. You can get versions with a modern English translation by the side to help you make sense of it all.

Early Modern English

In this topic you will:

- learn about the distinctive features of the Early Modern English period

- read and analyse examples of Early Modern English language.

Starter activity

Early Modern English is really the start of the language you know and use every day. Discuss what you think makes the way you speak and write today 'modern' and different from the earlier forms you have seen in the previous topic.

You will have realised by now that the Old, Middle, and Early Modern period of English cannot really be given definite historical dates for when they began or ended, but that they reflect periods that gradually seem to take hold of the language, and that collect together particular eras of development and change.

The wider context

From around the end of the 15th century through to the mid-18th century, levels of literacy were low, particularly among the poor, and there was little or no formal or widespread schooling. Women were socially subordinate to men and were normally defined by marriage or the raising of children. Advances in transport led to the development of international trade.

Extension activity

Many factors had an influence on the way language changed during this period. Carry out a little wider background reading and research to give you some idea of the backdrop against which the Early Modern English period took place, including:

- levels of literacy
- the position of women in society
- the development of international trade
- changes in the social class structure
- scientific developments
- religious changes.

💡 Caxton and the printing press

In 1476, Caxton set up the first printing press in England. The printing press helped to establish the future direction of the English language in two fundamental ways: first, a process was begun that meant that a form of the language would be able to be easily replicated; and, second, published books began to appear that were written in English, rather than in Latin or French. This made the written English word more accessible to the public, marking the beginning of more widespread education and literacy, and a meaningful debate about standardising English.

Fig. 4 *Printing presses began to revolutionise written texts across Europe during the 15th and 16th centuries*

Classroom activity 2

Discuss why being able to print texts made it easier to standardise the English language.

The English Bibles

Two Bibles of this time, the 'Tyndale' (1525) and 'King James' (1611) English Bibles, tell an interesting story. William Tyndale's Bible was the first to be published, at a time when it was illegal to translate the Bible into English. He was eventually executed, although much of his work, along with that of Myles Coverdale, appeared in 1539 as the first authorised English Bible under King Henry VIII. Later, King James I abolished the death penalty for this offence and commissioned an updated authorised version: the King James Bible of 1611. This King James Bible is still published and used to this day, and many expressions still in contemporary use are derived from it, including **idioms** like 'salt of the earth', 'the straight and narrow' and 'sign of the times'.

Classroom activity 3

Discuss why these English Bibles in particular would have had a great influence on the language of the people of England. Remember that many people were not literate at this time.

The Grammarians

The Early Modern English period saw the rise of the **Grammarians**. John Hart, in his 1551 text *The opening of the unreasonable writing of our Inglish toung*, set out the range of punctuation marks available to writers: the apostrophe, colon, comma, exclamation mark, full stop, hyphen, parentheses and question mark among them. The fact that these were not the names that Hart himself used (for example, his 'joiner' would become the modern hyphen) shows the experimental phase that English punctuation entered. William Bullokar's *A Brief Grammar of English* (published in 1586) began a rash of texts that sought to level grammatical rules upon the language, extending well into later modern English, with books like Lynne Truss's *Eats, Shoots and Leaves* (2003) perhaps even continuing the tradition into the 21st century. These represent a **prescriptivist** approach to the changing language, with many during the Early Modern period basing their rulings on attempts to map the English language on to the structure of Latin.

Many of the rules proposed by the Grammarian writers shaped the formation of Standard English. The 18th-century Grammarian Robert Lowth suggested that the practice of using a **preposition** that was unattached to an object was a **colloquialism**. An example of this **preposition stranding** is 'This chair was sat on'. This in turn contributed to the 'rule' that sentences should not end with a preposition, the basis for which was the fact that the Latin language was unable to accommodate such syntax – and Grammarians took it as their template for English.

Similar rules regarding 'incorrect' usage have included beginning sentences with a conjunction, double (or **multiple**) **negatives**, and the use of **'split' infinitives**, where an adverbial is placed in between the preposition 'to' and the base verb – as famously seen in 'to boldly go'.

There were set phrases constructed to express grammatical functions (periphrases), for example **irregular comparative** and **superlative** adjective and adverb forms: 'more beautiful' and 'most beautiful'. Verb

Key terms

Idiom: metaphorical or non-literal sayings common in their cultural context.

Grammarian: this term has come to refer to the writers of the Early Modern English period who published texts that set out prescriptive rules for the language.

Prescriptivism: an approach to language that seeks to impose particular rules for language use in order to maintain a specific standard form, and, in some cases, to restrict or prevent the use of non-standard forms of the language.

Preposition: a function word that expresses a relationship between words, phrases or clauses. Prepositions usually relate to space or time.

Colloquialism: a word or phrase from everyday spoken language.

Preposition stranding: using a preposition that is unattached to an object, e.g. 'The angry man was difficult to talk to' as a re-ordering of '[it] was difficult to talk to the angry man'.

Multiple negatives: the use of more than one form of negation in a phrase.

Infinitive: the 'base form' of the verb preceded by the preposition 'to', used to express its action without linking it to a specific subject.

Split infinitive: placing an adverbial in between the preposition and verb in an infinitive verb form.

Irregular: a word that doesn't follow the standard patterns of inflection for change of meaning or function, e.g. a verb that does not use the -*ed* suffix to create the past tense, or an adjective that does not use the -*er* suffix to create the comparative form.

Comparative: adjectives inflected with -*er* or combined with 'more' are in the comparative form.

Superlative: adjectives inflected with -*est* or combined with 'most' are in the superlative form.

Auxiliary: a verb that supports or 'helps' another verb.

Modal: a verb used to express possibility, probability, certainty, necessity or obligation: e.g. will, would, can, could, shall, should, may, might, must.

Periphrase/periphrastic: the use of several words to create a grammatical phrase, e.g. a verb phrase using an auxiliary verb in conjunction with a main verb.

Imperative: a sentence function that gives directives, commonly known as commands.

Affixation: modifying an existing word by adding a morpheme to the beginning or end of it.

Conversion: creating a new meaning for a word by using it to fulfil a different word class function, e.g. using a noun as a verb.

Borrowing: a word or phrase taken from another language and brought into English usage.

Lexicon: all of the words in a particular language.

Fig. 5 *Shakespeare symbolises the expansion and experimentation of English during the Early Modern period*

forms also followed this convention to express differences of time. The future tense was formed using the **auxiliary modal** verb of 'will' or 'shall' ('I will go to the theatre'), although some Grammarians took pains to distinguish precisely which of these two modals was appropriate in specific cases. A unique **periphrastic** feature found throughout the period was the use of 'do' as an auxiliary with other verbs to fulfil a range of functions. Its use was highly variable, but it can be found constructing tense ('the Lord did sheawe'), adding emphasis ('I ask only those that do sing the sweetest'), and as part of the **imperative** mood ('Do come when you are well again').

Some people even blamed the advent of printing itself for causing such diversity in the orthographical system of English. It is fair to suggest that the proofreading and printing process was often carried out by people with little education, and even with a first language other than English, so errors and idiosyncrasies came about, especially as spelling still very often reflected the spoken language of the writer. Standardisation efforts persevered, and the English language went through further phases of change. One example was the proposal to capitalise all nouns within sentences (a feature of modern German), which remains in modern English only in the form of titles of person (Sir, Duchess, etc.) and the proper noun system.

Lexical expansion

Lexical expansion was a feature of the Early Modern period and many writers played a significant part in it.

Shakespeare

Shakespeare (1564–1616) is often credited with introducing a great many words and idiomatic phrases into the language – cleverly expressed by the journalist, Bernard Levin:

> 'If you cannot understand my argument, and declare "It's Greek to me", you are quoting Shakespeare; if you claim to be more sinned against than sinning, you are quoting Shakespeare; if you recall your salad days, you are quoting Shakespeare; if you act more in sorrow than in anger, if your wish is father to the thought, if your lost property has vanished into thin air, you are quoting Shakespeare; if you have ever refused to budge an inch or suffered from green-eyed jealousy, if you have played fast and loose, if you have been tongue-tied, a tower of strength, hoodwinked or in a pickle, if you have knitted your brows, made virtue of a necessity, insisted on fair play, slept not one wink, stood on ceremony …'

And many, many more! Shakespeare's use of language is a good example of change using the processes of **affixation**, **conversion** and Latinate **borrowings**, and Shakespeare is responsible for coining words like 'gnarling', 'swashing', 'swasher' and 'abhominable'. Estimates vary as to Shakespeare's total contribution of words to the English **lexicon**, but it certainly involves many hundreds of words. It is interesting to reflect that, like the King James Bible, the works of Shakespeare, in their day, would have been received by most people as spoken (that is, performed at theatre), rather than written texts.

The inkhorn controversy

Many other writers, including Christopher Marlowe, Edmund Spenser and Sir Philip Sydney, borrowed words from the classical languages of Latin and Greek. Extensive use was made of processes like **compounding** (e.g. 'tragicomedy', 'thermometer'), conversion (e.g. 'essay', 'season'), **prefixation** (e.g. 'nonsense', 'amphitheatre'), **suffixation** (e.g. 'relaxation', 'alienate'). Not everyone saw this change as positive. These new words became known as '**inkhorn**' terms – a word that refers to the inkwells of writers that were made from horn – and the inkhorn controversy raged between writers throughout the period. Some writers (notably Thomas Wilson and John Cheke) complained about the addition of foreign words to the English language and saw the practice as creating an unnecessarily large and unwieldy language. They adopted a prescriptivist attitude towards English, and in some cases voiced a form of **linguistic purism**.

Dictionaries

Another form of prescriptivism saw the emergence of English dictionaries. None of the early dictionaries was particularly comprehensive, and they tended to favour the particular values and experiences of the writer in balancing the collection of words with records of the orthography, semantics, phonology and grammatical usage of the time. They do, however, mark another milestone on the way towards a standardised language. The first dictionary published solely in English was Robert Cawdrey's *A Table Alphabeticall*, published in 1604.

In Cawdrey's preface (see overleaf), you will notice the use of the **substitution** of some letters: s appears to be formed in a very similar way to f. Also, v and u are frequently interchanged. The reasons for this are to do with the gradual implementation of the Roman alphabet, which had been going on for many centuries: f is closer to the way that the Roman cursive lower case s was written, and the same is true for v, which was written as u. The use of v in the u position seems to come from the Latin upper case form of u, which was formed as a V. These minor orthographical variations can be found in written language as late as the 19th century, as the standardisation of the orthographical system continued. Another feature is the way that some characters are joined together, for example the s and t in 'understand' in Cawdrey's preface overleaf. This is known as **ligature** and often represents instances where letters form a common cluster, like st or ct.

Fig. 6 *The inkhorn controversy was sparked by a tendency in many 16th and 17th century scholars to bring terms into English from classical languages like Latin and Greek*

Key terms

Compounding: joining two or more words together to create a new word.

Prefixation: creating a new word by adding a prefix to the start of it.

Suffixation: creating a new word by adding a suffix to the end of it.

Inkhorning: bringing a new word into use by taking it from one of the classical languages of Latin, Greek or Hebrew. This term is usually only specifically used to describe this practice in writers of the Early Modern English period.

Linguistic purism: the view that one particular language, or language form, is the most authentic and must be promoted over other, inferior varieties.

Substitution: swapping a letter, cluster of letters, or sound with another in its place.

Ligature: a feature of printed text that uses a line to join particular common combinations of letters together, especially clusters of consonants like 'st' or 'ct'.

Data response exercise 1

Read the facsimile of Cawdrey's preface that follows.

1 Copy and complete a table like the one on page 10 to show differences in the orthography of this piece compared with present-day Standard English.

2 What patterns can you see in the orthographical variation? For example, in what position does the long s appear?

3 What explanations can you give for some of the variations?

■ Key terms

Long s: an archaic way of writing the modern letter 's', which looks a bit like an 'f'. Its usage began in Old English and can be found right through the Early Modern English period, including as part of a ligature between two letters.

Capitalisation: using an upper case letter form (for example, 'G' for 'g'), whether in standard or non-standard places.

Final e: a remnant from Middle English, where the written final e reflected that vowel being pronounced at the end of the word.

Feature	Example 1	Example 2	Example 3	Example 4
u for v				
v for u				
long s				
capitalisation				
ligature				
y for i				
final e				

Study tip

Often, one or more of the texts you are provided with in the exam will be a facsimile (a realistic copy) of the original text, rather than a modern, typed-out version. This is an excellent opportunity to bring in discussion of orthographical and graphological elements, and to link them to archaic features and background detail such as Caxton and the process of printing. However, always ensure you link your point to the development of language, rather than purely layout or typeface.

■ Looking ahead

Many of the texts you can use to find out about Early Modern English (and older forms) are literary. This is a good example of how studying English Language and English Literature can cross over and enhance each other. If you enjoy both, you will be able to find university courses that allow you to study units in each area, as well as some that combine the disciplines, for example, in learning Old English language forms and using them to appreciate the literature of Saint Bede (673–735).

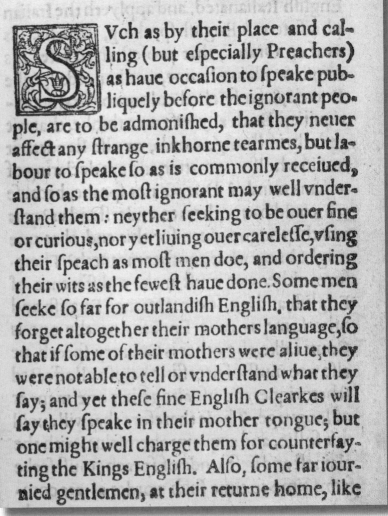

To the Reader.

Vch as by their place and cal-ling (but especially Preachers) as haue occasion to speake pub-liquely before the ignorant peo-ple, are to be admonished, that they neuer affect any strange inkhorne tearmes, but la-bour to speake so as is commonly receiued, and so as the most ignorant may well vnder-stand them : neyther seeking to be ouer fine or curious, nor yet liuing ouer carelesse, vsing their speach as most men doe, and ordering their wits as the fewest haue done. Some men seeke so far for outlandish English, that they forget altogether their mothers language, so that if some of their mothers were aliue, they were not able to tell or vnderstand what they say; and yet these fine English Clearkes will say they speake in their mother tongue; but one might well charge them for counterfay-ting the Kings English. Also, some far iour-nied gentlemen, at their returne home, like

Perhaps the most striking feature of Cawdrey's preface is the length of his first sentence! This grammatical feature in Early Modern English can be found in many texts, with multi-**clause** complex and compound-complex sentences that run to many dozens of words – or even clauses. Often, the opening clauses raise some grammatical or semantic point that doesn't make complete sense until much later in the sentence. As an example, look at the reference to 'some men', later identified as 'English Clearkes', in Cawdrey's second sentence. These kinds of sentence, which make use of multiple subordinated clauses, have become known as '**suspended sentences**'.

Cawdrey's dictionary pioneered such things as a full alphabetical system of listing words (for example, 'plume', 'pluralitie' and 'poeme' follow in sequence), although it numbered approximately 2,500 words only, and did not account for the letters G, L and S! Needless to say, dictionaries developed and expanded. Nathan Bailey's *Dictionarium Brittanicum*, published towards the end of the Early Modern period, in 1730, contained 48,000 words; its increased range is shown in the following **facsimile**.

> alio *Thymus*.
> FAG End [of ᵹeᵹan, *Sax.* to join together] the latter end of cloth, &c.
> FA'GOT [*Fagot*, F] a bundle of sticks or wood for fuel.
> FA'GGOT, a badge which in times of popery was worn on the sleeve of the upper garments, by such persons who had recanted and abjured herefy.
> FAGGOTS [with *Military Men*] are ineffective persons, who receive no regular pay, nor do any regular duty; but are hired occasionally to appear at a muster, and fill up the companies, and hide the real deficiences thereof.
> FAGGOT of steel, 120 pound weight.
> To FAGGOT *a Person*, is to bind him hand and foot.
> FAGOTTI'NG [in *Musick Books*] a single curtail, a musical

Data response exercise 2

1 Practise your understanding of word classes by defining each of the 'faggot'-related entries shown above as fully as you can.

2 What does this range of definitions for 'faggot' tell you about change in the Early Modern period?

The most comprehensive and formative dictionary of the period was Dr Samuel Johnson's *Dictionary of the English Language*, commissioned in 1746 and published in 1755. In his preface, Johnson reflects on the nature of change within the English language in his time, writing that it:

> 'has itself been hitherto neglected, suffered to spread, under the direction of chance, into wild exuberance, resigned to the tyranny of time and fashion, and exposed to the corruptions of ignorance, and caprices of innovation.'

His reaction to this situation was to try to set a standard for the orthography of the language, as well as provide his own definition of words. One of the prime features of Johnson's method was in his use of the language of literature to build his lexicon. He also scrutinised the etymology of a word to help decide upon the rules for its spelling.

Fig. 7 *Often known just as 'Dr Johnson', Samuel Johnson not only produced the influential 1755 Dictionary but was a prolific commentator on all aspects of the English language*

Johnson used many quotations from literature (around 114,000 across the 43,000 word entries) to evidence the usage of a word – a practice that you will see further developed in the modern *Oxford English Dictionary (OED)*. The following comment on etymology gives an insight into how he decided upon the 'true orthography' of a word, in which he stated that he had:

> 'referred them to their original languages: thus I write enchant, enchantment, enchanter, after the French, and incantation after the Latin; thus entire is chosen rather than intire, because it passed to us not from the Latin integer, but from the French entier.'

Johnson's approach adopted a thoroughness not seen in previous dictionaries: the word 'take' being an extreme example of this, containing over 130 definitions. Although, as you have read, his had not been the first dictionary, the combination of these features made it the first to begin to represent the language in actual, recorded use. This made Johnson's dictionary highly influential, offering the kind of prescriptivism that many Grammarians were calling for, and advancing the cause of standardisation. It can be seen to mark something of a shift in the development of the language – the Early Modern period was closing, and the burgeoning Modern English language was coming into its own.

Early Modern English text studies

The following extracts will give you a miniature tour of the kinds of writing happening across the Early Modern English period – from 1600 up to about 1750. Now that you have studied several of the main features of Early Modern English, use these texts and activities to practise your skills of textual analysis, to discover the distinctive forms of individual writers, and to place the features specific to this period in context.

The phrasing of the tasks in the Data response exercises is similar to that you will meet in your exam (although you will have a pair of texts, rather than one). The feedback which follows each example lists some of the main features worth analysing in each case. Your own analysis should deliberately quote, in support of each feature and idea, and build the points into a full discussion.

Language around you 1

Plan a 'language change walk' in your local area to look for evidence of archaic English words and phrases. Map out the older buildings and places nearby, including churches and graveyards, museums, National Trust or English Heritage sites, old streets, pubs or houses. Take photographs and note down examples of old words, phrases, typefaces and spellings that you find.

Data response exercise 3

The following extract is taken from *The Guls Horne-Booke*, by the playwright Thomas Dekker, in 1609.

Evaluate how Dekker creates humour through his style and analyse the distinctive Early Modern English features that you see in Dekker's writing.

Notes:

Ragga-muffins: 'common people' (line 4)

third sound: the start of a play was signalled with trumpets sounding three times (line 6)

it skils not: 'it matters not' (line 6)

flirt: to joke with or mock (line 11)

bastinado: a French/Spanish derivation for a 'beating' (line 14)

How a Gallant should behaue himselfe in a Play-house

Before the Play begins, fall to cardes, you may win or loose (as
Fencers doe in a prize) and beate one another by confederacie, yet
share the money when you meete at supper: notwithstanding, to gul
the Ragga-muffins that stand a loofe gaping at you, throw the cards   5
(hauing first torne foure or fiue of them) round about the Stage,
iust vpon the third sound, as though you had lost: it skils not if the
foure knaues ly on their backs, and outface the Audience, theres
none such fooles as dare take exceptions at them, because ere the
play go off, better knaues then they will fall into the company.   10

Now sir if the writer be a fellow that hath epigramd you, or hath
had a flirt at your mistris, or hath brought either your feather
or your red beard, or your little legs etc. on the stage, you shall
disgrace him worse then by tossing him in a blancket, or giuing
him the bastinado in a Tauerne, if in the middle of his play, (bee it   15
Pastorall or Comedy, Morall or Tragedie) you rise with a skreud and
discontented face from your stoole to be gone: no matter whether
the Scenes be good or no, the better they are, the more doe you
distast them: and beeing on your feete, sneake not away like a
coward, but salute all your gentle acquaintance, that are spred either   20
on the rushes, or on stooles about you, and draw what troope you
can from the stage after you: the Mimicks are beholden to you, for
allowing them elbow roome: their Poet cries perhaps a pox go with
you, but care not you for that, theres no musick without frets.

Data response exercise 4

The following extract is a letter written by Lady Brilliana Harley, to her son
who is studying in Oxford, at the time of the English Civil War, in 1642.

Evaluate the way that the personal and private nature of this text has shaped
the way that it is written as well as the use of distinctive features of the
period.

Aim to consider the following points, in addition to other distinctive aspects
of the text.

- Harley's letter is very individual in its style, creating a distinctive **idiolect**.
  Try to find features that make up her particular style and explain what
  they might show.
- Some of Harley's spellings reflect the way that she is likely to have
  spoken English, by changing certain consonant sounds, or shortening or
  elongating vowel sounds. Look for examples of this and discuss what they
  mean for Harley's use of language.
- Because her letter is relatively informal, Harley makes use of several
  features that are often found in speech, e.g. the use of the **coordinating
  conjunction** 'and' to list things and give information. Analyse some of her
  sentences in the light of this.

For my dear sonne Mr. Edward Harley.

My deare Ned – I longe to see you, but would not haue you come
downe, for I cannot thinke this cuntry very safe; by the papers I
haue sent to your father, you will knowe the temper of it. I hope
your father will giue me full derections how I may beest haue my
howes gareded, if need be; if he will giue the derections, I hope, I
shall foolow it. […]

Study tip

Practise the art of annotating the
texts on the exam paper – it can help
you select quotations and link them
to key terms quickly and accurately.
However, don't forget that the
question paper is not collected in, so
make it a quick and efficient process
that is done as you read, and – most
importantly – make sure all the good
points and terms make it onto your
answer paper!

Key terms

Idiolect: an individual style of
speaking, made up of choices in all
frameworks.

Elongated: used to describe a long
vowel sound.

Coordinating conjunction: a
conjunction that connects
main clauses together to form
compound sentences.

Fig. 8 *Lady Brilliana Harley was a prolific letter writer. Several hundred of her letters remain and are a valuable record of the English language during the Early Modern period*

■ Further reading

The Oxford English Dictionary Online has a number of interesting essays on different aspects of English at http://public.oed.com/aspects-of-english/. This site includes an 'English in time' section with several articles on Old, Middle and Modern English. Read through a selection of these to bring you up to the end of the Early Modern English period before moving on to the next topic.

■ Key terms

Anaphoric: a word or phrase that refers 'backwards' in a text to something mentioned earlier.

■ Topic revision exercise

1 Why did Caxton's printing press and books like the King James Bible have such an impact on English and standardisation?

2 Describe the idea of prescriptivism and the effect that the Grammarians had on the development of English.

3 What non-standard spelling patterns can you remember seeing in the Early Modern English texts in this topic?

Had I not had this ocation to send to your father, yet I had sent this boy vp to Loundoun; he is such a rogeisch boy that I dare not keepe him in my howes, and as littell do I dare to let him goo in this cuntry, least he ioyne with the company of vollentirs, or some other such crwe. I haue giuen him no more money then will sarue to beare his charges vpe; and becaus I would haue him make hast and be sure to goo to Londoun, I haue toold him, that you will giue him something for his paines, if he come to you in good time and doo not loyter; and heare inclosed I haue sent you halfe a crowne. Giue him what you thinke fitte, and I desire he may not come downe any more, but that he may be perswaded to goo to seae, or some other imployment. He thinkes he shall come downe againe. Good Ned, do not tell Martaine that I send him vp with such an intention. I haue derected theas letters to you, and I send him to you, becaus I would not haue the cuntry take notis, that I send to your father so offten; but when such ocations come, I must needs send to him, for I can rely vpon nobodys counsell but his. I pray God blles you and presarue you in safety, and the Lord in mercy giue you a comfortabell meeting with

Your most affectinate mother, Brilliana Harley.

■ Data response exercise 5

The following extract is a short biography from *Brief Lives*, by John Aubrey, published in 1680.

Evaluate the ways that the context of this biography has shaped the way that it has been written. You may find the term **anaphoric** useful.

John, Earl of Rochester:– he went to school at [Burford]; was of Wadham College, Oxford: I suppose, had been in France.

About 18, he stole his lady, [Elizabeth] Malet, a daughter and heir; a great fortune, for which I remember I saw him a prisoner in the Tower about 1662. His youthly spirit and opulent fortune did sometimes make him do extravagant actions, but in the country he was generally civil enough. He was wont to say that when he came to Brentford the devil entered into him and never left him till he came into the country again to Alderbury and Woodstock.

He was ranger of Woodstock park and lived often at the lodge at the west end, a very delightful place and noble prospect westwards. Here his lordships had several lascivious pictures drawn.

His lordship read all manner of books. Mr Andrew Marvell, who was a good judge of wit, was wont to say that he was the best English satirist and had the right vein. 'Twas pity death took him off so soon.

In his last sickness he was exceedingly penitent and wrote a letter of his repentance to Dr Burnet, which is printed. He sent for all his servants, even the pigherd boy, to come and hear his palinode. He died at Woodstock Park, 26 July 1680.

Modern English

Study tip

When you read widely and study the English language, you will find many terms used to describe different eras. 'Modern English' is often used to cover the whole period from about 1550 onwards. You may also come across labels like 'New English' and 'Present Day English', or, particularly when looking at literary texts, 'Elizabethan English', 'Victorian English' or 'nineteenth-century English'. All of these ways of defining particular times of English usage are valid, and they each tend to have a slightly different emphasis. Use them to help you deepen your understanding and describe what you are referring to more precisely in discussion and essays.

Key terms

Descriptivism: an approach to language that seeks to understand the varieties of a language and not to interfere with them.

Starter activity

Choose one of the areas of influence on the English language from the list below and discuss it in a small group. They are all important factors in shaping the Modern English period. Ask yourselves what role the area you have chosen would have played – and continues to play today.

- Schools and education
- Foreign travel and trade
- English novels and poetry
- Newspapers, radio and television

Expansion and development of the English language

If the Early Modern English period was characterised by the gradual establishment of the modern English language that you recognise today, then the two centuries that followed represent expansion, in terms of both the lexicon and literature of English, and its emerging role as a world language. Standardisation continued to grip the language, supported by the steady increase in education for children.

This section resumes the story of the modern development of English from the latter part of the 18th century, and continues into the late-20th century, before the emergence of computer-based new technologies.

Education and learning

In the early part of the 19th century, there were a number of contextual factors that resulted in some improvement in the chances of a child in England going to school. Restrictions were placed on child labour, the 'poor laws' were revised, and the creation of new schools was financially supported by the government. These measures built on school attendance rates of approximately 30 per cent of children at the start of the 19th century, leading towards the first Education Act, in 1870, that made schooling compulsory until the age of 12.

The principal aim of schooling at this time was to teach pupils how to read, and how to write in standard English, and this contributed to improving literacy rates. The publication of many 'grammars' followed; these attempted to impart the orthographic and grammatical rules of the standardised language. However, even within these texts, there was variation, with relatively minor local differences being reflected in alternatives that you will still find in the language today: '-ise' and '-ize' at the end of verbs, '-t' and '-ed' inflections to show the past tense in words like 'burn', and single/double letter variants when adding inflections to verbs like 'level' ('leveled' or 'levelled' are both 'correct') or 'focus'.

The Oxford English Dictionary

With the English language growing at this rapid rate, linguists towards the end of the 19th century began to take a more **descriptivist** attitude towards recording the new words, uses, and definitions emerging. Work

■ Key terms

Broadening: extending the range of meanings for a word by adding a new meaning and/or use to an existing word. For example, 'to boy' gaining a meaning as a verb meaning to humiliate someone.

Prop-word: the use of the word 'one' in place of a noun.

Utterance: the spoken language equivalent of a phrase or sentence.

Archaic: no longer in common modern use.

Obsolete: used to describe a word or part of the language that has disappeared from use entirely.

Relative pronoun: a word such as 'which' or 'who' when it is used to introduce a relative clause and give more information about another phrase in the sentence.

Objective case: this describes nouns or pronouns when used as the object of a verb or preposition in a clause. Some English pronouns have particular forms for the objective case, for example, 'me', 'him' and 'her'.

Language contact: the instance of speakers of different languages interacting, often resulting in some form of exchange or blending of the languages.

Fig. 9 *The BBC was formed in the first half of the 20th century and 'BBC English' was born*

began on the *Oxford English Dictionary* (*OED*) in the middle of the century and, by 1884, the first instalment (covering just part of the letter A!) was published, under the working title of *A New English Dictionary on Historical Principles*. The project was ambitious, and sought to log every word found in the written evidence of the English language since the 11th century and, in each case, to record its pronunciation, spelling, usage and meanings. Like Johnson's dictionary, the *OED* used the concept of quoting exact sources of the usages of a word from written material.

The changes charted by the *OED* also saw the meanings of existing words alter; in many cases **broadening** their meanings, and in a few beginning to narrow. Use of the word 'one' as a **prop-word** (which operates like a pronoun) to replace nouns in a sentence or **utterance** grew throughout the 19th century: for example, 'That green budgerigar is the one I would like.' This is now a common element in contemporary English usage, and so much so that 'one' has effectively been added to the lexicon as a form of closed-class, functional word.

■ Extension activity

Remind yourself of the distinction between closed-class and open-class words. Make sure you are clear about why closed-class words change so little.

By contrast, some words become rarer in their usage and may lose meaning altogether. The verb 'ecstasiate' (meaning, to go into an ecstasy) had a fairly short life from the early 19th century through to the mid-20th century, although it is currently very rarely used, if at all. **Archaic** usages, like the pronoun 'thou', decline in a similar way, although the sense of the word remains fairly commonly understood, even if the word is rarely used, preventing the word from becoming **obsolete** and disappearing from the language. The American linguist Edward Sapir predicted in 1926 that the **relative pronoun** 'whom' would fall out of use, based on the trend towards the word 'who' broadening to fill all uses where 'who' or 'whom' would have been placed. This followed and 'whom', as the **objective case** of 'who', is no longer in common current use.

The beginnings of a global language

As the British Empire expanded, particularly in the 18th and 19th centuries, so the use of English spread around the world, bringing it into contact with more diverse speakers than ever. For the language, this perhaps had two main consequences. One was the impact these opportunities for **language contact** had on English itself: in addition to the existing influx of words from European languages, the African and Asian languages of Britain's colonial territories added new borrowings to the lexicon, such as 'bungalow' (Urdu) and 'chimpanzee' (Bantu). The other was to lay the foundations of English as a 'world language' as smatterings of it were increasingly taken up by people worldwide for international trade.

Journalism and broadcasting

The first English newspaper had in fact appeared in the early 18th century, but it took the industrial revolution to provide the machinery for mass print production. *The Times* and other national newspapers emerged at the beginning of the 19th century, offering far more widespread availability to readers, which provided a context for accelerating linguistic change and powerfully influencing language use. Public broadcasting, under the banner of the British Broadcasting Corporation, emerged in Britain in the early 20th century. It brought the spoken word to the people, first through the medium of radio in 1922, and television 10 years later.

Modern English text studies

The extracts that follow are authentic examples of Modern English usage, in chronological order, showing something of the changes in the language across this time-span. As with the Early Modern English selection, use these texts and activities to practise your skills of textual analysis, to discover the distinctive forms of individual writers, and to understand the features specific to this period in context. Feedback on the main features is provided at the end of Section A.

Hans Place: Friday (Nov 24).

MY DEAREST CASSANDRA,

I have the pleasure of sending you a much better account of my affairs, which I know will be a great delight to you.

I wrote to Mr. Murray yesterday myself, and Henry wrote at the same time to Roworth. Before the notes were out of the house, I received three sheets and an apology from R. We sent the notes, however, and I had a most civil one in reply from Mr. M. He is so very polite, indeed, that it is quite overcoming. The printers have been waiting for paper – the blame is thrown upon the stationer; but he gives his word that I shall have no farther cause for dissatisfaction. He has lent us Miss Williams and Scott, and says that any book of his will always be at my service. In short, I am soothed and complimented into tolerable comfort.

[…]

He was out yesterday; it was a fine sunshiny day here (in the country perhaps you might have clouds and fogs. Dare I say so? I shall not deceive you, if I do, as to my estimation of the climate of London), and he ventured first on the balcony and then as far as the greenhouse. He caught no cold, and therefore has done more to-day, with great delight and self-persuasion of improvement.

[…]

Evening. -- We have had no Edward. Our circle is formed – only Mr. Tilson and Mr. Haden. We are not so happy as we were. A message came this afternoon from Mrs. Latouche and Miss East, offering themselves to drink tea with us to-morrow, and, as it was accepted, here is an end of our extreme felicity in our dinner guest. I am heartily sorry they are coming; it will be an evening spoilt to Fanny and me.

Another little disappointment: Mr. H. advises Henry's not venturing with us in the carriage to-morrow; if it were spring, he says, it would be a different thing. One would rather this had not been. He seems to think his going out today rather imprudent, though acknowledging at the same time that he is better than he was in the morning.

[…]

Data response exercise 6

This letter is written by Jane Austen to her older sister, Cassandra, in 1815.

It illustrates some of the features that are representative of English at this time. List and explain some of these features.

Study tip

Although you are presented with 'paired' texts that share a particular topic in the exam question, it is not compulsory to compare or contrast them. You can take this approach if you prefer, but it is equally valid to tackle them individually.

I send you five one-pound notes, for fear you should be distressed for little money. Lizzy's work is charmingly done; shall you put it to your chintz? A sheet came in this moment; 1st and 3rd vols. are now at 144; 2nd at 48. I am sure you will like particulars. We are not to have the trouble of returning the sheets to Mr. Murray's any longer, the printer's boys bring and carry.

I hope Mary continues to get well fast, and I send my love to little Herbert. You will tell me more of Martha's plans, of course, when you write again. Remember me most kindly to everybody, and Miss Benn besides.

Yours very affectionately,
J. AUSTEN.

Further reading

Visit The Advertising Archives website at http://www.advertisingarchives.co.uk/ to browse a collection of over a million high-quality facsimiles of advertisements and other texts from the mid-19th century to the present day.

Data response exercise 7

The following advertisement appeared on the front cover of a novel, printed in 1887.

Consider how the product, Beecham's Pills, has been represented in the text, and in what ways the language might have been affected by its context.

A WONDERFUL MEDICINE

BEECHAM'S PILLS

Are admitted by thousands to be worth above a Guinea a Box for Billous and Nervous Disorders, such as Wind and Pain in the Stomach, Sick Headache, Giddiness, Fulness and Swelling after meals, Dizziness and Drowsiness, Cold Chills, Flushings of Heat, Loss of Appetite, Shortness of Breath, Costiveness, Scurvey, Blotches on the Skin, Disturbed Sleep, Frightful Dreams, and all Nervous and Trembling Sensations, &c. The first dose will give relief in 20 minutes. This is no fiction, for they have done it in thousands of cases. Every sufferer is earnestly invited to try one box of these Pills, and they will be acknlowdedged to be

WORTH A GUINEA A BOX.

For Feamales of all ages these Pills are invaluable, as a few doses of them carry off all humours, and bring about all that is required. No female should be without them. There is no medicine to be found to equal BEECHAM'S PILLS for removing any obstruction or irregularity of the system. If taken accord-ing to the directions given with each box, they will soon restore femaes of all ages to sound and rebust health.

For a Weak Stomach, Impaired Digestion, and all Dicorders of the Liver they act like "magic," and a few doses will be found to work wonders upon the most important organs of the human machine. They strengthen the whole muscular system, restore the long-lost complexion, bring back the keen edge of appetite, and arouse into action, with the Rosebud of Health, the whole physical energy of the human frame. These are "facts" admitted by thousands, embracing all classes of society, and one of the best guarantees to the Nervous and Debilitated is BEECHAM'S PILLS have the largest sale of any patent medicine in the world.

Full Direction are given with each Box.
Sold by all Druggist and Patent Medicine Dealers in the United Kingdom, In Boxes at 1s, 1½d. ad 2s 9d. each.

A Wonderful Medicine, Beecham's Pills, Launceston Examiner, Saturday 11 June 1892

Data response exercise 8

The following letter was written to the parents of a young woman whilst she was serving in the Women's Auxiliary Air Force in 1943, during the Second World War.

Explain how the context has shaped the way the writer uses language to convey her experiences.

Notes:

(...)	Place name removed because of wartime censorship restriction
A.T.S.	Auxiliary Transport Services
N.C.O.	Non-commissioned Officer
Waaf	Women's Auxiliary Air Force.

March 1943

Well, isn't it all grand – Wednesday comes and Milly and I set off for (...) to have an evening in the officers!!! mess and then went round the village, even though it's all barricaded up. We had a Major driving us and he only had to say 'red herring' and then poodled through all the barriers, M.P.s and astonished general civvies.

Later on, we were left to our usual duties, this time on an empty golf course from about midnight on, doing wind observations with torches. Sirens sounded every so often, but nothing seemed to be dropped. A very nice Lieutenant, and the Major came by after an hour and were perfectly sweet to us. A bit later still (nearly 2am by then!!!!!) we headed back to the mess for hot Ovaltines, and the Major told us we were to be moved out to be billeted with some A.T.S.; he took us to a large house himself, took us to the N.C.O. and wished us goodnight. We were fagged out by then, so just had a quick wash – in the sergeant's bath! – and found our dorm for a jolly good sleep. Only a few hours, though, as we soon had to get to breakfast, and found out the Major was taking us away again to the station. An extraordinary day.

What fun! Having a superb time at the new place, even though the site is mostly marshland with 6 feet deep dykes. We carried on our training, doing some road work. I was on hard labour, swinging the pick-axe and shovelling – everyone mucks in together here. Then we began smoke sessions and did some trials. I also had to take on the obstacle course, across 19 dykes, with very few planks to save my damp feet. Next I have to draw up the report to be sent back.

The Waafs are friendly here, but last night we escaped the beer sessions and cycled out to a local dance. It was grand, with the men looking out for the gorgeous civvy girls. Our uniform is original here and the chaps all wanted a dance with us – and promised to give us skittle lessons at the local!

Topic revision exercise

1. How did education change during the late Modern English period, and what effect did this have on language use?
2. How was the *Oxford English Dictionary* put together, and why was it a more descriptivist project than previous dictionaries?
3. What two developments, one in the early 19th century and one at the beginning of the 20th century, played a major role in accelerating language change and influencing language use?

Study tip

It is important when defining a linguistic feature, such as a sentence type, to provide an exact example that shows you can securely identify it. However, you do not need to quote the whole sentence if it is long. Using ellipsis by quoting the first few words and the last few will be clear enough, for example, 'We carried on ... in together here.'

Further reading

Read Lynda Mugglestone's 'Nineteenth-century English – an overview' in the OED Online 'Aspects of English' section: http://public.oed.com/aspects-of-english/english-in-time/nineteenth-century-english-an-overview/.

Contemporary language change

In this topic you will:

- learn about the features of emergent forms in the English language
- read and analyse examples of the changes occurring in present-day English.

Key terms

Blending: joining morphemes or syllables from existing words to form a new word. For example, 'internaut' from 'internet' and 'astronaut'.

Clipping: the shortening of an existing word to leave a single part. For example, 'retro' from 'retrograde'.

Amelioration: a change in the meaning of a word that causes it to gain status. For example, positive, colloquial adjectives like 'sweet' and 'cool'.

Pejoration: a change in the meaning of a word that causes it to lose status. For example, 'lame' being used to describe something inept or inadequate.

Narrowing: the loss of the range of meaning for a word by a particular use becoming archaic or obsolete. For example, 'skyline' coming to be used only for a horizon with tall buildings.

Colloquial language: language used in informal, ordinary conversation.

Slang: informal vocabulary associated with a particular social group, more usual in spoken than written language.

Starter activity

Time to get your mobile phones out! In a small group, look through your recent texts, tweets, emails, Facebook posts, etc., and make notes on the non-standard language features in them: the unusual phrases, words, and ways of putting texts together and communicating.

Popular culture and social usage

Some of the largest and most influential cultural vehicles, like Hollywood, the internet, and the popular music scene, have been dominated by the English language at the close of the 20th century. This can have a global impact on language, with new lexical items, like the music genres 'rap' and 'hip-hop', becoming a part of forms of English used around the world, as well as being absorbed, often unaltered, into other languages.

Many different word formation processes create new words or alter old ones. Compounding involves combining existing words to form new phrases or words, for example, as separate words in 'muffin top' (overhanging flesh over a tight belt or waistband); hyphenated in 'drop-out' (this has several modern definitions, including the groove in the rear of a bicycle frame for fixing the wheel); and joined in 'radiodense' (added to the *Oxford English Dictionary* in June 2008, referring to a material that absorbs x-rays). **Blending** takes this a step further by **clipping** parts from an existing word before combining them into new lexical items, for example 'Brangelina', a blend of Brad Pitt and Angelina Jolie, coined in the wake of widespread media coverage of their relationship. Words also undergo semantic change, through the processes of **amelioration** ('sick' has gained status as a positive term); **pejoration** ('gay' is now commonly used in a negative sense as an adjective to imply a thing is deficient in some way, as in 'those trainers are so gay'); broadening ('pants' became a term for something of poor quality in the mid-1990s); and **narrowing** ('abacus' once had at least five different meanings, but only one remains in common, modern usage). Finally, words can change grammatically, where conversion takes an existing word use and translates it into another word class – the classic modern example being the creation of the verb 'to text' from the noun 'text'.

More radical changes tend to take place at a more localised level, within the usage of a particular country, region, or social group. In this sense, English can be seen to be proliferating at a considerable rate as the language enters the 21st century.

A good example of this sort of change occurs within **colloquial language** and, more particularly, **slang**. The noun 'chav', is used as a derogatory label, with the *OED* definition of 'a young person of a type characterised by brash and loutish behaviour and the wearing of designer-style clothes (esp. sportswear); usually with connotations of a low social status'. The *OED* cites the first recorded use as 1998, and it is a word that has become widely used in the first decade of the 21st century. Its etymology is intriguing, and shows the uncertain ways that new terms can be created. There are several theories for the origin of 'chav':

- an abbreviation of the north-east regional term, 'charver' (first recorded use: 1997 in the *OED*)
- an **acronym** formed from the words 'Council House, Alcohol and Violence', or similar, in fact an example of **folk etymology**
- a derivative from the Roman word 'chavo' for an unmarried Roman man, or Roman child.

Classroom activity 4

Colloquial insults, like 'chav', represent a rapidly changing area of the lexicon. Think of the most recent examples that you have come across, and research the possible etymology of them.

Classroom activity 5

Language that reflects people's identities is another way in which popular culture rapidly reinvents the language. Consider the recent words below. Produce a definition for each and describe how the word is used. Also try to define the linguistic process at work in the formation of the word:

- metrosexual
- smirt
- brand Nazi.

The usage of the word 'gay' illustrates how broadening of meaning can complicate attitudes within language. What was, originally, a word used to denote things that were merry, brightly coloured, or carefree, from Middle English times, has acquired many additional meanings. This original meaning remains in modern usage, although it is perhaps becoming a slightly archaic form. Several meanings of the word have come and gone, but the use of the word to denote homosexuality appeared in the first half of the 20th century, and a more recent usage, growing in frequency from the latter decades of the 20th century, and finding widespread use in the 21st century, is as an adjective to denote a quality of stupidity or disapproval for something. These contradictory usages can lead to homosexuality being given negative connotations, because the pejorative usage fuels the prejudice of homophobia.

Research point

A study by Tony Thorne of the colloquial language use at King's College London involved beginning a database of recorded terms and definitions in 1995. An analysis of the data that had been collected between 1995 and 2000 produced the following classification of the range of terms used. The first 13 semantic classifications are shown in Table 1, with a percentage of the frequency of words from that area in the database lexicon, and some of the main examples found.

Key terms

Acronym: a new word created by using the initial letters of a particular phrase. An acronym can be pronounced as a word, rather than said as a series of letters.

Folk etymology: a 'made-up' origin of a word, applied to it after it has been used for some time. Although folk etymologies are not the actual source of the word, they can sometimes reflect something about the way the word is used, and appear to 'make sense' linguistically.

Study tip

It is important to think about 'slang' in the right way. Slang is the common speech of a particular group in society, and not just any informal, colloquial language. Slang comes in specific varieties like the examples of Polari or Jackspeak discussed later in this unit, whereas colloquial language is a better way of referring to the more general, common forms of informal speech or swearing.

Fig. 10 *Colloquial terms for particular cultures and trends are constantly changing*

Table 1

1 Intoxication by drink or drugs (17.46%)	*hammered, langered, bladdered, rat-arsed*
2 Terms of approbation (15.23%)	*don, dope, det, safe, wick, fit, top, mint*
3 Romance, sex and related body parts (12.06%)	*on the sniff, out trouting, copping off, wabs, buns*
4 Insults and terms denoting misfits (11.42%)	*flid, minger, moose, smurf, swamp-donkey*
5 Terms of disapproval/disappointment (8.25%)	*cheesy, grievous, pussy, rank*
6 Greetings, farewells and exclamations (5.07%)	*easy, seen, yo, laters*
7 Social or ethnic categorisations (4.76%)	*bud-bud, bachelorette, arm-candy, catalogue man*
8 Relaxation (4.44%)	*chillin, vegging (out), hanging, gazing*
9 Money (3.80%)	*trust, squids, lookah, brassic*
10 Negative or unsettling states (3.49%)	*gutted, weirding, married alive*
11 Anger or excited states (3.17%)	*fanny-fit, (chuck a) hissy, throw a bennie*
12 Food (2.53%)	*scran, cane, Chicken McButtock*
13 Clothes (2.22%)	*kegs, shreddies, Claire Rayners*

Further reading

Tony Thorne's slang research and database is ongoing. Find out more by visiting his pages at http://www.kcl.ac.uk/study/elc/resources/tonythorne/index.aspx.

Thinking points

1. Which of these terms do you recognise as still being in use today?
2. What data do you think you would find if you carried out a similar study in your area?

Key terms

Non-standard: used to describe any word, phrasing or feature of language that does not adhere to the rules of Standard English.

Blog: (also weblog) a kind of online journal.

Webpage: an electronic page that can interlink text, images and **multimedia**.

Multimedia: texts with a combination of written language, audio and video material, and graphological elements such as photography, animation and other images.

Wiki: a collaboratively produced webpage; users switch between reading the material and editing/writing it.

New technologies and media

Perhaps the most visible form of language change that is occurring currently is the way that language is influenced by forms of new technology. The nature of these changes is far-reaching and still in process. New technologies like email and text messaging have fundamentally altered the distinction between spoken and written modes. The resulting mixed-mode forms of communication have caused the traditional distinctions of formality, manner and interaction to be blurred. This has resulted in a variety of **non-standard** forms emerging at several levels of the language, and the creation of entirely new genres and forms of text: **blogs**, **webpages** and **wikis** to name a few from a growing list. These forms of language become increasingly ubiquitous in terms of usage. Many companies, organisations and institutions now use email as their primary form of communication, with employees often receiving hundreds of emails during a week. There are billions of mobile phone users across the globe, with more than 2 billion using text messaging services regularly. The internet is increasingly becoming the first port of call for almost anything you can think of: arranging mortgages; catching up with friends and family; viewing classical paintings; watching television; selling antiques – even taking examinations! All in all, you can see why new technologies are perhaps the most significant influence on language use in the 21st century.

■ Features of new technology language use

From an orthographical perspective, written computer-mediated communications (CMC), including the short messaging service (SMS) of texting on mobile phones, have made particularly creative use of the range of alphanumeric and symbol characters. There are many reasons for this, including the use of language to support or represent:

- alternative **phonetic spelling**
- individuality and identity
- membership of a group
- emphasis and emotion
- quicker communication
- trends and fashion
- humour and playfulness.

Below is a selection of the main non-standard forms, with examples, from the research of the linguist, David Crystal, in his book, *The Stories of English*:

- unusual symbol combinations, as in personal nicknames which use upper and lower case letters unpredictably: daViD, aLoHA
- omission of capitalisation within sentences, even including i for I
- omission of internal sentence punctuation and full stops (though question marks and exclamation marks are usually kept)
- abbreviations, often involving **rebuses** (as in text messaging), such as sat for Saturday, C U for 'see you', l8 for 'late'
- emotive punctuation sequences, such as yes!!!!!!!!, Jim??!!??
- spellings, such as outta, 'out of', wanna, 'want to', cee ya, 'see you', seemz, 'seems'
- grammatical constructions, such as omitting a verb (he lovely), or breaking a **concord** rule (me am feeling better)
- **eye-dialect** forms, such as it wuz lotsa lafs, i got enuf
- **nonce formations**, such as running words together (igottanewcar) or abnormal hyphenation (what-a-helluva-mess)
- misspellings or lexical substitutions which achieve a fashionable privileged status in a particular group, such as the deliberate spelling of computer as comptuer (originating in an individual error which caught the group's fancy).

These examples presented by Crystal represent just the surface of a range of usages that are being coined at a rapid rate. **Emoticons** and **smileys**, acronyms and **initialisms** are particular forms (see Table 2 overleaf) that already run into thousands of individual lexical items – those commonly used online are in fact a blend of new coinages and existing items. Consider another interesting aspect of the way that these forms are written. In Standard English, initialisms are almost always written with capital letters, as are many acronyms (although, with time, these can be assimilated into the language as a standard, lower case lexical item, for example 'radar'). The rules for this in CMC forms are often guided by different principles. Using capital letters in an email, or on a web chat, is understood as meaning a word or sentence is 'shouted', and this is an element of the newly forming conventions of 'netiquette' – etiquette on the internet, a computer network or new technology forms. You will notice that emoticons and smileys need to be 'read' by imagining them being turned clockwise through 90 degrees – this in itself is a feature unique to CMC written forms, although many computer programs now have wide-ranging sets of emoticons, using colour and animation to produce **icons** that can be added into texts.

■ Key terms

Phonetic spelling: using letters to spell out exactly how a word is pronounced, rather than using its standard spelling.

Rebus: a way of representing a word or phrase by using letters, other characters and images in non-standard and imaginative ways.

Concord: the correct grammatical agreement of word classes and syntax, e.g. the use of the correct singular pronoun in 'I am feeling better.'

Eye-dialect: an unusual and non-standard way of spelling used to represent patterns of speech.

Nonce formation: a word created as a 'one-off' for that use and occasion only.

Emoticon and smiley: both words refer to the use of combinations of alphabetical characters to create a pictorial representation of an emotion or thing.

Initialism: the abbreviation of a phrase using the initial letters of the words within it.

Icon: a small graphical image used to represent or symbolise something. For example, computers use icons for files, buttons and programs, and they are used in websites to 'tag' content and represent particular categories such as the range of services a supermarket offers.

■ Key terms

Multi-authorship: texts with more than one contributor or author, often occurring simultaneously in social media formats.

Hashtag: the use of the number sign character (#), now more widely known as 'hash', to mark a particular word or phrase to show that it refers to another text. Rather than just a label, these are increasingly used in writing as a part of sentencing – even to the extent that 'nonce formation' versions are coined for humour (#NoReallyItIsTrue).

Asterisk: the word for this typographical sign (*) comes from the Greek for 'little star'. It is used in CMC to mark a word or phrase as a correction, or add emotional or physical commentary to a text, in a similar way to an emoticon.

Hyperlink: a connection from a textual element, like a word, phrase or image, to another text.

Intertextuality: a way of expressing the relationship between different texts and the way that texts can affect the meanings of other texts.

Further conventions have emerged with the rapid, mass-audience communications made easily accessible by global social-networking websites such as Twitter and Facebook. These include **multi-authorship** of texts, the use of the **hashtag** to denote a word or phrase that is a reference to another text, the prefixation of corrections with an Asterix (*asterisk – sorry!) and the insertion of paralinguistic or affective features through asterisk parenthesis (*sniggers*).

■ Classroom activity 6

From the non-standard forms that Crystal described above, choose one and use the seven bullet-pointed reasons on page 23 to explain how it might have come about.

Table 2

Acronyms		Emoticons and smileys		Initialisms	
LOL	laugh out loud	*<):o)	clown	@TEOTD	at the end of the day
IMHO	in my humble opinion	%-}	dizzy	ASL	age, sex, location
EM?	excuse me?	:-D	laughing	BTW	by the way
FAQ	frequently asked questions	+:-)	priest	FYI	for your information
WYSIWYG	what you see is what you get	8-0	shocked	HTH	hope that helps

Inevitably, new technological forms provide additional new items to the lexicon on a regular basis, across the range of the other word-formation processes. Examples of recent additions, added to the *Oxford English Dictionary* in its revisions published on 14 September 2007, are:

- 'darknet' (a blended term for a covert channel set up on the internet, often used for illegal purposes)
- 'microsite' (a broadened term which already had an ecological usage, to mean a small website)
- 'toolset' (a compound for a particular set of software tools or skills).

It should be noted, however, that some of these have been used over decades, only appearing in 2007 owing to the way in which the *OED* triggers new word entries. These 2007 entries focus on computer use; interestingly, new entries in early 2013 included many terms related to Olympic and Paralympic events, no doubt following the extensive coverage of the London 2012 Olympic Games over the previous year or so. For example:

- 'boccia' and 'goalball' (a borrowing and a compound term for Paralympic sports)
- 'medal' and 'podium' (both entered as verbs, converted from existing nouns, to mean winning a medal and appearing on a medal ceremony podium).

The structure of new technology communication forms, particularly those based on the internet, has become increasingly complex, with the ability to merge many different textual segments, link to other texts or media instantaneously, and enable the authoring and editing of texts to take place in real time, rather than the traditional method of a single publication on to paper.

The main device for enabling this form of complex cohesion is that of the **hyperlink**, enabling the concept of **intertextuality** to be realised by

■ Link

See the details about the *OED* on page 104. There is information on how to access the most recent *OED* revisions in Further reading on page 27.

a reader at the moment of reading – creating an entirely new model of text production and reception, perhaps best termed **hypertextuality**. Hypertextuality is the ability of a text to be interconnected with many other textual and media sources at one time, with the reader able to call upon these while 'reading' the text. This can mean that the reader has control over the sequence that he or she follows, and perhaps even the ability to edit and influence them.

In terms of cohesion, this means that the standard format of anaphoric, **cataphoric** and **exophoric** referencing still applies to texts, but that the connections themselves can be realised within the text – usually by clicking a computer mouse on particular hyperlinked words or images – rather than be constructed mainly in the mind of the reader. New forms of web-based texts like **forums**, wikis and blogs have emerged that allow readers to become writers, and texts to be authored by many people at any time – so these kinds of texts are ever-changing and do not have a definitive version.

Contemporary English text studies

The following extracts present examples of some of the more dramatic changes at work in the English language. Use them to practise identifying contemporary and emerging features, and to evaluate their effects and meaning according to the audience, purpose and context of each case. As with the previous two Data response exercises, an overview of the main features is provided in the feedback at the end of Section A. Try to incorporate and build on it in your own analysis.

English as a foreign language

Dnt u sumX rekn eng lang v lngwindd? 2mny wds & ltrs? ?nt we b usng lss time & papr? ?nt we b 4wd tnking + txt? 13yr grl frm w scot 2ndry schl sd ok. Sh rote GCSE eng sa (abt hr smmr hols in NY) in txt spk. (NO!) Sh sd sh 4t txt spk was 'easr thn standrd eng'. Sh 4t hr tcher wd b :) Hr tcher 4t it was nt so gr8! Sh was :(& talkd 2 newspprs (but askd 2 b anon). 'I cdnt bleve wot I was cing! :o'-!-!-! OW2TE. Sh hd NI@A wot grl was on abt. Sh 4t her pupl was riting 'hieroglyphics'.

Edu xperts r c:-&. Thy r wrrd tht mobile fone spk has gn 2 far. SQA (Scot Qual Auth) has sd txt spk oftn apprs 'inappropriately' in xms. Dr Cynthia McVey (Glasgw Cal Univ Psychol lect) sez 'Yng pepl dnt rite ltrs so sitng dwn 2 rite is diff … txting is more aTractve'. (Sh is COl).

But Judith Gillespie spokeswmn 4 Scot parent/tcher assoc sez we mst stmp out use of txtng 4 eng SAs (Y not hstry, geog, econ, etc? she dnt say). no1 can rite. no1 can spel. 'u wd b :-o @ nos of 2ndry pupls wh cant distngsh btwEn 'ther' & ther''. R tchrs a prob? 2 mny tchrs (she sez) thnk pupls 3dom of xpreSn shd nt b inhibtd.

B frank. Do u care? Wot if all eng bcame txt spk? AAMOF eng lits gd in txt spk. '2BON2BTITQ.' '2moro & 2moro & 2moro.' C? Shakesprs gr8 in txt! 2da he wd txt all hs wk. May b. Nethng is psble in txt spk.

2 tru. 13yr grl noes wots wot. I say 2 hr URA*! KUTGW! 10TD yr tcher wll b tching txt. I say 2 edu xperts, 4COL! Gt rl! Eng lang must b COl 2 b xitng. Eat y <3 out! @TEOTD ths is 24/7 wrld! IIN! 01CnStpTxtng. Hax shd tke hEd I no 10TD Gdn wll b in txt. JJ. John Mullan

Key terms

Hypertextuality: the phenomenon of a text that does not possess a single sequence that it is intended to be read in, and makes use of linkages to combine it with other texts, images or sounds.

Cataphoric: a reference that links a word or phrase to a word or phrase that is further 'forwards' in the text and yet to come, e.g. the way the pronoun 'It' links to the noun phrase 'my new bicycle' in the sentence 'It was the best ever, my new bicycle.'

Exophoric: a reference that links to something 'outside' of a text and not described or explained within it, e.g. the way that the noun phrase 'that article' is used in the sentence 'I have never read anything as biased as that article.'

Forum: an online message board, representing messages as linked to each other in threads.

Elision: the missing out of sounds or parts of words.

Abbreviation: a word shortened by removing a letter or clusters of letters.

Data response exercise 9

This article (left) appeared in *The Guardian* on 7 March 2003, as a reaction to the use of 'txt speak' by a student in a school assignment. Evaluate how the writer has used contemporary English features to discuss the topic of modern language use. You may find the terms **elision** and **abbreviation** useful.

Link

For an example of many of these orthographical and phonological variations, look at the example of Leet on page 49.

Data response exercise 10

The following extract is taken from a **liveblog** by Tim Jonze on *The Guardian* website, covering the 2013 Brit awards ceremony on 20 February 2013. Evaluate the way that language is used to serve different purposes and manage cohesion within the text.

9.24pm GMT — So now you know …

> **Boris Becker** ✔ @TheBorisBecke 🐦 Follow
>
> Cant stand Taylor Swift…
>
> 9:20 PM - 20 Feb 2013
>
> 551 RETWEETS 188 FAVORITES   ← ↻ ★

9.25pm GMT — **Best international group** … as presented by someone or other … oh, Dave Grohl … goes to … **the Black Keys!** And they can't even be arsed to do a video acceptance speech.

Updated at 9.27pm GMT

9.28pm GMT — Reading the posts below, it's hard to see how Mike Scott from the Waterboys could possibly have taken issue with the "intellectual depth and rigour" of my writing … still I guess you get bitter when you haven't written a good song since Dark Side of the Moon.

> **Mike Scott** ✔ @MickPuck   🐦 Follow
>
> Sometimes I'm blown away by the intellectual depth & rigour of rock journalism
>
> guardian.co.uk/music/2013/feb…
>
> 1:55 PM - 19 Feb 2013
>
> **Brit awards 2013: 10 things to expect**
> Tim Jonze: Watching the Brits on Wednesday night? From spurned lovers to flashy after-parties, here are 10 things to look out for …
>
> 🇬 The Guardian @guardian
>
> 3 RETWEETS   ← ↻ ★

Updated at 9.34pm GMT

9.31pm GMT — Muse had fireworks. Swift had dubstep. Robbie had a suit too blue for most standard issue retinas. Now it's Ben Howard and he's only gone and topped the lot by bringing a bloody guitar along #ThinkingOutsideTheBox

Updated at 9.33pm GMT

9.34pm GMT — People are emailing me saying that Mike Scott actually wrote The Whole of the Moon. I am officially retiring from Jokes until 2018.

Updated at 9.36pm GMT

Data response exercise 11

This screenshot shows part of an entry on the Geological Society of London's blog, posted on 8 March 2013. Evaluate the way that the writer has used the contemporary format of a blog to detail the use of mobile phone software in geological field trips.

Smart apps in the field

There are those who say the Earth sciences are the most visual science of all. Yet, whilst there are heavyweight visualisation software applications (ESRI's ArcGIS to name one) to aid professional geologists carry out their **office** tasks, there is little to aid geology students carrying out their **field** tasks – despite the fact that the same packages are 'offered' to students in their laboratories.

Student tasks in the field can be categorised into: capturing data, viewing data and analysing data. For each of these tasks, there's an app.

◼ Capturing data: As of 6 February 2013, a search in Google Play app store returns 25 results for 'strike and dip'. The top two apps are Rocklogger and GeoClino.

◼ Viewing data: We've had applications for this since the age of PDAs (Personal Digital Assistants). Again, if we search Google Play we get over 96 results for the same date when querying 'geological maps'. The top two are RockLogger and BGS iGeology – ignoring WolphramAlpha, which is not free and not a specialist geology application. It should also be noted that RockLogger's main purpose is not data viewing.

Tags

Aberdeen activities AGI Anniversary Antarctic art BGS British Science Association British Science Festival Captain Scott christmas climate change communication Darwin earth science week education energy environment eruption etna expedition explorers filming fossils geography geology geoscientist hazards history Ice islands krakatoa maps Mars media mining outreach palaeontology penguins pioneer productions Poetry stromboli technology volcanoes water

Follow Blog via Email

Enter your email address to follow this blog and receive notifications of new posts by email.

Sign me up!

Twitter Updates

◼ RT @MelJLeng: Nice review by Bryan Lovell of @geolsoc on "The Serpent's Promise:The Bible Retold as Science" by Steve Jones http://t.co/uq... 4 hours ago

◼ Because good weather can't last: Rite in the Rain notebooks on sale in the Burlington House Bookshop and online! bit.ly/ZMFl3H 5 hours ago

◼ RT @RosalieTostevin: Still

Topic revision exercise

1 How has modern popular culture influenced the English language in recent times?

2 What distinctive non-standard features are used in the mobile phone SMS 'text' language?

3 How have new internet-based texts, with features like hyperlinks, altered the nature of written texts?

Further reading

Use the OED Online's 'Previous updates' page (http://public.oed.com/the-oed-today/recent-updates-to-the-oed/previous-updates/) to browse back through the words that have entered the English dictionary over recent years. Use John Simpson's 'commentary' pieces for an overview of the trends for that quarter.

The Macmillan Dictionary offers something similar on its 'BuzzWord' pages (produced by Kerry Maxwell). Start with the list of archived words (http://www.macmillandictionary.com/buzzword/AtoZ.html), and also follow the links to essays reviewing the new words entered in 2011 and 2010.

Attitudes towards language change

In this topic you will:

- learn about some of the major debates about change in the English language

- engage with a variety of attitudes towards the English language.

Debates surrounding language change

When you discuss language change features in the exam, it is important to link them to the attitudes towards language change that form part of the debate. This is particularly useful in Section B of the exam where you will need to evaluate these attitudes in the texts you are presented with, and engage with the debate yourself.

Starter activity

What is your attitude towards the English language? Score your reaction to the statements below: 1 if you strongly disagree, through to 4 if you strongly agree with each one. See how high your score is and try it out with some other people. A low score suggests you might have more of a prescriptivist attitude towards some aspects of language while a high score suggests a more descriptivist view; you will find out about these concepts in this topic.

- I like different accents and they don't put me off people when I hear them.
- Sometimes I play around with language for fun or to make it fit how I want to use it.
- Different groups of people should be allowed to develop their own ways of communicating.
- I think it is fine if English changes all the time, and that it will be very different in 100 years.
- I am interested in different varieties of speech and writing and like to find out about them.

Prescriptivism and descriptivism

The concepts of prescriptivism and descriptivism have been briefly explained earlier in this unit, and they represent useful extremes of attitudes towards change. We have seen how the Early Modern English period saw the rise of individuals who decided to impose rules upon the English language, to try to shape and standardise its usage, particularly in terms of spelling and grammatical construction. Their 'prescriptivist' model came largely from the example of classical languages. Prescriptivism, however, is a wider concept than this, and you should use it to refer to any form of attitude towards language that seeks to:

- restrict variation
- control future changes
- impose standardised rules
- reject existing non-standard forms
- view non-standard varieties as inferior.

It would be a mistake to see prescriptivism as entirely negative. It has practical benefits for the language: for example, it provides a central Standard English form that helps English users from across the world to learn the language and communicate reliably. Nonetheless, prescriptivist attitudes have sometimes been criticised for placing too much emphasis on technical aspects of the language, and even discriminating against users of non-standard forms.

Study tip

Be prepared to write about the models of both prescriptivism and descriptivism. Avoid the temptation to treat one as 'right' and one as 'wrong', but instead evaluate them yourself in the context of the text or idea that you are discussing.

Descriptivism approaches language differently, and you should be able to identify its arguments in examples of use that you encounter. Key features of a descriptivist attitude include aiming to:

- describe forms of variation
- present varieties without preference
- record change as it happens
- avoid interference with change and variation
- understand use in context.

Again, it is important that you use these features to debate language use, and descriptivist models are at the heart of much of the research by linguists mentioned in the What is language variation? topic of this unit. Remember, though, that some descriptivist attitudes have received valid criticism: for example, the standard form of the language can be negatively affected by the use of non-standard varieties in written publications, school or the workplace.

🔍 Political correctness

'Political correctness' (PC) is a term that describes an approach that seeks to reduce and remove the offence caused to particular individuals or groups through prejudice and discrimination. You have already encountered the PC debate in your Unit 2 work at AS Level and you know that language can play a large part in causing offence and reinforcing inequality. Political correctness is now an undoubted influence within the field of language change, and encapsulates a particular attitude towards language use.

Although it had occasionally appeared in the preceding two centuries or so, the modern usage of the phrase 'politically correct' emerged in 1970s America and shared ground with the feminist movement of the time, making gender representation its main focus. The profile of PC grew, and its influence spread to the UK. By the early 1990s, it was being used as a general tool for rendering language 'neutral', involving not only gender but issues of representation in many social groupings.

PC was heavily satirised and by the late 1990s the term had lost much of its credibility, undermined by **mock-PC** terms like 'vertically challenged' for 'short'. Table 3 shows examples of words that were attached to the PC debate at that time.

> **Classroom activity 7**
>
> Now apply these two attitudes to some of the more familiar examples of non-standard English usage given below. Describe the view that each would be likely to take on the example of language use given.
>
> - Using 'txt' spellings such as 'gr8' (great), or 'c u ltr' (see you later).
> - Using 'Americanisms' such as spellings like 'color' (colour), or words like 'pants' (trousers).
> - Blending languages to form new varieties like London Jamaican and MLE (explored on pages 54–6).

> **Key terms**
>
> **Mock-PC:** satirised examples of politically correct terms designed to make fun of and discredit more genuine forms of PC.

Table 3

PC term	Original term	Comments
chairperson	chairman	Designed to remove part of the '**generic masculine**' problem in English, where the suffix 'man' is used to refer to all people in that position but, semantically, excludes the female gender
Ms	Miss/Mrs	An alternative title for women, to redress the imbalance of this system which indicates female marital status but not male
herstory	history	An extreme example in the eyes of many but put forward as a form of positive discrimination by some feminists to counter the appearance of the male pronoun 'his' and the symbolic interpretation of the patriarchy of 'his-story'
hearing impaired	deaf	A phrase suggested in response to negative connotations that had become associated with wider uses of the word 'deaf'
to vocationally relocate	to sack/to fire	An example of one of the many satirical, spoof PC terms coined

Key terms

Generic masculine: the practice of using masculine forms of English to refer to all people.

Gender-marked: a word or phrase that has been modified to show the specific gender it refers to.

Extension activity

Carry out some research into some of the classic works around sexism in language, for example:

- Muriel Schulz's 'The Semantic Derogation of Women' in Thorne and Henley's *Language and Sex: Difference and Dominance* (1975)
- Dale Spender's *Man Made Language* (1980)
- Dwight Bolinger's *Language, the Loaded Weapon: The Use and Abuse of Language Today* (1980).

Use what you have found out about them in a group discussion based on the question 'Is the English language sexist?'

Fig. 11 *Political correctness has become muddied by satire and mock-PC terms*

Wider grammatical structures of the language came under fire from supporters of PC. For example, the absence of a non-**gender-marked**, third-person singular pronoun results in the masculine form being used as the default to refer to an individual of unspecified gender, as in 'Every student must bring a pen to his examination'. Kate Swift and Casey Miller suggested new pronouns to tackle this problem – to become third-person singular gender-neutral pronouns which refer to both and either gender: 'tey', 'ter' and 'tem'. This proposal effectively took the structure of the existing gender-neutral plural form 'they', 'their' and 'them', and modified it. 'Tey', 'ter' and 'tem' have not caught on, but it is interesting to note the increasingly common and grammatically incorrect use of the plural forms in singular positions, as in 'Every student must bring a pen to their examination.'

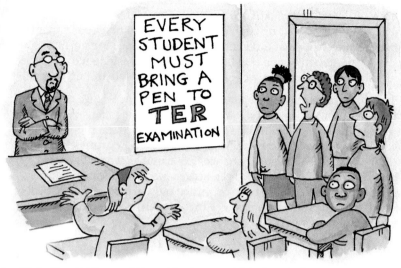

Fig. 12 *Swift and Miller sought to tackle a long-established gender bias*

As an expression of an attitude towards language, PC is the aspiration to remove negative, offensive connotations from language use. The backlash towards PC represents a fear of the loss of freedom of expression in language. Other critics of PC have pointed to the danger of making the language unwieldy by creating much longer PC substitutions for terms deemed 'politically incorrect' (e.g. the two-word, six-syllable 'visually impaired' for 'blind'), or of 'criminalising' certain words.

■ Colloquial language and pronunciation

The use of colloquial language and some non-standard pronunciation forms provokes strong opinion, and there are many long-standing, colloquial register features that most of us will have been 'corrected' for in the past (e.g. saying 'ain't', dropping 't's, referring to a 'bloke').

In 2005, the UK children's television channel CBBC was criticised for a programme *Dick and Dom in Da Bungalow*. It made use of colloquial, non-standard items like 'ain't', non-standard grammatical constructions like 'you was', pronunciation forms that included abbreviated elisions like 'd'ya', and non-standard, regional patterns like /faverit/, which mimics the shortened vowel sounds of northern English accents. Specifically, the show was criticised for having a negative effect on children's literacy, by making it difficult for them to spell words not pronounced clearly or that had been contracted in this way.

While there is certainly a valid debate to be had about the relationship between spelling patterns and phonetic patterns, it is important for you to consider the relationship linguistically. For example, English has a wide range of spelling patterns, both regular and irregular, formed largely by the variety of influences on the language charted earlier in this unit. Consider the following words, and the relationship between orthography and pronunciation: 'cough', 'bough', 'though', and 'through'. It is perhaps difficult, in a language with so many irregular patterns, to find a standard form of **grapheme–phoneme correspondence** that represents phonetic patterns and spellings in a standard way – let alone to impose it.

■ Key terms

Grapheme–phoneme correspondence: the relationship between letters and sounds in words and, consequently, the way we write them and say them.

■ Link

For more information on the status and prestige of different forms of English language, see pages 4 and 41.

Key terms

Great Vowel Shift: a general change to the pronunciation of a range of vowel sounds in English that took place between the 13th and 16th centuries. The vowels involved were generally more fronted or raised in the way they were pronounced, to become the vowels that we are using today.

Language around you 2

Investigate the attitudes people have towards colloquial language use. List 20 examples of language use that people define as 'rude', 'impolite' or 'slang', and rate them in terms of offensiveness from 1 (mildly impolite and the least offensive) to 20 (the most offensive).

In this light, strong opinions about pronunciation are perhaps mostly expressing an attitude towards the status and prestige of different forms of the language (explored in detail later in this unit). We have already seen how the English language has quite different dominant pronunciation forms at different times. They change considerably without necessarily impairing literacy rates or damaging the coherence of English (e.g. the **Great Vowel Shift** in the Early Modern English period).

These language forms are defined in dictionaries in a range of ways, from 'informal' to 'colloquial', 'vulgar', 'coarse' and 'offensive' through to 'swearing'. These definitions can themselves be seen to represent different attitudes towards language, and reveal how attitudes towards the acceptability of language change. For example, words like 'crap' or 'bloody' would once not have been acceptable in broadcast media at all; then they would have been permitted only in certain 'watershed' or controlled situations; whereas now they are fairly widespread, with some few remaining restrictions.

Progress or decay?

The debate about whether the ongoing process of change in the English language is one of progress or decay is often an extension of the argument between prescriptivists and descriptivists. In her appearance at the BBC Reith Lectures in 1996, linguist Jean Aitchison suggested three models for the, often prescriptivist, view that language is in decay. In the following text from the lecture, it is important to note that Aitchison herself does not take the view of the three metaphors given, but offers them as a critique of common 'decay' attitudes.

> Above all, three overlapping accusations recur, which can be called the "damp spoon" syndrome, the "crumbling castle" view, and the "infectious disease" assumption. The "damp spoon" image comes from a newspaper writer, who has a "queasy distaste" for the "vulgarity" of some current usages, "precisely the kind of distaste I feel at seeing a damp spoon dipped in the sugar bowl or butter spread with the bread-knife". She implies that sloppiness and laziness cause much of language change …
>
> But let's move on to the "crumbling castle" view. This treats the English language as a beautiful old building with gargoyles and pinnacles which need to be preserved intact, as implied in statements by the writer John Simon: Language, he argues, should be treated like "parks, national forests, monuments, and public utilities … available for properly respectful use but not for defacement or destruction". This view itself crumbles when examined carefully. It implies that the castle of English was gradually and lovingly assembled until it reached a point of maximum splendour at some unspecified time in the past. Yet no year can be found when language achieved some peak of perfection, like a vintage wine. Nor have those who claim that English is declining ever suggested what this date might have been …
>
> But let's move on to the "infectious disease" view. In an article entitled Polluting Our Language, the writer expressed a widespread view that we somehow "catch" changes from those around us, and that we ought to fight such diseases: "The wholesale spread of corruption may surely be ascribed to mere infection, to the careless, unthinking assimilation of the floating germs which envelop us." Change is indeed brought about through social

contact, so the catching notion is not entirely wrong. But the "disease" metaphor falls down. People pick up changes because they want to. They want to fit in with social groups, and they adapt their hairstyle, clothes, and language, to those of people they admire …

J. Aitchison, The Language Web: The Power and Problem of Words: The 1996 BBC Reith Lectures, *1996*

To translate Aitchison's three metaphors for prescriptivist attitudes towards the way that language changes: 'the damp spoon' implies laziness in language use; 'the crumbling castle' suggests an elitist approach to preserving forms like Standard English and **Received Pronunciation (RP)**; and 'the infectious disease' sees non-standard speakers of English as 'catching' from others an unhealthy, inferior form that we should all steer clear of.

■ Key terms

Received Pronunciation (RP): the prestige form of English pronunciation, sometimes considered as the 'accent' of Standard English.

■ Extension activity

Think about how specific examples of change, like those discussed in this topic, would be viewed from the perspective of Aitchison's three metaphors. The table below includes an example of each.

Start by copying the table and slotting examples A, B and C into their appropriate column, and then try to think of some more examples yourself.

A: using contractions in written language considered lazy

B: language contact: for example Americanisms entering British usage seen as an unhealthy influence

C: the use of 'inkhorn' terms in Early Modern English seen as corrupting the purity of the language.

'the damp spoon'	'the crumbling castle'	'the infectious disease'
liaison and elision in pronunciation of words as an example of sloppy pronunciation	using conjunctions to begin a sentence seen as grammatically incorrect	'txt' speak use of non-alphabetic characters seen as a degrading influence

Adopting the view that the English language is not decaying is perhaps a less easy standpoint. You can either take the 'neutral' attitude that language does change with society but that this is a form of neither progress nor decay, or you can suggest that language is evolving into a better form over time, and progressing. These attitudes are often aligned with a descriptivist view – and both see the process of language change positively, in the sense that it in some way changes to meet the needs of society over time.

 Topic revision exercise

1 What are the main features of the prescriptivist and descriptivist attitudes towards language?

2 What problems in the English language has the PC movement become connected with?

3 What do Aitchison's three metaphors for language change describe?

■ Further reading

Search for Stephen Pinker's article 'False Fronts in the Language Wars' on his webpage (http://www.slate.com/authors.steven_pinker.html) for an alternative view of the descriptivist-prescriptivist debate.

An extract from Robert Lane Greene's *You Are What You Speak* is also available online (http://www.visualthesaurus.com/cm/dogeared/a-brief-history-of-sticklers/), with some further discussion on the idea of 'declinism' that he raises, from Nancy Friedman (http://nancyfriedman.typepad.com/away_with_words/2011/04/word-of-the-week-declinism.html).

Language change theory

In this topic you will:

- learn about some of the main theories that have been developed in the study of language change

- evaluate language change theories and begin to shape your own ideas about language change.

Starter activity

Time for something of a 'chicken and egg' debate. Discuss with other students which comes first – thought or language. It can become quite a circular argument, but it will help you think about some of the issues of how and why language changes. For example:

- Do children 'think' of things before they use language to define them, or do they need language to develop their thought?

- Does the language you use reflect your attitudes, or have your attitudes been shaped by the language you are exposed to?

Linguistic determinism and reflectionism

In the first half of the 20th century, Edward Sapir and Benjamin Lee Whorf put forward the Sapir–Whorf Hypothesis (SWH), which has remained an influential theory, and summed up the concept of linguistic determinism. Sapir and Whorf each studied Native American languages, but the principles of determinism have been applied to many languages – not least English! The main principle of the SWH is that language precedes thought and controls it – in this pure form, known as the 'strong version', human thought is only possible through language; that is, we can only think things which we have the language to articulate.

This strong version has been criticised as too rigid, and seems to negate the possibility of language change at all, as it would be impossible to coin or invent the many new words and language forms that we see emerging all of the time in English. The 'weak version' of the SWH theory has been put forward as more usable: that revises the force of 'determinism' and suggests that language can only influence thought but does not have complete control over it.

Some linguists have tackled the problem of the relationship between language and thought from the other way around: in linguistic reflectionism, language is shaped by our thoughts and is simply a result of the way that we are and think. This reflectionist argument has been criticised for dismissing the value of trying to shape or change language: for example, to prevent the use of racist language, as it supposes that the racism is a reflection of the way people think and will only re-emerge in the newly changed forms.

Lexical gaps

The theory of lexical gaps provides a way of seeing likely paths that language change may take in the future. The 'gaps' referred to are words and usages that are not currently used in English, but that fit the existing linguistic patterns well. For example, the words 'pap', 'pip', 'pop' and 'pup' each had at least one meaning going into the 20th century – but the word 'pep' did not, even though its phonological structure would make perfect sense to an English speaker. It could easily be used as either a noun or a verb in the same ways that the other four are: it would fit the inflection rules of finite verbs or plurality, for example. It made some sense then when the word 'pep' appeared in the 20th century, in US usage at first, as an abbreviation of 'pepper', to refer to energy or high spirits.

Study tip

In your own assessment of language, it is sensible to view the influence of language and thought as interdependent, with elements of determinism and reflectionism both in evidence.

Link

For more on Leet, see page 49.

Alternative forms of existing words can be generated by 'filling' these lexical gaps by using **derivational morphology**. The following abstract nouns each have a verb counterpart that is formed without the *-ion* suffix: transgression (transgress); impression (impress); confession (confess). The words aggression and compassion are similarly constructed, but do not have an equivalent verb form of aggress or compass – again, suggesting a logical gap in the language that could well result in those words coming into existence. An example of this is the use of *-age* as a suffix to create a noun from a verb stem (as in 'breakage' from 'break') in the sociolectal form Leet and in modern colloquial forms, which may coin words like 'eatage' for food.

A third way in which the phenomenon of lexical gaps operates is in converting an existing word. In modern usage, a version of this process has been dubbed 'verbing' (itself an example of conversion or verbing!), where verb forms are created from existing nouns, often in the field of technology, to fill the need for a word that denotes using that particular technological item. In this way, the verb (to) 'text' came about, as well as other examples like (to) 'DVD' or (to) 'click', from the noun of the sound a computer mouse makes.

Random fluctuation and cultural transmission

The anthropologist and linguist Charles Hockett put forward a theory in 1958 that laid stress on the significance of random error and events within the language system. In this model, language changes owing to its instability. Rather than their being particularly an example of 'progress' or 'decay', as discussed in the Jean Aitchison material, the theory of random fluctuation sees the changes that occur in language as responses to the ever-changing context of language use and its users. These contextual factors themselves may well be understood as more or less random occurrences (a period of years of unseasonably warm weather, for example), and the linguistic changes that follow (for example, newly coined words and idiom), although fitting, are random successes from a range of plausible responses: for example, another language and group of users may well deal effectively with a similar change in a different way. A classic recent example has been the creation of the word 'book' as a synonym for 'cool', due to the fact that typing in C O O L in the predictive text feature of some mobile phones brought the word 'book' up instead as the first option – a pretty random way of acquiring a new word!

Substratum theory

This theory focuses on the influence of different forms of language that come into contact with English, through speakers of other languages or English dialects.

As a concept of change, substratum emphasises the way that words, meaning, structures, written forms, or sound may change the shape of the English language over time. Many of the examples charted so far can be seen to have changed English in this way: the influence from the languages of the various forces that invaded Britain throughout the Old English period; or the words borrowed from foreign countries in the later Modern English periods when it became the invader, during colonial expansion.

An example from English usage in the USA, researched by the linguist William Labov, noticed the ways that the Jewish community in New York, who were speakers of Yiddish, altered the pronunciation patterns of words when they **hypercorrected** their use of English. The word 'door'

Fig. 13 Jewish immigrants settled in New York and brought Yiddish into contact with American English there

became /do-er/, and 'coffee' /caw-fee/, which are recognisable features of the distinctive New York accent today.

Classroom activity 8

List and briefly discuss a range of situations where contact between different language forms might take place.

Functional theory

The central concept of functional theory can be identified in many other, more specific theoretical models put forward by linguists: that is, that language changes according to the needs of its users. Evidence of this is most readily seen in the way that the English lexicon digests words, on what seems like a daily basis.

Words become obsolete and so drop out of usage and, in time, of existence – the changing worlds of technology and industry reveal this keenly: terms from the age of sailing ships like 'oakum' (fibre from old rope) have all but gone, but even 20th-century words like 'vinyl', 'LP', 'cassette' and '12 inch' are on the wane as music technology advances. Even in recent times, failed inventions or formats can have this effect, for example 'Betamax' as a video cassette format from the late-20th century – and perhaps even 'floppy disk' is slipping out of usage.

Conversely, huge numbers of words enter the language to fulfil the needs of its users. In technology, the words described above are replaced by 'MP3', 'DVD' or 'flash drive' and 'USB'. Colloquial usage, and the slang of individual groups, also coins and discards words at a rapid rate, to fulfil the need for identity and expression among users – and it can even recycle itself, with words that have fallen out of use being brought back into circulation.

These examples are primarily lexical, but functional change can shape all dimensions of the language. Consider the pronunciation difference between 'witch' and 'which' emphasised by some speakers, using an **aspirated** initial /hw/ to fulfil the need to distinguish between these otherwise **homophonic** words. Grammatically, unnaturally complex constructions are often used to fulfil the need for distinctions of politeness, as in 'I'm sorry to be a pain, but would you mind if I asked you to close the door, please?'

Key terms

Aspirated: pronouncing a word with the 'h' sound added to it, to create a 'breathy' sound.

Homophone: a word which sounds the same as another word or words.

Study tip

Prepare material on specific language change theories for the exam, including the names of linguists and key terms. You should aim to bring these into your essay, linking them to features of the texts you analyse.

Wave and S-curve models

In the 20th century, linguists increasingly began to view language change as a highly organic process. That is to say that linguists became much clearer about the fact that, when a particular variation of the language occurred (for example, a historical change like the Great Vowel Shift), it was not simply 'switched on' across a wide body of language users, who then proceeded to use that form from then on in their speech. Instead, change happened gradually, and the S-curve and wave models tried to explain the way in which this took place.

Chen (1968 and 1972) put forward the assertion that change entering the language would be taken up by its users at a certain rate. At first, the effects would be minimal – in the instance of a phonological change, only a few words would be affected. The change would then accelerate, expanding the majority of matching pronunciation patterns in a user's language. Finally, the pace of change would slow as the few remaining vocabulary items unaffected would be converted to the change over time. The result is that the pace of change, measured in a chart that maps vocabulary against time, would be shown as a roughly S-shaped curve – as shown in Figure 14.

Other linguists developed this concept of the way in which a change is adopted by the users of a language. Bailey (1973) explored the impact of geographical distance and social strata on language change. Figure 15 illustrates his 'wave theory', that a language change beginning at the point marked X would move across a particular geographical region, and across different social groups. As it did so, its effects would become weaker and less pronounced, to the point where the variation would be hardly distinguishable. The effect of this would be that the further away a person was, both socially and/or geographically, from the origin of a particular change, the less impact it would have on his or her language use. This is evident in the way that examples of change cited in this topic have occurred but is also useful to understand the way that language variations occur, which is explored in the next topic.

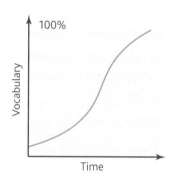

Diagram taken from Crystal text in AQA ENA 6, June 2004

Fig. 14 *S-curve model*

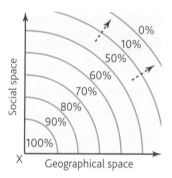

Diagram taken from Crystal text in AQA ENA6, June 2004

Fig. 15 *Wave model*

Topic revision exercise

1. What are the determinist and reflectionist theories of the relationship between language and thought?

2. How does functional theory explain the way that language changes?

3. What does the S-curve theory explain about the way that changes take place within the language?

Further reading

Scope, the cerebral palsy charity, changed its name from 'The Spastics Society' in 1994. Search the 'Publications' section (under 'Help and information') of their website, www.scope.org.uk, for 'name change' and you will find a booklet explaining the context for the decision: an interesting case study for linguistic determinism and other change concepts.

What is language variation?

In this topic you will:

■ learn about the relationship between Standard and non-standard English

■ consider some of the major causes of language variation

■ find out about how a language variety is formed and maintained.

Key terms

Sociolect: the language variety used by people with a shared social background.

The range of variation in a language represents all of the different ways in which its users have modified it to fit their particular needs, preferences or identity. A language variety, then, retains an identifiable core of the standard language to mark it out as a part of it, rather than a different, separate language. These varieties are called dialects and **sociolects**, and understanding and identifying the possible forms these take in English are the main focus for this part of the unit.

Causes of variation

Variation in English is generated by the way in which social groups are formed by shared experience or community. This can be a very physical process, like living within the same, contained geographical region, or working in the same environment; or quite an abstract one, like enjoying similar cultural interests, or specialising in a particular field of learning. These ways of creating and maintaining a language variety can be understood in terms of Jean Lave and Etienne Wenger's 1991 theory of 'communities of practice'. This theory suggests that participating with others in using a language variety is central to learning and strengthening it.

Starter activity

An individual's particular style of speaking is known as an 'idiolect'. Begin your thinking about language variation by focusing on your own idiolect. Make a mind map with yourself in the middle. Build it out, noting the different varieties of English you hear around you and the people who use them. Then add in other influences, such as interests you have, the sport you play or the music you listen to. An example of a simple mind map is shown below.

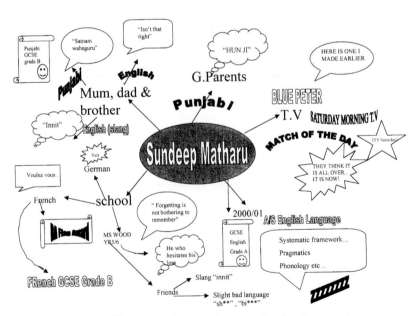

Fig. 16 *A mind map of language influences shows the diversity of a person's exposure to different linguistic varieties*

Social influences on language

The following social factors influence the way we use language.

■ **Age**: Different age groups have been exposed to entirely different trends in language during their lifetime, and an age group's language may well vary compared with the language of people much older or younger than them; people may share particular varieties of English with people of a similar age to them. Colloquial youth language is a particularly vivid example of this.

■ **Sexuality**: Different sexualities are often strongly linked to a person's sense of identity and this can cause particular social groups to form their own distinct variety of language to express this. An example of this is Polari, used by some members of the male homosexual community in the mid-20th century.

■ **Gender**: Like sexuality, gender is closely linked to shared identity and behaviour. The particular ways that men and women have been found to use language have been the subject of much research, like Deborah Tannen's theories of male 'report' and female 'rapport' language.

■ **Social class**: In Britain, social class is a particularly strong determinant of identity and social groups, and the way people speak has long been one of the prime factors people have used in discriminating between the upper, middle and lower classes. RP is an example of an extreme prestige form of 'upper class accent'.

■ **Ethnicity**: Britain has always been strongly influenced by cultures and languages from other parts of the world. The intermingling of people with different cultural, linguistic and ethnic backgrounds has produced the ideal conditions for the processes associated with **creolisation**, which in turn leads to the creation of new language varieties. A modern example would be London Jamaican, researched by Mark Sebba and others in the late 20th century.

■ **Deviance**: Illegal or anti-social practices often bring groups of people together, with an explicit need to use language to support their activities and forge a form of covert prestige. Examples of this might be the language associated with drugs, or archaic **argots** like Thieves' Cant, or the origins of Cockney rhyming slang.

■ **Occupation**: The job that a person does can often be one of the more formative influences on their identity, social environment, and their individual interests. Occupational dialects emerge to support the jargon and identity of a particular profession, for example, the language used in the courts and the legal services.

■ **Region**: Regional accents are perhaps traditionally one of the most dominant forms of variation in Britain. They are formed by the shared pronunciation patterns of a particular part of Britain. There are a great many examples, but strong regional accents that are still prominent in modern Britain are Brummie, Scouse, and Scottish, although local users would be likely to recognise even finer subdivisions of variation within their area.

■ **Hobbies**: People's social lives can become defined by the cultural interests or specialisms that they like to be associated with and involved in. This can range right across countless areas, such as sports, music genres, crafts, scientific interests, engineering, and often sociolects spring up to support these. An example would be the computer-hacker-originated form, Leet, or the sociolect developed by joining in with an online gaming project.

Link

For more information on these influences, see pages 42–62.

Key terms

Creolisation: the creation of a new language variety by language contact and new speakers growing up using it.

Argot: the particular jargon or slang-based language variety used by a social group.

Link

For more information on Leet, see page 49.

Fig. 17 *Many professions rely on a distinctive blend of occupational slang and technical jargon*

Classroom activity 9

Think of a word or phrase of language variation related to each of the influences listed on page 39, and write a note on their usage or origin. Set them out in a table like the one below. Compare and discuss your notes with other students.

Aspect of social variation	Examples of language and their usage or origin
Age	The terms 'emo', 'townie' and 'goth' are almost exclusively used by teenagers and youths.
Sexuality	
Gender	

Forms of variation

There are six main forms of language variation.

- **Phonological**: differences in pronunciation patterns, often focused upon particular **phonemes**, for example the use of the **glottal stop** as a replacement for the /t/ sound

- **Lexical**: alternative and additional words within a particular variety, for example the word 'mush' as a colloquial word for 'friend' in some Southern regional dialects

- **Semantic**: changes of meaning to established Standard English words, for example 'weed' or 'stoned' within the sociolect surrounding the drug culture in the UK

- **Grammatical**: the use of unusual syntax patterns or using rules of grammar different to Standard English, for example the use of double or multiple negation in many dialect and sociolect forms

- **Orthographical**: although the variants in this topic are predominantly spoken varieties, some forms may make explicit use of the written mode to represent their variation – for example, the use of a wider range of orthographic characters in a sociolect like Leet.

- **Pragmatic**: reflects social meaning and usage, including variation in the way politeness, humour and conversation are managed through language.

Some dialect forms are long established and their roots pre-date any real notion of Standard English, or conscious variation from it. The established regional forms throughout Britain are examples of this, where their phonological, lexical and semantic differences in particular can in many cases be attributed to the long histories of speakers of that region, going far back to the social and historical context of the Old English era, described in the How does language change? topic.

Other dialects, particularly more recent sociolect forms, can be based on an existing form. Some creole forms caused by users being a part of bilingual or multilingual communities exhibit this, particularly in large cities like London, Birmingham, Bristol and Manchester. The emerging variety of multi-ethnic youth dialect (MEYD) explored later, is an example of this, where English is the main source of the vocabulary of the language (its **lexifier**) and provides its predominant grammatical structure, with additional variants from the creole language.

Key terms

Phoneme: the smallest unit of sound in a language.

Glottal stop: a sound produced by stopping the flow of air in the throat, often used in place of the consonant /t/.

Lexifier: the language that provides the majority of words and structural elements in a dialect created by combining two or more language varieties.

Study tip

When you study different varieties of English, try to build a 'rounded' view of their features, including several framework areas. For example, consider phonological accent features but also look at the wider associated dialect features of non-standard lexis and grammar.

Link

For more information on multi-ethnic youth dialect, see page 55.

Non-standard English

The 'variation' part of the varieties of English not only implies the range of different forms of the language but also how they tend to be measured – by their variation from Standard English. As such, the forms of English in this section, and those you will discuss in your exam, are all 'non-standard' in some way, by this definition. It is important to consider how to study non-standard English before getting into the detail of particular varieties. As the prescriptivist/descriptivist debate in the language change section showed, there are, perhaps, two main attitudes with which to approach language. In studying language variety, it is best to adopt a descriptivist perspective when you encounter new forms of variation – at least until you understand a variety well enough to form any valid judgements about it. In short, non-standard does not mean 'wrong' or 'inferior' because it differs from Standard English. In fact, when you investigate non-standard features, you are more than likely to discover that they have developed to deal efficiently and successfully with a particular sociolinguistic challenge faced by the users of that form.

The linguists whose work is briefly discussed in this section – Peter Trudgill, David Crystal and Mark Sebba, for example – are predominantly descriptivist in their attitude towards language, which is precisely what has allowed them to investigate and understand variation: you would be well advised to follow the same path. Indeed, Crystal, in his 2004 book *The Stories of English*, suggested that linguistics is moving away from the established 'prescriptive era' and called for 'a new intellectual sociolinguistic climate' to match this.

Prestige

The other way of measuring the nature of a particular variety is to consider the status that it holds within society. The American linguist William Labov developed the idea of prestige and put forward the concepts of **overt prestige** and **covert prestige**. These distinguish between the standard prestige form accepted and promoted by society (like that ascribed to Standard English, for example), and language forms that acquire prestige precisely because they were different to those accepted values – covert prestige. In this model, a general English dialect form like Scots English may be seen to have an overt prestige, related to the mainstream national identity of Scotland and Britain. Dialect forms that are attached to deviant activities or groups may well acquire a covert prestige among users.

In his research into the different pronunciations in New York City in the 1960s, Labov focused on particular **linguistic variables** – in this case, the specific phonemes used to produce a particular sound. He identified the way that particular forms seemed to be attached to socio-economic class. For example, in pronouncing the /th/ sound in 'thirty-third street', the most affluent New Yorkers would pronounce this /th/, while the least affluent would use a /t/ form. Even more interesting was the way in which he observed a continuum whereby users at different points between these two social-economic class extremes, would produce a sound somewhere between the two – a kind of blend between /t-th/. Labov's methods were successful and many similar types of investigation have been carried out, including studies in Britain, discussed later in this section.

Key terms

Overt prestige: a form of status valued and shared by mainstream society and culture.

Covert prestige: a form of status shared by minority groups in society, usually with alternative or opposing values to mainstream society.

Linguistic variable: a specific language feature that linguists test or observe in use to see how it varies between different people or contexts.

Link

For information on Malcolm Petyt and social climbing in Bradford, West Yorkshire as well as information on Peter Trudgill and vernacular in different registers in Norwich, see pages 50–2.

Topic revision exercise

1 List three of the main areas of variation described and an example of a language variety influenced by each one.

2 What is meant by non-standard language?

3 Describe the main details of Labov's concepts of overt and covert prestige.

Further reading

Read 'How we study language variation' on The Open University website (http://www.open.edu/openlearn/) for another perspective on the main areas of language variation.

Social variation

In this topic you will:

- learn about the main areas of social variation and the ways they are represented in the English language

- encounter and evaluate the findings of research into social varieties.

Starter activity

Before reading the language and gender theory that opens this topic, draw up a table with the headings 'male speech' and 'female speech'. List on each side as many stereotypes for the way the sexes speak that you can think of. These could be characteristics that you have observed in men and women, or just well-worn clichés. When you have your list, see how many of the features are borne out by particular researchers – and which are contradicted.

Key terms

Stereotype: an often widely held view in society about the nature or behaviour of a particular group or type of person. The word is derived from an 18th-century word from the development of printing: a kind of plate used to make duplicate copies of text.

Minimal response: a single word, very short phrase or non-verbal filler used in response.

Variation in the way that English is used occurs right across the spectrum of society. In addition to linguistic variables, researchers focus on studying the impact of key social variables, like gender, age or ethnicity. It can be difficult to isolate a single social aspect: in the case of gender, for example, it might be easy to state whether people are males or females, but how can you be sure that another factor, like social class, is not influencing their language use just as much?

Research into social variation

What follows are details of differences and a range of studies carried out by researchers in recent decades, broken down into the main social variations. Although most of the studies mainly focus on one particular social variable, be aware that they may well reveal something about the language use of another social group. Some of the examples given represent a clear example of a fairly defined sociolect form, with a relatively closed group of users, like an occupational dialect, for example. Some of the research presents findings about variation more widely evident in the language commonly used by major cross-sections of society, like the divisions of socio-economic class in Britain.

Gender

There has been a great deal of research into the way gender affects language variation. You may well believe that women speak more than men in interaction, and researchers have found this to be a common **stereotype** that people hold. Researchers have also found that this is largely a stereotype only. For example, some findings – including those of Pamela Fishman, and Dale Spender in the late 1970s – have suggested that men talk for approximately twice as long as women in mixed-sex conversations.

Pamela Fishman and the 'division of labour in conversations'

Pamela Fishman looked specifically into the way in which men and women interacted, in research stretching across the 1970s through to the 1990s. Her conclusion was that the way in which men and women contributed to conversation varied – and that women tended to 'work hardest' to help enable a conversation to take place. She analysed several hours of the conversation of three white, American, middle-class heterosexual couples and categorised the variation between men and women across four main features of interaction including **minimal responses** (Table 4).

Table 4

	Women	Men
Questions	Asked three times the number of questions asked by men	Asked one-third of the number of questions asked by women
Minimal responses	Used supportive minimal noises to show interest	Delayed giving or didn't give minimal responses
Attention-getters	Used phrases like 'D'ya know what?' to gain husband's attention	Made little or no use of attention-getters
Topic initiation	Topics initiated by the women were not always taken up in the conversation	Topics initiated by the men were always successful, and were supported by the women

The conclusions drawn from this were that women became drawn into lower-status work in the conversation, sustaining and encouraging the men's utterances and topics. In turn, women's topics were not always taken up and were not encouraged by men. Fishman saw her findings in these husband–wife interactions as reflective of a wider dominance model of society.

> Louise Kessler and the descriptive language of university students: Kessler set an equal number of both male and female art history students and physics students a task that involved producing description from photographic stimulus. She found that, although the art students provided the longer descriptions, it was the males in both subjects who used more words than the females on average. In addition, the male students used the most colour terms overall, although there were differences in male and female usage: more adverb modification of adjectives from males (e.g. 'unusually green') and more evaluative adjectives from females (e.g. 'beautiful').
>
> Matthew Hassan and prestige forms between a brother and sister: Hassan recorded a telephone conversation between the two siblings and then followed this up with an **elicitation task** containing words commonly pronounced in a non-standard way: e.g. 'better', 'water', 'have' and 'horn'. He found that the sister reproduced the higher prestige standard pronunciations in both casual conversation and the word list; the brother glottalised 'better' and 'butter' and dropped the /h/ in 'have' and 'has'.

*Adapted from **P. Stockwell**, Sociolinguistics: A Resource Book for Students, 2007*

Extension activity

Use the Kessler and Hassan research paragraphs to further explore some of the gender research you have read about so far. Discuss the implications of each with a partner and identify what aspects of which gender researchers they seem to challenge or support, and whether they suggest the idea of definite **genderlect** differences.

Lakoff and 'women's language'

Robin Lakoff is another American linguist who has researched language and gender – in particular the way that women's interaction differs from men's. In her book, *Language and Woman's Place*, drawn from her work in America in the 1970s, Lakoff put forward her understanding of how the language women use is indicative of their position in society. Her work explained the ways in which women's language varied by reference to their subordinate role in society.

Lakoff put forward specific features of speech that she suggested characterised the way that women spoke and revealed the impact of this subordinate role on their language. Adapted from a summary in Mary Talbot's *Language and Gender*, these include:

- **affective adjectives**: adjectives that describe feelings or emotional responses to things, for example 'a charming house'
- **emphatic stress**: using explicit, exaggerated pitch or volume stress on particular words
- **hedges**: phrases such as 'you know' or 'sort of' that can be seen to make an utterance more tentative
- **hypercorrect grammar**: a tendency to stick more closely to Standard English forms than men (this is a different use to the concept of hypercorrection explored elsewhere)

Key terms

Genderlect: a term to describe distinctive language differences attached to gender, as described and reported by some linguists.

Elicitation task: a data collection method that sets respondents pre-planned tasks (e.g. reading out a list of words) designed to give them the opportunity to produce particular standard or non-standard features of language.

Hedge: a word or phrase used to pad out or soften what's being said.

Further reading

Professor Robin Lakoff's 1975 book *Language and Woman's Place* helped to further the field of language, gender and power. Much of her subsequent writing has developed and extended her work on these themes, including *Talking Power*, first published in 1990 and *The Language War*, published in 2000.

Hyponym: a word that is more specific than a word with a related but more general meaning: e.g. 'azure' is a hyponym of 'blue'.

Euphemism: a word or phrase used in place of something considered taboo in a particular context, to soften or disguise its meaning.

Taboo language: words that cannot or should not be said in their context. Historically, taboo words tend to relate to body parts, urination and excretion, religion, sex and death. Currently some of the most taboo words are racist terms.

Intensifier: a word used to strengthen the meaning of another word or phrase.

■ Extension activity

Test Janet Holmes's findings in a different way. Record (using your mobile phone, for example) a mixed group (male and female) of your friends or family having a 'normal' conversation. Then listen back to the interaction and try to fill out a table for male and female speakers, with a count of how many times each use the three kinds of tag question described by Holmes. Your findings will not be representative, but are they similar?

- **precise colour terms**: a greater range of **hyponyms** within a particular colour, for example using specific terms like 'scarlet', 'burgundy', 'vermilion' as more specific forms of 'red'
- **rising intonation**: adding a rise in pitch at the end of an utterance, making its effect more like that of a question
- **superpolite forms**: the use of **euphemisms** and a lack of words considered to be swearing or **taboo language**
- **tag questions**: the addition of short phrases like 'do you?' or 'shall we?' to the end of an utterance to turn it into an interrogative form
- **the intensifier 'so'**: using the word 'so' to add to the strength of meaning in a phrase, as in 'I think that is so weird'
- **vocabulary of women's work**: defined in the context of Lakoff's research as words like 'shirr' and 'dart' (both US terms particular to dressmaking), used to describe activities typically carried out by women.

■ Extension activity

Lakoff also referred to affective adjectives as 'empty' adjectives – what do you think she could have meant by that?

Janet Holmes and referential/affective tag questions

Many linguists responded to Lakoff's work by exploring her ideas more fully. A New Zealand linguist, Janet Holmes, broke down the distinction of tag question use even further by defining the kinds of tag question used by women, in her research from the early 1980s. She defined two main kinds of tag question, referential and affective, and broke the latter down into two further sub-divisions:

- **referential tag questions**: signal factual uncertainty or a lack of information, e.g. 'The film is on Channel Four, isn't it?'
- **affective (facilitative) tag questions**: expressing solidarity or intimacy, e.g. 'We've never liked musicals, have we?'
- **affective (softening) tag questions**: weakening the tone of a criticism or command, e.g. 'Give me that hairbrush, would you?'

Her findings supported Lakoff's assertion that women used more tag questions in their speech, but it also provided further insight into the way in which they were used (Table 5).

Table 5

	Female	Male
Referential	18 (35%)	24 (61%)
Affective (facilitative)	30 (59%)	10 (25%)
Affective (softening)	3 (6%)	5 (13%)
Total	51	39

Deborah Tannen and 'difference' models

Various theories have been put forward to explain the variations between the language use and identity of males and females. Deborah Tannen's work during the 1980s and 1990s has mostly supported the approach of difference, emphasising separate, unique linguistic characteristics for men and women, reinforced since childhood.

Table 6 is a summary of the ways in which Tannen has built up opposites to describe the different language use of women and men, taken from Mary Talbot's *Language and Gender*.

Table 6

Women	Men
Sympathy	Problem-solving
Rapport	Report
Listening	Lecturing
Private	Public
Connection	Status
Supportive	Oppositional
Intimacy	Independence

Officer A: 'You feel like you belong to a kind of club. No one cares how long you've been in, it's seen as a special role and you feel special for taking on the training. Everyone likes to feel their job is important, don't they? And the danger is something you accept as part of the job.'

Officer B: 'I was told I was the right sort for the programme, my face fitted. You have to be a solid character. Others might be jealous of what you're doing and so you might get a bit of mick taken at first. But within the team itself, it's very tight – you can talk to anyone and they look after their own once you're in.'

5

Deborah Cameron, the 'myth of Mars and Venus' and the 'gender similarities hypothesis'

Cameron challenges the assertion put forward by many researchers that men and women are essentially different – that they think differently, communicate differently, and are suited to different roles in life. In describing the 'myth of Mars and Venus' (the title of her own 2007 book) she is referring to pop psychologist John Gray's 1992 bestseller book *Men are from Mars, Women are from Venus* and stating that the idea of fundamental gender differences is misleading, suggesting that there are more differences within the genders, rather than between them.

In summing up the claims made by linguists like Tannen (described earlier), Cameron describes the 'myth of Mars and Venus' as suggesting the following common assertions about male and female language, as presented in a 2007 *Guardian* newspaper article.

1 Language and communication matter more to women than to men; women talk more than men.

2 Women are more verbally skilled than men.

3 Men's goals in using language tend to be about getting things done, whereas women's tend to be about making connections to other people. Men talk more about things and facts, whereas women talk more about people, relationships and feelings.

4 Men's way of using language is competitive, reflecting their general interest in acquiring and maintaining status; women's use of language is cooperative, reflecting their preference for equality and harmony.

5 These differences routinely lead to 'miscommunication' between the sexes, with each sex misinterpreting the other's intentions. This causes problems in contexts where men and women regularly interact, and especially in heterosexual relationships.

'What Language Barrier?', The Guardian, *1 October 2007*

Data response exercise 12

Read the two transcripts (left) from two army officers talking about their involvement in bomb disposal training. One is female and the other male. Can you identify any of the characteristics suggested as being distinctively male or female by Tannen in either extract that would lead you to choose which is which?

Further reading

Search second-hand online booksellers for a copy of John Gray's *Men are from Mars, Women are from Venus* – you should be able to pick one up very cheaply. Read Gray's ideas on gender, specifically those parts that refer to communication and interaction, but be prepared to think of them in the context of the work of other linguists – in particular Deborah Cameron.

Study tip

One way you can bring language and gender theory into question 2 is to identify a language feature that has appeared in one of the texts and is attributed as a 'male' or 'female' usage by a particular researcher; then discuss how well it fits the context of that person's research.

Fig. 18 *Cameron's language and gender research challenges many of the 'difference' models proposed by pre-eminent linguists*

In fact, what Cameron anticipates is that the more linguists investigate the similarities in gender interaction, the more they will find the idea that men and women 'speak different languages' is false. She puts forward, as evidence for this, **meta-analysis** research by Janet Hyde published in 2005 that provides an argument for just such a 'gender similarities **hypothesis**'. Hyde compared the results from several hundred existing studies into male and female language use going back over several decades. Her findings are summed up in Table 7, where the 'Value of d' represents the difference in language use between the genders: Hyde usefully sums this up in the last column by translating the figure into how much of a difference it can be understood to be.

Table 7

Focus of search	No. of studies analysed	Value of d	Effect size
Reading comprehension	23	−0.06	Close to zero
Vocabulary	44	−0.02 – +0.06	Close to zero
Spelling	5*	−0.45	Moderate
Verbal reasoning	5*	−0.02	Close to zero
Speech production	12	−0.33	Small
Conversational interruption	70	+0.15 – +0.33	Small
Talkativeness	73	−0.11	Small
Assertive speech	75	+0.11	Small
Affiliative speech	46	−0.26	Small
Self disclosure	205	−0.18	Small
Smiling	418	−0.40	Moderate

Note: asterisks indicate cases where the small number of studies analysed is compensated for by the fact that they were conducted with very large controlled samples.

Source: *J. Hyde*, *The Gender Similarities Hypothesis*, American Psychologist, *60, 6*

As you can see, Hyde's research found a small or negligible difference in most areas of communication between the genders, supporting Cameron's stance. What Cameron also asserted, though, is that the perception that people have of this 'myth' is very real – and even though research may prove that the language of men and women is not drastically different, people may well continue to hold this stereotype.

Occupation

There are several reasons why a person's occupation is likely to have a significant impact on the language that he or she uses. First, it is likely that the job will involve spending time being with and communicating with people that person would otherwise not have mixed with. Second, the area of business or expertise of an occupation will have, to a greater or lesser degree, its own lexicon of subject-specific vocabulary. And, third, in many cases, an occupation represents something that a person has aspired to be, or has an interest in that contributes to his or her individual identity.

For the purposes of presenting a variety of occupation-based sociolects, it is best to think of occupation more widely – not just as a job or employment, but also to include hobbies, or interests that a person may devote a similar sort of commitment to.

Classroom activity 10

There are many occupations that have a specific variety of language attached to them. Discuss different examples and come up with three professions with examples of specific language they use.

The Royal Navy and seamen

So well-defined and deeply rooted is the sociolect of the Royal Navy (known as Jackspeak) that it has been the subject of comprehensive 'slang dictionaries'. There are even collections of poetry and prose written in it.

Jackspeak's main non-standard features are lexical, as shown by some examples below from *The Pusser's Rum Guide to Royal Navy Slanguage*.

- Abeam – adjacent to, or just opposite something
- FOD-plod – a line of personnel walking slowly across the area around an aircraft to pick up any debris, to prevent Foreign Object Damage
- Queen Mary – large articulated lorry and trailer used to move an aircraft by road
- Ring off – to finish a task, derived from the old engine telegraph system of bell signals
- Turk's head – ornamental and decorative rope-work

These examples show the range of ways that Jackspeak has formed as a variety. A term like 'abeam' represents a long-standing technical term, used from at least the early 19th century, and is part of the **jargon** that can develop to support the practices of an occupation. 'FOD-plod' reveals the way that the processes of change detailed in the previous topic can be utilised to create new lexical items, to simplify the terms for procedures or equipment. To 'ring off' is interesting as it is an example of a **phrasal verb** with a specific origin that has entered into mainstream usage. Similar to this is the idiom 'to let the cat out of the bag', which also derives from Royal Naval usage and refers to the cat o' nine tails (a whip used for punishment) being taken out of its storage bag, ready for use on some unfortunate sailor.

Fig. 19 *Sometimes the language is left with words for items that have long slipped out of use*

Key terms

Jargon: technical language in any field.

Phrasal verb: a verb that is made from a lexical verb like 'put' and a smaller word like 'out' (making 'to put out').

■ Language around you 3

Visit a nearby health centre and gather some leaflets aimed at a range of different people. Use them to collect examples of the kinds of jargon, slang and euphemism (and perhaps dysphemism) used to describe various medical matters.

Key terms

Dysphemism: a word or phrase used to present something with a harsh, more extreme or offensive tone. They can appear in tabloid newspaper headlines, swearing, taboo or politically incorrect language, and insults.

Medical jargon and medical slang

Looking into the language that surrounds medicine is interesting as it reveals the way that an occupational dialect can adopt more than one register. The first example in the extract below shows the technical, scientific lexis that you might expect to find and which is possibly associated with the overt prestige of the medical profession.

What are Chromosomes?

The chromosomes are like the wrapping around the genes. We cannot see individual genes under the microscope but we can see the chromosomes. There are 23 pairs of chromosomes making 46 chromosomes in all. Men have an X and a Y chromosome while women have two X chromosomes. The other chromosomes are the same in men and women.

Chromosome Terminology:
Aneuploidy
Individual whole chromosomes are missing or extra; i.e. having less than or more than the normal diploid set of 46 chromosomes.
Autosome
The term used to denote any of the 22 paired chromosomes, excepting the sex chromosomes.
Biparental
Involving, or inherited from both parents.
Centromere
The specialised area of a chromosome at which it is divided into its short and long arms.

Newlife Foundation for Disabled Children

Words like 'biparental' are examples of the high-frequency use of Latinate forms, and 'aneuploidy' the Greek-derived forms, that dominate the technical register of medicine. The extract from this website shows something of how precise these terms need to be, how inaccessible they are to people outside of familiarity with this medical sociolect, and why they require a 'plain English' translation.

There is evidence of a slang register in use in the medical profession. The following terms are taken from an article that appeared in the *British Medical Journal* in 2002, which presented a list of medical slang compiled by a London paediatrician, Adam Fox.

- *Ash cash* – money paid for signing cremation forms
- *Buff* – applying spin to a patient's history to facilitate a transfer
- *Code brown* – incontinence-related emergency
- *Departure lounge* – geriatric ward
- *FTF* – Failure To Fly, for attempted-suicide victims
- *House red* – blood
- *Wrinkly* – geriatric

Fox explained that these terms (and many others) were not only used in the spoken interactions of medical personnel but also in doctor's notes and medical reports. What they reveal is how sociolects often arise to deal with the more taboo areas of society – in these examples, those to do with subjects like illness and death. There is a kind of grim humour involved in many of the examples, which supports the idea of a sociolect helping form a kind of solidarity between medical workers. In the case of 'wrinkly', you can see how this word has entered into mainstream colloquial usage, perhaps because it is one of the simpler, less specialised and least abstract terms.

Leet and the language of 'haxxors'

The phenomenon of Leet is unique as an example of a sociolect, as it is almost exclusively a written mode form, with its non-standard features being predominantly lexical and orthographic. It is, perhaps, the first example presented here that could truly be referred to as an **anti-language** – a concept explored in more detail later in this topic.

Leet originated in the 1980s and takes its name from the bulletin board systems (BBS) that were one of the ancestors of the modern-day internet. On these an 'elite' user would be allowed to have full access, and 'Leet' is formed as a clipping of this word down to the second syllable and re-spelled to represent the new term phonetically. This context was a highly specialised one, and Leet forms became associated with computer experts and, more specifically, hackers who used computers and networks for illegal and deviant activities, suggesting a kind of covert prestige. As the use of the internet has become more widespread, as have other text-based communication systems like mobile phone texting, many of the non-standard features of Leet have entered into mainstream usage.

The orthographical non-standard features of Leet involve using an extended range of alphanumeric characters (letters, numbers, punctuation marks and special characters) to redesign the way that letters and words are represented. The result of this gave users the freedom to create their own combinations of letters, as the examples, taken from Wikipedia, show in Table 8.

Table 8

				Examples of letter respellings					Lexical items	
A	C	E	G	L	O	T	Y	Words		Affixes
4	[	3	1	0	7	j		n00b		-xor
/\	¢	&	&	£	()	+	`/	haxxor		-age
@	<	€	(_+	1_	oh	-|-	ψ	Leetage		-ness-
/-\	(	£	9	|	[]	1	f	b&		-'d
^	{	ë	C-	L_	¤	'][''	λ	ROFL		-& / &-
aye	©	[-	gee	lJ	□	†	Ч	w00t		
ə		|=-	(γ,	¬	Ω		¥	phreaking		
			(_-							

This selection shows the depth of Leet as a sociolect form, as well as its potential for covert prestige – serving its purpose as a **cryptolect**, a language used specifically for its secrecy. The combination of ways a word can be spelled seems almost limitless, reflecting the way that Leet had been used in the past to dodge attempts to track online communications, by searching for particular words, which would be almost impossible given the ever-changing way they may be spelled. The only rule seems to be the creative use of a symbol or combination of letters that in some way represent the basic graphological shape of a letter, or that reproduce its sound phonetically.

The lexical items are examples of simple letter combinations and the affix forms in use. Some of these mirror standard forms, like *-age* or *-ness* as bound morphemes used to create (usually abstract) noun forms. The

■ Key terms

Anti-language: a variety of language intended to prevent non-users understanding it.

Cryptolect: a secret language devised for use by a particular group of people.

■ Link

Contrast the graphological nature of Leet letter formation with the phonetic spellings of 'txt speak' on page 25.

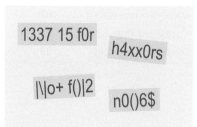

Fig. 20 *The internet has had an enormous influence on contemporary English, including its very own varieties like Leet*

Agent noun: a noun describing a person who 'does' something, usually derived from the verb describing the action involved, for example an 'adviser' being the agent noun for someone who 'advises'.

Trend: a pattern or definite tendency suggested in the data and results of research.

■ **Classroom activity 11**

Compare the Leet forms shown in Table 8 with your own use of non-standard orthographical forms in texting and online chat or email.

Study tip

When referring to studies that include quantitative results, like Petyt's percentage of class-based H-dropping in West Yorkshire, don't just memorise the whole results set in isolation. It is better to prepare particularly significant statistics alongside a qualitative detail or interpretation of the findings.

Table 9

Socio-economic class	% of H-dropping
Upper-middle class	12
Lower-middle class	28
Upper-working class	67
Middle-working class	89
Lower-working class	93

way in which they are used is non-standard and results in newly coined words, like 'Leetage', a noun meaning the concept of communication through Leet. The -*xor* suffix is unique to Leet, and is used to create an **agent noun** from a verb stem, in the same way that -*er* or -*or* might be used in Standard English: 'haxxor' being a similar structure, but a different spelling of 'hacker'. Phonologically, the ampersand character, '&', pronounced 'and', is used to replace that syllable, with a word like 'band' or 'banned' being spelled 'b&'.

It is easy to see how many of these principles have influenced the emerging 'e-languages' of texting and other forms explored earlier. Some of these principles have entered mainstream modern colloquial language, with the term 'n00b' (an abbreviation of 'newbie': a new-comer to a particular subject or pursuit) in a spoken form, and the wider use of the -*age* suffix in coined words like 'foodage' or 'eatage'. The interjection 'w00t', to show excitement, follows similar trends to 'n00b' and was named 'word of the year' in 2007 by the US Merriam-Webster dictionary. Other examples from Table 8 include the acronym 'ROFL' (Rolling On Floor Laughing); the respelling of 'phreaking' (freaking) is a substitution for the swear word 'fucking' which mimics its phonetic structure; and '-d' is an affix that reintroduces an archaic way of writing the standard -*ed* suffix for past tense verbs and past participles.

Social class

Socio-economic class, the idea of different 'levels' in society based on a complex combination of income, cultural preference, occupation and education, has historically been a dominant source of division in British society. Like gender, this has resulted in a considerable body of linguistic research, of which examples from Malcolm Petyt, Peter Trudgill and Jennifer Cheshire are presented here, with a guide to areas for further independent study.

Malcolm Petyt and social climbing in Bradford, West Yorkshire

Petyt (1985) focused on the use of a common linguistic variable in many northern English accents, that of the omission of the initial /h/ sound in words like 'hat', 'happen' or 'horrible', known as H-dropping. He measured the frequency of instances of H-dropping across social classes.

This study is a good introduction to the idea of the relationship between non-standard dialect use and social class as its results follow the basic **trend** of greater regional accent use in the working class, diminishing as you move up the social class scale. In this case the Bradford, West Yorkshire accent feature of H-dropping was shown to be highly varied in usage at the two extremes of the social scale, with lower-working class speakers using it in almost all instances of /h/ initiated words, while upper-middle class speakers only used it in approximately 1 in 10 opportunities. The results in between are revealing, by showing a clear 'curve' of the usage rate dropping off – but showing a clear divide between middle and working class usage within that, with a sharp drop from upper-working class at 67 per cent to 28 per cent of lower-middle class speakers.

Petyt added further conclusions to his findings, suggesting that, in instances of social mobility, where individuals may have moved up the socio-economic scale, they would modify their speech a bit further towards RP, and make less use of features like H-dropping. He developed this by looking at a further linguistic variable, in distinguishing between the vowel sounds /u/ (as in RP 'put') and /uh/ (as in RP 'putt'). In many northern English accents, the /u/ vowel is used in place of both RP pronunciations, and the /uh/ vowel does not appear – making it a good test against social class in the region. Furthermore, this variable revealed more clearly speakers who had moved up the social scale and tried to implement this modification in their speech. This resulted in hypercorrection, by using both /u/ and /uh/ forms, sometimes resulting in the use of the wrong form, as in using /uh/ in the first vowel sound of the word 'cushion'.

Peter Trudgill and vernacular in different registers in Norwich

Trudgill's research (1974) into class-based use of regional accent forms (**vernacular**) in Norwich followed similar lines to that of Petyt's but produced a more complex set of findings by introducing the distinction between males and females in each social class. He employed a more complicated **methodology**, using four different contexts to gather his data: reading a word list; reading a passage; formal conversation; and casual conversation. This range of collection methods seemed to construct a sliding scale of formality, which is borne out by the results. Respondents responded to the word list as a highly formalised activity, which perhaps had the effect of making them highly conscious of their pronunciation, and therefore reporting lower non-standard usage frequencies. At the opposite end of the scale, the casual speech created the most informal context. This could be seen to be an illustration of the influence of the **observer's paradox** and demand characteristics in the investigation.

The linguistic variable focused on by Trudgill was the frequency of pronunciation of words ending with the **velar nasal** /ng/ sound, being pronounced as the non-standard, regional variant /n/. For example, saying /walkin/ rather than /walking/. Trudgill's findings (percentages) are shown in Table 10 (abbreviations: U = Upper; M = Middle; L = Lower; W = Working; C = Class).

Key terms

Vernacular: the language form naturally spoken by the people of a particular region or country.

Methodology: the design of a particular experiment.

Observer's paradox: this states that the results of an experiment can be affected by the presence of the observer, or the unnatural context of an experiment.

Velar nasal: a type of consonant sound produced by stopping the flow of air with the back part of the tongue pressed against a part of the roof of the mouth.

Link

There is more information on the observer's paradox on page 149, and on demand characteristics on pages 155–6.

Table 10

	Word list	Passage	Formal	Casual
MMC				
- Male	0	0	4	31
- Female	0	0	0	0
LMC				
- Male	0	20	27	17
- Female	0	0	3	67
UWC				
- Male	0	18	81	95
- Female	11	13	68	77
MWC				
- Male	24	43	91	97
- Female	20	46	81	88
LWC				
- Male	60	100	100	100
- Female	17	54	97	100

Classroom activity 12

Look at Table 10 again and work out which of the results given seem to go against the general trend. Can you propose any reasons for why this might be?

Overall, Trudgill's findings mirror those of Petyt in Bradford very closely: a similar curve of the frequency of non-standard usage in relation to social class can be identified, with a 'drop-off' from the middle to the working class groups.

The inclusion of gender showed that women generally used the non-standard variant less frequently than men in all social classes and contexts, with the two exceptions being in the upper-working class word list elicitation task, and the middle-working class passage task.

The use of different contexts allowed Trudgill to show some evidence of the effect of context on the use of non-standard variant forms. A similar 'curve' appears, with the least non-standard usage coming in the most 'unnatural' and formal way of using language – reading out a list of specific words. The most non-standard usage came from the most natural and informal context, in casual conversation. This trend roughly followed a curve across the middle tasks, the reading of a passage aloud, and formal conversation, with the exception of the **anomaly** of male lower-middle class results.

Jennifer Cheshire and peer groups in Reading

Cheshire's study in the southern English town of Reading in the early 1980s differs from Trudgill's and Petyt's in that it made use of a much wider range of linguistic analysis, focusing on grammatical variants. She identified 11 non-standard features and measured the frequency of the use of these in the speech of boys and girls in Reading adventure playgrounds.

To focus on the girls' findings, Cheshire constructed her own concept of social class by establishing two groups of girls: Group A expressed disapproval for participation in minor criminal activities, carrying weapons, fighting and swearing; whereas Group B was formed of girls who approved of these things. Eight of the variables she chose, and her results, are shown in Table 11.

Table 11

Variant	Example	Group A girls %	Group B girls %
non-standard '-s'	They calls me names.	25.84	57.27
non-standard 'has'	You just has to do what teachers say.	36.36	35.85
non-standard 'was'	You was with me, wasn't you?	63.64	80.95
negative concord	It ain't got no pedigree or nothing.	12.5	58.7
non-standard 'never'	I never went to school today.	45.45	41.07
non-standard 'what'	Are you the ones what hit him?	33.33	5.56
non-standard 'come'	I come down here yesterday.	30.77	90.63
'ain't' as **copula**	You ain't no boss.	14.29	67.12

If you consider the Group A girls to represent a middle-class cohort, and the Group B girls a working-class cohort, Cheshire's results were less clear-cut in their distinction between the two social groups than the findings of Trudgill and Petyt. There are clear instances of higher use of non-standard forms in the Group B 'working class' girls in five of the eight grammatical variants, a roughly equal share in two and lower use in one. Perhaps this shows the increased variability of younger language users – and certainly shows that both groups of girls used a significant amount of non-standard language. Cheshire's findings for groups of boys

Fig. 21 *Teenage girls in town – do they have their own distinctive form of language?*

returned similar results and showed that, for all of the children, patterns of non-standard usage were an important part of the identity of each group, to which members conformed.

Extension activity

Other key studies into language and social class include:

- Lesley Milroy and social networks in districts of Belfast
- William Labov's 'Department Store' study in New York
- Basil Bernstein and restricted and elaborated code, 1971.

Milroy's work is described briefly on page 77. Use the internet to look into the findings and results in more detail, and to explore the work of Labov and Bernstein.

Ethnicity

The diversity of the population in Britain has led to increasing variation in the usage of English speakers with different ethnic backgrounds, largely due to the phenomenon of language contact, described earlier.

Pidgins and creoles

When language contact occurs between two or more languages, new language forms appear by the exchange of grammatical, lexical and phonological elements. For example, Chinese Pidgin English (CPE) is an important example of this phenomenon – in fact, the word 'pidgin' comes from the pronunciation of a CPE word for 'business'. CPE began as early as the 17th century as a language used between English and Chinese speakers in trade. The results are known as **pidgin** and **creole** forms, which can be distinguished as follows.

- **Pidgins**: Pidgins have evolved from a main source language, usually taking from it the majority of their vocabulary, but are less grammatically developed. In terms of use, pidgins are spoken by people placed in particular social contexts, rather than having any native speakers, and tend to fulfil **transactional** purposes primarily. Non-pidgin speakers who do speak one of the source languages that have contributed to it are unlikely to be able to understand the pidgin without experience of it.

- **Creoles**: Creoles grow out of a pidgin, as it becomes more established and begins to be used by second generation, native speakers – people who are born into and grow up speaking the creole language. The grammar of a creole is usually derived from the source languages, in a simplified form. Creoles serve a wider range of language needs, including **phatic** purposes.

In the fullness of time, fully mixed languages can appear, which are as grammatically complex as the individual source languages that have contributed to them – as English itself has done over many centuries.

Ethnic variation in writing

Before getting into the detail of specific research into particular ethnic varieties, it is interesting to explore the use of creole forms in writing and literature. Use the following extracts to explore some of the features of these varieties, as well as something of the context of creole forms.

Key terms

Pidgin: a simplified language form created as a result of language contact, usually to support some sort of activity like trade.

Creole: a language variety created by previous language contact and then developed over successive generations of users.

Transactional: (speech) used to facilitate some kind of exchange, for example of goods, services or information.

Phatic: (speech) used to fulfil social purposes such as greetings, and small talk and humour.

Data response exercise 13

Read each of the following extracts from creole-influenced literature, and make notes in response to the following question for each: What non-standard features can you identify being used by the writer?

Look in particular for the use of additional **particles** to construct some verb phrases, with the words 'a' and 'fi' used to achieve this. In addition to the other non-standard features you can find, try to find an example of particle use and explain the way that it is used in the verb phrase.

Key terms

Particle: a word used in a verb phrase to provide meaning, e.g. an adverb or preposition in a phrasal verb.

Code-switching: a term for the way speakers with several strong linguistic influences will form a variety that mixes features of pronunciation, grammar and vocabulary from them, and will then 'switch' between these forms as they speak.

Research point

Loreto Todd, in *Pidgins and Creoles* (1990), counters the assertion that creole-influenced varieties are 'lazy' forms of English. She points out that features that are commonly criticised in this way, such as the omission of Standard English inflections, are simply an influence of one of the other grammatical sources of creole forms: West African languages, for example, do not use such an inflection system.

Thinking points

1. Why do you think creole and similar varieties of English have attracted criticism from some linguists?

2. Is there such a thing as a 'better' or 'worse' grammar?

Maybe next time he tell me he get married. You tell him no need be Chinese girl. Now modern days, okay marry Japanese, maybe haole, anykine girl okay.

*From Darrell Lum's play, Oranges are Lucky. Extract taken from **D. Crystal**, The Stories of English, 2005*

That day when my Palm-wine Tree Wife did die was the baddest most worstest day of my life. Her tree-trunk body did fall for ground making sound like atomic nuclear explosion.

*From Karen King-Aribisala's novel, Kicking Tongues. Extract taken from **D. Crystal**, The Stories of English, 2005*

Mama,
I really dont know how fi tell yu dis,
cause I did mek a salim pramis
fi tek care a likkle Jim
an try mi bes fi look out fi him.

*From Linton Kwesi Johnson's verse letter, 'Sonny's Lettah'. Extract taken from **D. Crystal**, The Stories of English, 2005*

Mark Sebba and London Jamaican

London Jamaican is a particular variety that has evolved due to the language needs of immigrant communities that have settled in England, and produced second-, third- or further-generation speakers. Several researchers have looked into the speech of Caribbean communities within the UK and London itself. Mark Sebba identified the main choices of young, new-generation speakers born into London's Caribbean communities as effectively being between Caribbean creole forms; Cockney forms that he summed up as 'London English'; and Standard English/RP forms. He used the concept of **code-switching** to describe a London Jamaican speaker's ability to change between these forms in speech.

Sebba defines London Jamaican as a language with a combination of phonological, lexical and grammatical elements from all three of these sources. For example, from his work in the 1990s, Sebba details the following possible range of pronunciation variables available to a London Jamaican speaker (Table 101 is adapted from Sebba's research).

Table 12

	Creole-derived pronunciation	Cockney (London English)	Received Pronunciation
/l/ as in 'well'	/l/	/u/	/l/
/th/ as in 'with'	/d/	/v/	/th/
/ow/ as in 'how'	/oh/	/a/	/ow/
/uh/ as in 'love'	/o/	/uh/	/uh/

It is easy to see how different varieties of English are created when faced with such diversity. Much of Sebba's research involved interviewing and recording the speech of young, British-born teenagers, who had Jamaican parentage. Look at the examples of transcription of conversation between two girls, from a group known as the 'Catford Girls' Possee' on page 55.

Data response exercise 14

When you read the transcript below, copy out the parts that you think 'belong' to each of the three varieties of language mentioned above: Jamaican Creole, London English and Standard English. A full commentary appears in the feedback to this activity on page 99.

Key:
%   Glottal stop
(.) (1.0)   **Micropause** and pauses with length in seconds

C   all right, we went to this party on Sa%urday night you know Jane and I (.) and I tell you boy de par%y was well rude, you know, well rude (1.0)

J   whe you a seh?

C   mi seh dis party well rude! (0.6)   5

J   that good, was it?

Key terms

Micropause: a period of silence of less than half a second.

💡 Sue Fox and 'multi-ethnic youth dialect'

Sue Fox's research is focused on the dialect of youths from a variety of different ethnic backgrounds across London (a city with highly diverse ethnic communities) at the start of the 21st century. Her findings suggest a variety of 'multi-ethnic youth dialect' (MEYD), which she has termed 'Multicultural London English' (MLE) with strong characteristics drawn from the influences of several other language, creole and cultural sources.

The project suggests that MLE is identified with by adolescent users in the wider city environment of greater London – although evidence suggests that forms of multicultural dialect are gaining ground with youths in other large UK cities like Bristol and Birmingham. The influence of settled immigrant speakers is significant (notably West Indian, West African and Bangladeshi), but Fox has found that the speakers of the dialect are drawn from white, black and Asian communities alike. The emergence of MLE is viewed as a fully functioning dialect in its own right – the gelling of a common culture among the culturally diverse youth population of London has formed particularly fertile conditions for the growth of the variety.

Table 13

Feature	Usage	Source
Shortened vowel sounds	Found particularly in words like 'face', pronounced /fehs/, or 'go' pronounced /goh/	Primarily similar to Jamaican phonology, but also found in Asian and African speakers
'blud'	To mean a mate or friend	Thought to be derived from the word 'blood', as in 'blood brother'
'nang'	To mean 'good'	An Australian-derived colloquial term, used also in Indian subcontinent varieties
'duppy'	To mean being attacked or killed – also can be a pejorative term for white people	Jamaican patois for a kind of ghost
'grime'	Describes a genre of UK rap music performed by artists like Dizzee Rascal and Lady Sovereign	The influential London music scene and music press

Fig. 22 *Sacha Baron Cohen used a mock form of MLE in the speech of his Ali G character*

Another quality of MLE is that it is a rapidly changing dialect. Words, phrases, and even pronunciation features that are adopted by its speakers may only remain current for a relatively short while, before being replaced by new trends or lexical items. This is perhaps reflected in the semi-parodied forms of the language used recently by the likes of Sacha Baron Cohen's Ali G caricature, or DJs like Tim Westwood, termed 'Jafaican' – a term which implies an in-authentic mimicking of black-origin language forms by white speakers. However, the research by Fox, and other linguists like Kerswill, suggests that MLE is a genuine and evolving dialect, and belongs to black and white speakers alike.

Extension activity

A number of other studies into British Black English (BBE) varieties (as London Jamaican and others tend to be termed) have been carried out, expanding into more recent immigrant communities and Asian influenced variation. Use internet and library resources to research the work of these additional researchers into ethnicity-related variation in English.

- Viv Edwards
- Roger Hewitt
- Michelle Straw

Sexuality

The influence of different sexualities on language use has changed over recent decades, in tandem with changing attitudes towards sexual diversity in society. Different sexualities exist on a more equal footing in many aspects of mainstream culture now – although it would be wrong to suggest that true equality and freedom of sexuality exists in society. However, there has been a shift from the mid-20th century and earlier, when homosexuality was a mainstream taboo, and homophobia was more openly exhibited and tolerated than in 21st-century Britain.

The study of the language surrounding sexuality, and particularly the relationship between language and homosexuality, and language and homophobia, is perhaps underdeveloped. Looking at the changes that the word 'gay' has undergone (through to playground insult in the 21st century) reveals how important research in this area might be. Paul Baker's study of Polari is one particular, well-developed example of an investigation into an example of a language variety defined by sexuality.

Paul Baker and Polari

Baker's research focused on a variety that was most commonly used between the 1930s and 1970s and that differed mostly from Standard English in the inventive lexicon it developed. It was predominantly used and developed by gay men and centred around London, travelling out into the British Merchant Navy, and the theatre scene. As a variety, it can be considered a form of slang within the English language, and shows many of the properties associated with the concept of anti-language, not least to support the gay subculture prior to the decriminalisation of homosexuality in 1967.

Baker estimated its lexicon to be in the region of 500 items, although he suggested that most users would have only drawn from a fraction of these in their speech. The Polari lexicon included borrowings from other languages (Italian, Occitan – broadly speaking, a language found around the mutual borders of France, Italy and Spain – and French); other sociolects (American air force slang, Thieves' Cant – an Early Modern English anti-language used by criminals) and drug slang. It included terms coined by using the process of rhyming slang or **backslang**.

Classroom activity 13

Look at the list of Polari words below. Using information in the Language change topics, try to describe the process that has been used to create each word. Check your ideas against the feedback at the end of the section on page 99.

- **bevvy** – drink
- **bitch** – to complain
- **bona** – good
- **camp** – effeminate
- **ecaf/eek** – face
- **fantabulosa** – wonderful
- **mangarie** – food
- **scarper** – to run off

You may well have heard all of these examples – but particularly 'bevvy', 'bitch', 'camp' (although probably not in its original form). These show the exchange between Polari and mainstream language: although some of these words can be traced in use prior to the heyday of Polari, it may well be the case that the changes in social attitudes towards homosexuality mentioned earlier resulted not only in the demise of the language as a 'secret' form but also saw some of its lexicon enter into mainstream use and culture.

Topic revision exercise

1 Describe three of the features that Robin Lakoff defined as 'women's language'.

2 What main relationships do the researchers considered in this topic tend to find between non-standard forms and social class?

3 What is MEYD?

Further reading

Try to get hold of a copy of John Ayto's *Twentieth Century Words* (1999). It is often available very cheaply second-hand. Use it to explore the kinds of slang, jargon and other variations that entered English usage in waves throughout the 1900s.

Key terms

Backslang: the creation of a new word by spelling and pronouncing an existing word backwards.

Link

Look back at page 21 to see the way the word 'gay' itself has undergone language change over time.

Looking ahead

The different forms of language discussed in this topic are all part of a major area of language study: sociolinguistics. If you are particularly interested in the kind of issues raised here, there are lots of study and research routes you could follow in this field after your A Levels.

Regional variation

The effect on language variation of living in different regions of the British Isles is a dominant one. Here, you will be able to look at the features of a few major varieties in detail, before moving on to consider the role of English at a global level.

Scouse

In terms of its geographical location, in and around the city of Liverpool, Scouse is considered to be on the northern side of the clear and dominant north–south divide of English language variation. As such, it shares some of the common northern accent features, like the widely known short /a/ vowel sound in words like 'bath' and 'class'.

Scouse is an accent with a distinctive and easily recognised set of phonological patterns, ranging from the almost melodic, sing-song patterns of its **prosody**, exhibiting a fairly wide pitch range, through to the particular consonant and vowel patterns, and dialect forms. In these aspects, Scouse is seen as being a particularly unique regional accent, with less of the homogenous northern accent features found widely across the north west, Lancashire, and large cities like Manchester. Many researchers have pointed to the influence of prolonged and significant language contact with Irish speakers historically, giving rise to the modern form of the accent, seen thriving in the 20th and 21st centuries. Indeed, the work of Kevin Watson in the 21st century, in defining some of the pronunciation variants of Scouse, has suggested that it is an accent that is resisting the pressures of **dialect levelling** and exists on a 'dialectal island of its own'.

Several researchers have explored the features of Scouse, and the following typical pronunciation characteristics have been identified.

- There is a harder pronunciation of the /g/ sound in words ending in 'ing'.
- There is merging of the vowel sound represented in the words 'fur' and 'fair', pronounced somewhere between /air/ and /uhr/.
- The pronunciation of /k/ in words like 'back' is similar to Scottish pronunciation of the word 'loch', so 'back' becomes /bakh/.
- There is an elongated vowel sound in words like 'look', pronounced /look/ rather than /luk/.
- Final /t/ consonants can have several distinct pronunciations, either replacing it with a soft /h/ or /r/ sound as in the word 'what' becoming /woh/, or as an /s/ or /ts/, as in 'light' becoming /lys/.

Scouse exhibits lexical and grammatical features distinctive to its dialect form. It shares some of the more common non-standard regional forms like the use of multiple negation, but also:

- apparent non-standard pluralisation of the second person pronoun 'you' to 'yous' (although this may be a pronunciation feature, rather than the adding of an '-s' plural inflection)
- lexical items like 'abnabs' (sandwiches), 'bap ossie' (an empty house), 'midder' (to pester).

- learn about the features of specific regional varieties of English within the British Isles
- examine data and examples of regional variation from researchers and writers.

Key terms

Prosody: the elements of pitch, pace and volume that can be altered in the intonation of a human voice.

Dialect levelling: a phenomenon in which dialect forms lose their distinct differences and begin to share common language forms.

Starter activity

Visit the 'Voice Recordings' page of the BBC Voices website (http://www.bbc.co.uk/voices/). Click on the various regional forms dotted around the map, to listen to examples of different accents in the UK, before you read about some of the more particular forms in this topic. Use a blank map of the UK to note the location of different varieties you hear, and go on to add those you read about in this topic, and any others you know of.

Extension activity

Record some television footage of a famous Scouse speaker (e.g. the footballer Steven Gerrard or the actress Jennifer Ellison) and make note of the Scouse features you hear them using.

Irish English

Irish English, sometimes known as Hiberno-English, is a term for the collection of different forms of English spoken and used throughout Ireland. The variations from mainland English forms have historically come from the interplay between the English spoken in the Republic of Ireland and the features of the Celtic Irish Gaelic languages also spoken (which have been subject to a level of containment owing to the geographical nature of the island and its sea borders). Particular pronunciation patterns, dialect terms, grammatical constructions and idioms have created a unique form of English, with individual flavours of Irish English being found in the major cities and areas of the country.

This contact between the Irish and English languages led to an inevitable transfer of lexical items, as well as other instances of borrowing and coinage. The words below are drawn from the wider dialect lexicon of Irish English.

- Banjaxed – used only in the **past participle** form (not as a fully functioning verb) to describe something broken.
- Dingen – an adjective meaning 'very good' from Gaelic.
- Feck – slightly popularised in the UK by the comedy show *Father Ted*. (It is primarily a colloquial verb form, meaning 'go', 'steal' or 'throw' in different usages. 'Fecking' can be used as an intensifier roughly equivalent to 'damned' or 'bloody' in English.)
- Gansey – (noun) a jumper or jersey.

Characteristic idiomatic forms and grammatical constructions are as follows.

- 'Arra' is used as an **interjection**, not dissimilar to 'ah' in English in utterances like: 'Arra, look on the bright side', or similar – especially implying a more positive or comforting outlook following something negative.
- 'Amn't' is used as a **contraction** of 'am not' by analogy with the contractions 'isn't' and 'aren't'.
- 'So', as a tag of agreement, is used at the end of utterances in the same way as 'too' or 'as well', as in 'Let's go so'.
- 'So' can be used to emphasise and join **reduplicative** forms, where the subject pronoun and auxiliary or primary verb is repeated, as in 'I can go, so I can', or 'It is bad, so it is'.
- There is less use of 'yes' or 'no' as direct responses to questions (perhaps due to a lack of direct translations in Irish). Instead, a form that repeats the question verb is favoured, as in: 'Are you coming to town?' – 'I am.'
- There is more frequent use of the **definite article** in noun phrases, as in, 'I came home for the Christmas'.
- The verbs 'do' and 'be' can be paired as an auxiliary form as part of the construction of the **present continuous tense**, as in, 'They do be running very fast'. This is extended to 'does be' for the singular form ('He does be talking strangely').
- Because of the influence of Irish, which does not have a **past perfect tense**, 'after' is used in conjunction with the present continuous verb form to construct this form, as in, 'The car was after hitting the wall and crashed through the barrier', for 'The car had hit the wall and crashed through the barrier'.
- The singular and plural forms of the second person pronoun are distinguished using the archaic form 'ye' and 'youse' respectively (compare the use of 'youse' with this feature in Scouse).

Key terms

Past participle: a past tense verb form used with an auxiliary to express something that has happened ('had broken'), or as a modifier in describing a noun ('the broken vase').

Interjection: a spoken word or phrase used to express emotion.

Contraction: a word shortened in speech or spelling.

Reduplicative: the repetition of a word, phrase or sound pattern for effect or to create a new term.

Definite article: the determiner 'the' used to show a noun is referring to a particular thing.

Present continuous tense: a verb form used to express an action that is still happening.

Past perfect tense: a verb form used to describe an action that completed before a particular time, e.g. 'the man had stopped laughing'.

Extension activity

Write a short piece of narrative, including dialogue, to illustrate some of the features of Irish English described on pages 59–60.

Key terms

Closed vowel: a vowel sound that has consonants 'either side' of it, as in the /a/ sound in 'cat', which has a /c/ and /t/ sound enclosing it.

Diphthong: a vowel sound with 'two parts' to it, e.g. the sound in 'bear', 'care' or 'air' where the sound is 'eh-uh', if you exaggerate the way you say it a bit!

Deletion: the non-pronunciation of a sound from the normal, standard pronunciation pattern.

Retraction: used to express the movement of the place in which a particular speech sound is produced towards the back of the mouth. Also referred to as 'backing'.

There exist more localised differences in Irish English forms within Ireland. The dominant regional areas can be seen as those of the north of the island, including Northern Ireland, the south-western region around Cork and the central and eastern region around Dublin.

Dublin English

Looking into the use of English in Dublin, the capital city of the Republic of Ireland, is particularly interesting as it contains implications for the concept of standard and prestige forms. Owing to the national identity of the Irish, most speakers in the Republic of Ireland would measure themselves against Dublin English as their standard, and prestige form, rather than any notion of RP or Standard English.

Raymond Hickey studied Dublin English to chart the way that the accent has been seen to be changing since the 1980s. He used recorded speech data from the 1990s to explore the increasing gap in the city between the stronger local pronunciations of the Dublin English accent and those used by speakers in the areas of the city deemed more fashionable.

Dublin English pronunciation data set

The following examples are some of the main features of the local, predominantly working-class, Dublin English pronunciations.

- Breaking of **closed vowel diphthongs** into two separate syllables: for example, in 'clean' this would become /klee-un/, with a clear separation in the way the two halves are said. Similarly, 'fool' would become /foo-ul/. This does not hold true for open vowels at the beginning or end of a word.
- Changing /th/ consonant sound to /t/ or /d/: for example, 'thought' becomes similar to /tort/ or /dort/.
- **Deletion** of /t/ or /d/ sounds that come after /l/ or /n/: for example, 'bend' would become /ben/, or 'melt' becomes /mel/. This is quite similar to the idea of a glottal stop, and in some cases a glottal may be used after the /n/ or /l/ in the place of the deleted /t/ or /d/.

In researching these features of the local accent, Hickey proposed evidence for a Dublin Vowel Shift, taken up by middle class speakers forming what he termed a 'fashionable' variety of the accent. This fashionable form was taken up by non-locals, and served to distinguish them from the working class local accent, described above, and its users. Hickey concluded that this change was motivated by social factors within Dublin and summarised the central features of this shift as being the vowel **retraction** or backing of the diphthongs in words like 'time' and 'toy' – that is, sounding the vowel sound further back in the mouth to create a different pronunciation form closer to RP. These same middle class speakers of the 'fashionable' variety would deviate from other forms in the data set above, including removing the breaking of vowel sounds into two distinct syllables.

Estuary English

Estuary English was brought into prominence by the work of David Rosewarne in the early 1980s, together with the prediction that it may well in time replace RP as the standard pronunciation form of English. Whether that has taken place is a matter for debate, but Estuary English is a variety that is growing out of its original regional roots, influencing more speakers, and spreading into wider areas of usage in the UK.

Even if you are not aware of it, you are very likely to be familiar with Estuary English. It is often described as being something of a midpoint between RP and the Cockney-related forms of London and the south east – along the Thames Estuary, in fact, from which the name of the variety derives. As such, the non-standard accent and dialect features are best understood as those that have been influenced by Cockney and the south east, as the remainder of the dialect is 'standard' in the sense that it adheres roughly to the prestige form of RP.

Rosewarne stated certain dialect features involving non-standard grammatical forms, including the contracted word 'ain't' as a verb and non-standard past tense forms like 'come' for 'came' in a usage like 'I come back home yesterday'. The use of double negative forms has been put forward as another dialectal feature derived from Cockney; although not all research has found this, some have described the non-standard negative constructions involving the **primary verbs** 'to be', 'to do', and 'to have', usually in the past tense. In these instances, the adverb 'never' is used to construct forms like 'I never did' or 'He never went', rather than the standard use of 'not', for example in 'I did not'.

Perhaps even more distinctive is the pronunciation profile of Estuary English. This has been the subject of the work of many researchers, and some typical phonological features for the accent include:

- **yod-coalescence**: the use of the consonant sound /j/ in place of /dy/ in the initial sound of a word like 'dune'
- **t-glottalling**: the consonant /t/ sound being pronounced by a glottal stop, instead of the full **plosive** sound, as in /wha-/ for the word 'what', or /waw-uhr/ for 'water'
- **l-vocalisation**: the replacement of the consonant sound /l/ with a vowel or semi-vowel sound, as in the /l/ in 'milk' shifting to make the word sound similar to /miwk/
- **vowel fronting**: the movement of the pronunciation of vowel sounds further forward in the mouth, resulting in the long vowel sound in a word like 'shoe' being articulated more like the vowel sound in 'drew'. Similar shifts occur in other longer vowel sounds, like those in 'kite', and 'home'.

Key terms

Primary verb: a small group of verbs that can be main or auxiliary verbs: be; have; do.

Yod-coalescence: merging the /y/ phoneme with consonant phonemes adjacent to it.

T-glottalling: replacing the /t/ phoneme with a sound made by a glottal stop.

Plosive: a sound that is created by a sudden release of air (like an explosion) from the mouth.

L-vocalisation: substituting the /l/ phoneme with a vowel or semi-vowel.

Vowel fronting: moving the place in which a vowel sound is generated towards the front of the mouth.

Classroom activity 14

Why might the utterance 'Alright, Duke!' be considered an ideal example of these Estuary English pronunciation forms?

Joanna Przedlacka produced research on the accent forms of Estuary English in the late-1990s from the Greater London area, covering an area approximately 50 miles in diameter (see Figure 23 on page 62). She used male and female informants aged 14–16 from four areas representing the spread of London to the north west (Aylesbury), north east (Little Baddow), south east (Farningham) and south west (Walton-on-the-Hill). Her findings suggested a tendency towards some of the pronunciation features described above, although Przedlacka concluded that there was no definite homogeneity of accents across the area. Where Estuary English trends were appearing these seemed to be led predominantly by the female speakers in the sample.

The phenomenon of Estuary English moving more widely across southern England, and even beyond, has been the subject of research, most notably by Paul Kerswill. Estuary English is a dominant pronunciation form in much of the spoken broadcast media, and from prominent public figures like politicians, business people, sportspeople, actors and musicians. This is one of the factors for the spread of Estuary

ASKHAM BRYAN COLLEGE

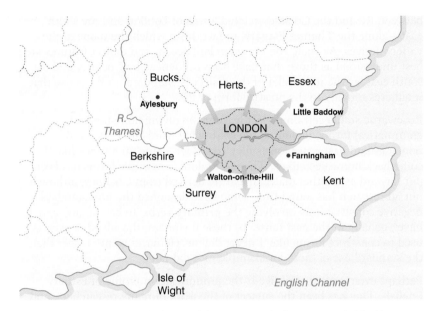

Fig. 23 *Przedlacka's research examined the extent to which Estuary English had become established in London's neighbouring counties*

Study tip

Estuary English is an important variety to revise and know well because it relates to many other areas of variation and change. For example, it highlights issues about the influence of the media, and the concept of dialect levelling.

Further reading

Visit the 'Your Voice' section of the BBC Voices website (http://www.bbc.co.uk/voices/) and read some of the feature articles collected there.

English beyond its regional heartlands of the south east. Kerswill's research into the city of Milton Keynes found vowel fronting, perhaps indicating the influence of Estuary English forms there as the population of the city has grown, with significant migration there from London and the south east. The emergence of Estuary English forms increasingly further afield from London signals something of the spread of the variety – and hints at its potential role in the concept of dialect levelling, in which regional and local dialect differences begin to decrease.

Extension activity

Some of the earlier sociolectal studies presented reveal regional accent and dialect trends, so you could reassess them to add to your map of regional forms around the British Isles. In relation to maps, Professor John Wells has done just this, and further reading on this topic could include his published atlas of British accents. You could also look at:

- Edinburgh English – Deborah Chirrey
- Yorkshire Dialects – Barrie Rhodes.

Publication details are given in the Further reading on page 127.

Topic revision exercise

1 What was Watson suggesting about Scouse when he described it as a 'dialect island'?

2 Describe two of the distinctive pronunciation features of the local Dublin accent.

3 Describe one of the non-standard grammatical forms often associated with Estuary English.

English as a world language

In this topic you will:

■ learn about the extent of English as a world language

■ use examples of usage to consider the ways in which English has influenced, and is influenced by, other varieties of language.

English is a language that has spread across the globe during its modern period and has been adopted as the first common language of several countries – and the first language of business in many more, in every continent. In the 20th century, the far-reaching voice of English language broadcast media contributed to the presence of English, if not as a first language, then as an influence on people's lives across the globe. In the 21st century, the expansion of internet usage to millions of users has contributed to the global visibility of English as an international language – although other languages, notably Chinese and Spanish, also operate on this worldwide scale.

As you now know, language is evolving constantly, and it is difficult to measure the exact extent of the use of English around the world, the varieties it exists in, and (even more so) to predict its future. One useful model is Tom McArthur's 'Circle of World English', drawn up in 1987, shown in Figure 24.

Starter activity

Print out a large, blank map of the world and use an online or text atlas to help you mark on some of the different English-based varieties in McArthur's 'Circle of World English'.

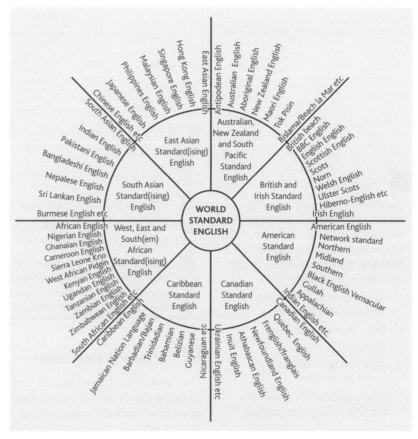

Fig. 24 *McArthur's Circle of World English shows the interrelated nature of English's many diverse forms*

Within Figure 24, McArthur moves outward from a central concept of a 'World Standard English' into eight main regions, each with a main Standard English variety, and many non-standard, derivative forms. This notion of a 'World Standard English' seems purely theoretical as no one standard form has emerged to unify the eight main regions suggested by McArthur – although it is clear that English itself is at the core of them all, in some way. This topic will discuss some of the implications of this wide variety of different Englishes and look in detail at some particular forms.

 Research point

Braj Kachru developed an alternative model of world English known as 'The Three Concentric Circles of Englishes'. Look at his model, given in Figure 25, and contrast it with McArthur's model, particularly in the way it presents the different English-based varieties of the world in relation to one another.

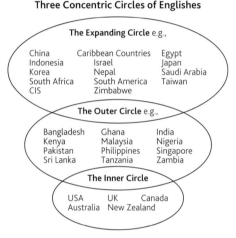

Three Concentric Circles of Englishes

The Expanding Circle e.g.,

China	Caribbean Countries	Egypt
Indonesia	Israel	Japan
Korea	Nepal	Saudi Arabia
South Africa	South America	Taiwan
CIS	Zimbabwe	

The Outer Circle e.g.,

Bangladesh	Ghana	India
Kenya	Malaysia	Nigeria
Pakistan	Philippines	Singapore
Sri Lanka	Tanzania	Zambia

The Inner Circle

USA	UK	Canada
Australia	New Zealand	

Fig. 25 *Kachru's 'Three Concentric Circles of Englishes'*

Extension activity

Use the internet to listen to clips of the following well-known English speakers (see Figure 26). What similarities and differences do you think that they share in their use of the English language?

- Barack Obama, President of the United States (American)
- Billy Connolly, comedian (Scottish)
- Kylie Minogue, actress and singer (Australian)
- Queen Elizabeth II, Queen of the United Kingdom (English)
- Sir Vivian Richards, cricketer and commentator (West Indian)
- Nelson Mandela, former President of South Africa (South African)

Thinking points

1. What do you think the sizes of Kachru's circles represent?

2. How does the nature and usage of English differ between the 'inner', 'outer' and 'expanding' circles?

3. Compare Kachru's model to McArthur's model. What different perspectives do they adopt in categorising English usage around the world? Do you think one could be classified as more 'prescriptivist' or 'descriptivist' than the other?

Different Englishes

On a global level, English can vary in any and all of the ways discussed so far in this book. What becomes more complicated, when you step outside of thinking mainly about English as the language used in the British Isles, is the concept of a standard form. McArthur's model in Figure 24 suggests eight main standard forms, representing the eight major regions of English usage that he perceived – although he, too, acknowledged that varieties may not always fit perfectly into this model. Other models organise these different Englishes in alternative ways – one being to see them as descendants of either British English or American English, as the two dominant forms, put forward in the early 1980s by Peter Strevens.

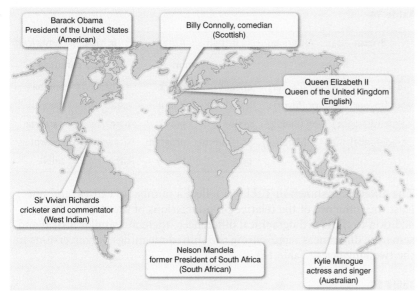

Fig. 26 *Six well-known international English accents from around the world*

The many different forms of English mentioned in McArthur's model may in fact lead to less, rather than greater, language diversity. Many of these forms are pidginised or creolised forms, mixed with other, more local languages. In a similar way to that of dialect levelling in Britain, the expansion of English across the world may well lead to the extinction of many languages – perhaps even hundreds or thousands of the roughly 6,000 in current usage.

Others point to the changing nature of the way in which languages exchange features with one another, due to the increase in travel and international communication and media forms, and suggest that dominant forms have arisen in the past and then fragmented. An example of this is the emergence of **high rising intonation** (HRI) in British English usage (sometimes simplified and termed 'uptalk'). This feature seems to recreate a rise in pitch similar to that used to indicate an **interrogative** in standard British English, but applied to a **declarative** utterance. It has been attributed to a similar pattern found in Australian English, and various theories have been put forward as to how it has arisen in UK usage: through the popularity of Australian soaps on UK television in the 1990s, for example, although some think this link is exaggerated, and it certainly cannot be the only factor.

■ American English

The distinctive sounds of an American accent are probably instantly recognisable to an English speaker in the UK, yet there are more subtle ways that the two main standard varieties differ. The two forms can influence each other and cause change at all levels of the language, often by a slow process of diffusion, without any immediate or obvious consequences. For example, spelling rules, and the spelling of individual words, regularly vary between the languages. Look at Table 14 for a comparison of some British and American spellings.

■ Key terms

High rising intonation (HRI): or high rising terminal, referring to the use of higher pitch at the end of an utterance to indicate it is being delivered as a form of interrogative.

Interrogative: a sentence that functions as a question.

Declarative: a sentence function used to make statements.

■ Research point

In the late-1990s, William Labov reported his findings of a shift in the vowel pronunciations of North American cities, which illustrated a feature that came to be known as 'the Northern cities shift'. Labov's research suggested that the accents spoken in cities such as Philadelphia and Chicago were diverging rapidly, particularly among white English speakers, with the trend being led by women. This went against the widely held assumption that the American accent – like the British – was 'levelling' and becoming more homogenised.

Fig. 27 *Labov noted that white speakers in relatively close, large US cities, were diverging in their accent*

Thinking points

1 Why do you think people of different regions might diverge in the way they speak?

2 What regional examples can you think of in British English that still seem to be unique and diverge from other accents?

Table 14

British	American	British	American	British	American
Rules		Common		Less common	
-re (centre)	-er (center)	cheque	check	amoeba	ameba
-our (favour)	-or (favor)	doughnut	donut	carat	karat
-ogue (dialogue)	-og (dialog)	grey	gray	paralyse	paralyze
-c- (defence)	-s- (defense)	programme	program	snowplough	snowplow
		tyre	tire	titbit	tidbit

The differences shown in Table 14 reflect a number of causes, and not least the influence of the relative pronunciations of the two varieties. In addition to these orthographical differences, there are similar lexical and semantic differences representing the shifted meanings or conversions in the two languages (Table 15).

Table 15

British	American	British	American
flat	apartment	rubber	eraser
plaster	band-aid	torch	flashlight
tin	can	chips	fries
biscuit	cookie	football	soccer
nappy	diaper	post	mail
lift	elevator	dummy	pacifier

Key terms

General American: Like British Standard English and Received Pronunciation forms, General American (GA) is the standard form of English in North America and surrounding regions. It is similar to a generalised form of Midwestern accent, and is the form most commonly used in the American media and film industry.

These lexical differences also exist in phrases with different idiomatic uses in the two forms and in American idioms that have not become a part of British English use, such as 'to talk turkey' (to talk seriously). More common are instances of transmission between the two varieties, particularly from dominant American media and culture entering into the UK, with 'Americanisms' like 'corny', 'guy', and 'jail' entering into common English usage and replacing older items.

Perhaps more subtle still are the prosodic differences between the language – in the pitch, pace and volume patterns used to create the stress emphasis within words. Look at Table 16 showing the comparative stress patterns in RP and **General American** (GA – the standard American accent form), with the stressed part of the word underlined.

Table 16

RP	GA	RP	GA
address	address	garage	garage
cigarette	cigarette	inquiry	inquiry
controversy	controversy	research	research

The respective rhythms of the GA and RP accents have some influence on these prosodic differences. They become a more complex phenomenon when you look for definitive patterns and investigate the effect of word function. For example, although a potential pattern seems to emerge with GA bringing the stressed syllable in a word forwards, to the initial position, the word 'garage' does not follow this rule, and there are others (e.g. 'ballet') that buck the trend. Three of these words can function as both a noun and a verb ('address', 'garage' and 'research'), in which the distinction between the two stress patterns on RP/GA grounds can become further muddled by speakers in each variety using the two forms to toggle between the two different word classes. These complications point to the subtlety of the difference, and to how easily one usage may be interchanged with another from 'across the pond' – the stress patterns shown in Table 16 for 'address' and 'research' being examples where it is not uncommon to hear both forms in both accents in modern usage.

Many aspects of the American language have their roots in centuries of history, with usages that are now rare or archaic in the English used in the UK still in contemporary US currency. Examples of this are typically lexical items, with words like the past participle 'gotten', 'fall' for 'autumn', and 'platter'. Other contextual factors have come to bear, including borrowings from contact with the language of the Native American tribes, especially when confronted with entirely new creatures and plants.

From there, American English was well on its way to forging its distinctive identity. In the 21st century, American English on the one hand continues to proliferate into a wide variety of forms, not least by the process of creolisation discussed next. The diverse nature of American society has seen prolonged and mutual contact between the American and Spanish languages, as well as historical forms from immigration, like the African-American language of Gullah, spoken in some southern states. On the other hand, it is part of a quite different direction in world English, with American and British English growing more similar, frequently occupying the same space on the world wide web and mainstream popular culture – with both exerting more influence and pressure on less affluent and visible forms of language.

Creole and pidgin forms

The ways in which pidgins and creoles come about has already been discussed under the topic of social variation and has been explored in relation to the UK-based form of London Jamaican. Creole and pidgin languages arising out of contact with English come in many shapes and sizes across the globe, and form the majority of the non-standard varieties occurring under the eight standard regions proposed in McArthur's model (Figure 24 on page 63). As these are languages often formed by convenience (particularly in the case of pidgins), they can appear and disappear in a relatively short space of time, if the conditions that made them useful no longer exist. Creole forms tend to be more culturally significant, and take on a more deeply rooted life in the speech of a community and its identity.

Pidgins and Creoles represented in literature

Written texts can also be a source of evidence for pidgin and creole language varieties. Authors use non-standard orthographical conventions to represent phonological patterns and can present nuances of syntax and individual lexical items.

Classroom activity 15

Read the following example of Hawaiian Creole English and describe a non-standard feature of each of the following kinds:

- phonological
- lexical
- grammatical.

Study tip

You can write examples of speech sounds using phonetic spelling of your own devising. It is a good idea to represent them in forward slash marks, /liyk this/.

My Ungko ... he tink my Antee steh going deaf. My Antee ... she no like go doctor, but.

One time ... my Ungko wen go look da doctor. My Ungko wen tell da doctor ... 'Hoy, doctor. I tink Mada steh going deaf. She no like come doctor, but. What can do, eh?'

Da doctor wen tell my Ungko ... 'We will need to determine the seriousness of her hearing loss.'

'How can, but?' My Ungko wen tell da doctor again. 'Mada no like come look you.'

Da doctor wen scratch his chin. 'Perhaps we can try something without her noticing.'

'Shoots!' My Ungko wen ansah. 'What you like try?'

N. Oribio, 'Deaf Ear', in Mark Sebba, Contact Language: Pidgins and Creoles, *1997*

Classroom activity 16

To look at specific examples of language variation, create a table like the one shown on the right for the three versions of the cartoon dialogue.

What does your table show about the way that the cartoon has chosen to represent Jamaican Creole?

Standard English	Kowaiti Bay cartoon	Jamaican Creole
my father	mi father	mi faada

Yes, a car knocked down Tata!

My father!

And we were just talking about him a little while ago!

So where is he now?!

Looks like a doctor knocked him down so ... He took him into his car and carried him to the hospital!

Translation into Frederic Cassidy's phonemic spelling system for representing Jamaican Creole pronunciation:

Yes, kyar lik doun **Tata**!

Mi faada!

An wi jos a taak about im a likl wail!

So we him de **nou**?!

Luk laik a dakta man lik im doun so ...

Im tek im intu im kyar an kyari im gaan tu di **haspital**!

*Jamaican cartoon Kowaiti Bay, and detail in **Mark Sebba**,* Contact Languages: Pidgins and Creoles, *1997*

Jamaican Creole

On pages 54–5 you were introduced to the Cockney/Standard English/ Jamaican Creole hybrid, 'London Jamaican', put forward by Sebba in researching 1990s London boroughs. Now you can look at one of those source varieties, Jamaican Creole, in more detail. Like those of American English, the roots of Jamaican Creole stretch back to the impact of the British colonists of the 17th and 18th centuries, and the use of West African slaves to work the sugar plantations on the Jamaican island. The slaves that came into Jamaica would have spoken mostly African Bantu or Kwa languages, and the language contact that ensued over the centuries shaped the Jamaican Creole form, as an English-lexicon-derived variety. After the abolition of slavery in 1833, Jamaica remained under British colonial rule until 1948. In the 21st century, most Jamaicans speak a version of Creole with a varying degree of Standard English forms, owing to the retention of Standard English as a prestige form in the country. Details of the main features of the stronger, **basilect** Creole form follow – but as a result of the influence of Standard English as the prestige language, it has fewer speakers than diluted forms.

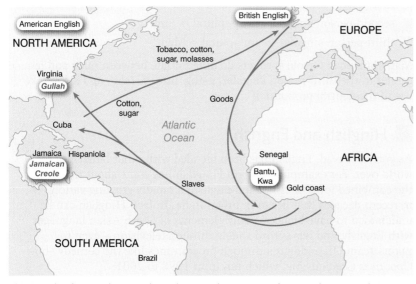

Fig. 28 *The slave trade routes brought several European, African and American language varieties into contact, leading to the development over time of several creole forms*

In the Creole verb system, different tenses and **aspects** are shown by adding additional words or particles to the main verb, rather than by adding the inflectional suffixes found in Standard English. In this sense it compares with the Hawaiian Creole English feature of 'wen + main verb' to create the past tense seen earlier – in fact, researchers looking into many of the creole forms across the world have noted that they share core features of this kind, despite being very distant geographically.

Table 17 shows some examples of tense and aspect forms in Jamaican Creole.

Table 17

Past tense	mi ben taak	I talked
Present progressive aspect	mi a taak	I am talking
Past progressive aspect	mi ben a taak	I was talking

Key terms

Basilect: the variety of language with the lowest status in a speech community.

Aspect: a verb form relating to the duration of an event.

Progressive aspect: a grammatical construction of a verb used to express an action that is in progress.

In these instances, there can be variation in the actual particle used: 'ben' may be pronounced as /bin/ or /ben/ by Jamaican Creole speakers, but the function and verb phrase structure remains the same.

Other Jamaican Creole verb constructions include the use of small words or particles in a copula verb position. For example, from the earlier cartoon, the use of 'deh' in 'Wey him deh now?!' replaces the verb 'is' in Standard English, in the context of the non-standard syntax. The word 'a' is similarly used to replace a form of the verb 'to be' in a statement like 'Mi a di dakta', which would translate word for word as 'I am the doctor' in Standard English. The verb 'to be' is also used as a copula in Standard English to link an adjectival phrase, as the complement to a noun phrase: in Jamaican Creole, this form of copula is not replaced, but is omitted altogether, leaving 'dem likl' in place of 'they are little'.

The pronoun system is one of the more prominent differences in Jamaican Creole, with simplified case and number distinctions across the first- and third-person forms. However, the second-person form does distinguish between singular and plural forms; something Standard English doesn't do. The basic system is:

- first-person singular = 'mi'; plural = 'wi'
- second-person singular = 'yu'; plural = 'unu'
- third-person singular = 'im'; plural = 'dem'.

Many Jamaican Creole speakers do differentiate between male and female gender in the third-person singular, using 'im' and 'shi', and also make use of the neutral pronoun 'it'.

Hinglish and Engrish

As you have read, English has been blended with other languages the world over. For example, the term Hinglish has come about to describe the combined form of Hindi and English, a rapidly growing variety in recent decades that began in urban India. In fact, Hinglish can be understood to have blended many elements of South Asian languages with English, and has spread widely through television – even to mainstream UK audiences through programmes like the comedy show *Goodness Gracious Me*, which ran from 1998 to 2001.

Some examples of Hinglish are:

- **accha**   used to mean 'okay', or 'is that so?'
- **badmash**   a dishonest man
- **buck**   a rupee (the Indian currency)
- **chuddies** underpants
- **filmi**   something related to the Indian Bollywood film industry
- **haina**   similar to the tag question 'isn't it?' (or 'innit')
- **kati**   'I am not your friend any more.'
- **timepass** a distraction for a period of time.

The ways that these words enter into Hinglish can take two forms: as an existing Indian-language word being borrowed; or as a translation of an Indian phrase or idea into English words.

These ways of creating new varieties can be found in particular right across Asia, and the term Engrish has been coined as a 'tongue-in-cheek' term covering the often quite idiosyncratic ways that east-Asian

Study tip

Don't feel that every example you discuss in your essays has to come from a named researcher. It is important to use named research findings, but it is also valuable to include your own examples of contemporary language variation that you may have experienced – make sure you can describe a few features of it accurately and linguistically though.

Classroom activity 17

Sort the words in the list above into the two main sources mentioned: Indian-language source and English-translation source.

languages in particular translate concepts of the Asian source language into English, or the pronunciation patterns used. This process of **assimilation** is because the phonetic patterns in east-Asian languages are very different from those used by English, and so there is little common ground, which means that certain phonemes are hard to reproduce. Also, the semantic and grammatical structures of east-Asian languages (many of which use symbol-based written systems) are similarly incompatible with English. These blended languages include a whole range of varieties, including:

- **Japlish**: Japanese and English and other influences
- **Konglish**: Korean and English and other influences
- **Chinglish**: Mandarin and English and other influences (spoken in China)
- **Taglish**: Tagalog and English and other influences (spoken in the Philippines)
- **Singlish**: Malay and English and other influences (spoken in Singapore)
- **Honglish**: Cantonese and English and other influences (spoken in Hong Kong).

The structure of Asian languages is very different from English in many ways, and this results in different pronunciation, spelling, semantic and grammatical forms taking shape. This has resulted in some quite amusing, even bizarre translations.

Link

Look back at McArthur's 'Circle of World English' on page 63 to see how some of the English varieties fit into his model.

Classroom activity 18

Read the following examples of 'Engrish' and try to work out the Standard English word or phrase that each translates as:

- friend-friend
- hom-reon
- inner clothes
- ryukkusakku
- siyampu.

Topic revision exercise

1. Describe two ways that American English and British English differ.
2. How does the pronoun system of Jamaican Creole work?
3. Why do strange 'Engrish' phraseologies and pronunciations tend to come about when Asian and English languages combine?

Further reading

There have been many ways of exploring the different forms of English in the world. Search for articles that will tell you more about alternative world English models from Peter Strevens, Manfred Gorlach, Marko Modiano and Mario Saraceni. Jane Setter's chapter on World Englishes in *Language: A Student Handbook on Key Topics and Theories* (2013) gives an accessible introduction to the topic and offers different models for the development of Englishes around the world.

Attitudes towards language variation

In this topic you will:

- learn about the main areas of debate involving language variation

- engage with the attitudes of others towards language variation and begin to form your own response.

Key terms

Accent: the specific way words are pronounced according to geographical region.

Starter activity

Carry out a survey using the statements below, with respondents answering 'true' or 'false' to each one. Record the number of people you ask, and their responses, and then count the results overall and for each statement: 'true' answers suggest a prescriptivist attitude towards language, and 'false' answers a descriptivist one.

- It's wrong to 'change' Standard English.

- English is the best language in the world.

- The only 'proper' kind of English is the one spoken in England.

- Some ways of speaking are better than others.

- People who speak non-standard English are usually not very intelligent.

Classroom activity 19

Read the two extracts and discuss the detail of the attitudes displayed by Mr Houston and the caller to a radio talk show.

The different attitudes of prescriptivism and descriptivism can be as equally applied to language variation as they were to language change in the first topic of this section. In terms of variation, prescriptivists would seek to control, and perhaps even prevent, the development of alternative forms to Standard English – with the overall aim of preserving and upholding the status of the standard as the prestige form of the language. Descriptivists would not seek to interfere with variation in this way, but to understand it within its local and global context – although many descriptivists, like David Crystal and Steven Pinker, would uphold the value of Standard English as a core form of the language.

Pronunciation and status

An aspect of non-standard language variety that prescriptivists might choose to object to is that of different **accents**, and the negative connotations that have sometimes been attached to them. These include any number of subjective associations over the years, with regional accents supposedly signifying a lack of intelligence, criminality, a lack of education, or untrustworthiness, amongst other assertions. On the other hand, the late-1990s and the 21st century saw an increase in the appearance of regional accents in national broadcast media and in companies using telephone call centres staffed by operators with regional voices – these instances promoting a positive view of accent variation, connected to values of friendliness, informality and trustworthiness.

Of course, it is difficult to see how either of these positions can really be based on objective, linguistic features. Similar attitudes are applied to other forms of variation, including social and ethnic dialects. It is true that people are constantly subject to sociolinguistic and psycholinguistic pressures that are likely to perpetuate attitudes of all kinds towards language.

Extract 1

'What is the more usual name for H_2O, Ballantyne?' I realise that the teacher has spoken my name. I look up to see Mr. Houston's thin face peering expectantly at me through his thick round glasses. He is almost smirking with anticipation. Does he think I don't know the answer?

Surely not! What has he planned for me, I wonder frantically.

'Wa'er' I answer confidently, in my distinctive Dundee accent.

Houston's smile grows slightly wider.

'Pardon?'

He puts a hand behind his ear and cocks his head.

'Wa'er' I say again, thinking perhaps I had mumbled the first time [...] I look over and see Caroline Patterson leaning towards me [...]

'James, it's water!' she whispers, and suddenly I understand I am not speaking correctly, at least not in the opinion of Mr. Houston. He is mocking my Dundee accent.

G. Rew, 'Wa'er', 1990

Extract 2

Caller: Hey, Jack?

Host: Hello, what's your point?

Caller: Well, I wanted to point out that blacks seem ignorant to me in the way that they talk. I mean they don't seem to see it's spelt A-S-K because they say it as A-X.

Host: But why is that a problem, if you understand what is being said, whoever says it?

Caller: But I don't know. Saying it that way gives it another meaning completely. It makes black people seem stupid.

Host: But, I'll ask you again; why is that a problem if you know the word being said means 'ask'? It's no different from all the other weird pronunciations we all have, is it?

The two extracts raise further debates: the 'them' and 'us' approach to social difference, perhaps particularly in the way that the caller refers to black speakers as 'they', which can result in language becoming a vehicle for personal prejudice – and even racism. The debate over pragmatic use is evident in the host's response to the caller's query, posing the question of what the purpose of language is. Of course, language is many things to many people, but fundamental to that is communication – and, as the host's question points out, if a person's usage is still fulfilling that purpose, the grounds for objection to its forms may not be purely objective or based on functionality. That is to say, objections may be motivated by a particular attitude towards that language variety.

Standard English

Different varieties can receive support or criticism based on their lexical, semantic and grammatical dialect features. The attitudes displayed can be similarly understood within a prescriptivist–descriptivist model, with a typical distinction being that prescriptivists seek to promote the superiority and prestige of Standard English. Perhaps the title of a book by John Honey (a figure associated with prescriptivist attitudes towards English) illustrates the attitude that some adopt in relation to standard and non-standard forms: *The Story of Standard English and its Enemies*, using the negative metaphor of opposition to describe the relationship between Standard English and its related social and regional varieties (its 'Enemies' in Honey's language).

You encountered some examples of the grammatical change objected to by the Grammarians in previous centuries. In modern times, a particular complaint has been the use of informal, non-standard language over Standard English – and this has been complicated by the advent of new technology forms and the non-standard features they have introduced into common usage.

National identities

English has become a significant or dominant language in such a number of countries that it is itself at the heart of several different national identities. England, Scotland, America, Australia and Jamaica are some examples of just such countries – and each has its own distinctive variety of English. With this comes a distinct concept of the standard variety of a country, and you have already explored some of the details of several of these forms.

This can become complicated when these national forms come into contact with each other, or other non-English languages. The debate, already raised in this section, around the relationship between British

Link

Turn to page 75 for examples of the kinds of attitude researchers like Howard Giles have found people to have towards different accents.

Link

Look back at pages 65–7 for more detail on British and American English variation.

English and American English forms, is an example of this, and shows how relatively minor differences like the difference between the spelling pattern 'favour' or 'favor', can become attached to attitudes of correctness in language. The use of high rising intonation is another example mentioned earlier – this time suggesting contact between British English and Australian English forms. The nature of the relationship between these and other forms is clearly very complex – with one variety originating from another, and developing its own identity.

Sometimes this contact can lead to strong opinions of the type discussed earlier, especially when this involves contact with languages foreign to English. Consider the following perspectives on the way English usage is being shaped, both within the UK and around the world.

Extract 1

Statement from the Home Secretary

Theresa May said, 'I believe being able to speak English should be a pre-requisite for anyone who wants to settle here. The new English requirement for spouses will help promote integration, remove cultural barriers and protect public services.

… 'This is only the first step. We are currently reviewing English language requirements across the visa system with a view to tightening the rules further in the future.

https://www.gov.uk/government/news/migrants-marrying-uk-citizens-must-now-learn-english, 9th June 2010

Extract 2

The prestigious *Politecnico di Milano*, a world leading school of engineering, announced in April 2012 that with effect from 2014 all postgraduate courses and a large number of undergraduate courses will be taught and assessed entirely in English. According to the university's rector: "We strongly believe our classes should be international classes – and the only way to have international classes is to use the English language."

In an age of globalisation and internationalisation of higher education, the only way to attract overseas students from the emerging economies of India, China and Asia, and fund ongoing research, is to have courses in English. As the *Politecnico* put it, there is "no other choice".

http://www.timesofmalta.com/articles/view/20120729/opinion/English-is-world-s-lingua-franca.430532, 29th July 2012

Extract 3

… improvised, speech-like forms of written English are proliferating on Facebook, Twitter and elsewhere. This means that non-standard dialects (Hinglish, Singlish, southern white English, black American English) are being written more than they used to. We might even see "standard" written forms of these, or something like them, emerge.

… English is undergoing a novel experiment. I can't think of a standardised living language that has been spoken by more non-native-speakers than natives for a long time. Natives consider the language "theirs", and will resist deep structural changes. The influence of foreigners is likely to cause annoyance. But such changes will come, inevitably, if slowly.

http://www.economist.com/blogs/johnson/2012/12/internet-and-language-change#, 18th December 2012

Further reading

Read Matthew Engel's online BBC News 'Viewpoint' article, 'Why do some Americanisms irritate people?' (http://www.bbc.co.uk/news/14130942). Then look at the list of reader examples sent in to the BBC about American English after the article was published (http://www.bbc.co.uk/news/magazine-14201796).

When languages overcome the potential barriers to language contact, and create new pidgin and creole varieties, it is interesting to note the implications often involved. Somewhat ironically, it can be the fact that a creole form contains 'too many' features of its source, lexifier language that can leave it exposed to criticism from standard speakers who regard it as no more than a lesser dialect form. As a result, pidgins and creoles tend to be of low status.

As a creole form distinguishes and establishes itself within a community of users, it can develop, and acquire status and even more tangible forms of recognition. For example, some pidgin and creole forms are used as a main language in some schools, and some have limited official status and uses nationally and internationally: e.g. Hinglish is used in many Indian schools and Tok Pisin (an English-derived language) is widely used by the government, primary schools and public services in Papua New Guinea). What is perhaps clear is that immediate attitudes on both sides of the variation debate may be strongly held, but that language forms generally need much longer periods of time to flourish and reveal their true worth.

Q Testing attitudes to variation

Linguists have long been engaged with trying to work out the sort of attitudes people have towards different varieties of English, and particularly accent. Accents are often attributed with stereotypes, which are in turn often reinforced by the media. These impressions can be created by 'unscientific' modes like satire, such as Harry Enfield's 'Scousers' shouting 'Calm down! Calm down!' in the 1980s and 1990s, or by scientific methods like the University of Aberdeen reporting in 2006 that the Brummie accent is the best at delivering comedy (think of Jasper Carrot, Lenny Henry and Frank Skinner – each with a distinctive 'Midlands' accent).

The approach taken by the University of Aberdeen took the form of telling the same joke to people, but in different accents. This is known as a 'matched-guise' methodology, where every attempt is made to isolate different accents as the only thing changing in the experiment, and then finding ways to record the response people give. One of the founding examples of this technique being used was carried out by Howard Giles in the 1970s, when he tested the perception of 'trustworthiness' that people interpreted in different accent forms. At that time, Giles found that RP was rated as being a mark of a person who was reliable, well educated and confident. Regional varieties scored more highly on traits such as friendliness and sincerity and were perceived to be more persuasive than RP – which compares well with the theories of status and solidarity discussed on pages 79–80.

More recently, in 2003, the image consultant firm the Aziz Corporation researched the perception amongst leading business people along similar lines of the status and solidarity model. Almost half of the respondents saw a strong regional accent form as a disadvantage in the business world. Their findings also differentiated between regional accents, with 43 per cent rating a Scots accent user as successful – and at the other end of the scale, findings showed 16 per cent to consider a Cockney accent to be a potential sign of dishonesty, with similar, negative, attitudes being levelled at the Scouse, Brummie and West Country accents.

Fig. 29 *Lenny Henry is one of several high profile comedians using a distinctive accent from Birmingham and the Midlands*

Study tip

When writing about attitudes to language varieties, aim to present a balanced view. For example, RP is seen as a prestige form but also has negative associations; regional forms provoke a range of attitudes, so avoid polarising the RP/regional variety debate.

Topic revision exercise

1 How does the status of international forms of English, like pidgin and creole, differ across the globe?

2 How did RP and regional forms compare in Giles's findings in his research into the attitudes towards different accent forms?

Further reading

Search the internet for 'BBC Voices poll results' to read about the findings of a survey of 5,000 people and their attitudes to language variation in the British Isles.

Language around you 4

RP is a useful reference point when writing about language variation and change. Like Standard English, it is a form against which non-standard forms are measured. RP has variously been known as a BBC, King's, Queen's, Oxford and public-school accent. What does this tell you about its status and usage?

Language variation theory

In this topic you will:

- learn about the main variation theories that have arisen out of the work of linguists

- evaluate the implications of some of these theoretical models.

Several of the case studies that you have encountered so far have made reference to related theoretical models proposed by their researchers. In this topic, theories that can be applied to the concept of variation of language are set out briefly, with some discussion of the context in which they were proposed.

Social variation theory

Anti-language

The theory of anti-language is used to explain the forms of sociolect that arise to support subcultures that seek some sort of covert identity, for example Leet and the lexicon employed by drug users to describe their habit. Often, this is related to the idea of deviance – of behaviour that is against the normal practices of society, and sometimes criminality.

The linguist, Michael Halliday, identified nine features common to anti-languages.

1 It is the language of an anti-society that exists within society as an alternative to it.

2 Word lists often form the main evidence of anti-languages.

3 Anti-languages are mostly formed by relexicalising existing vocabulary items.

4 Anti-languages have a different lexicon but use the same grammar as the main society.

5 Anti-language users communicate meanings that are inaccessible to a non-user.

6 Subcultures with an anti-language view it as a fundamental part of their identity.

7 Conversation is the main form of communication used to uphold the anti-language.

8 Anti-language is a vehicle of resocialisation.

9 There is continuity and exchange between language and anti-language.

Starter activity

Look back through the previous topics on language variation and make a list of different variation forms by taking the one you know the most about from each one (for example, Polari, Scouse, Leet, etc.). Use these to test Halliday's anti-language model on this page. Give each of your varieties a score out of 9 for the number of Halliday's anti-language features you think it fulfils.

Difference and dominance theories

The terms 'difference' and 'dominance' have been applied to attitudes towards language differences between men and women. As mentioned earlier, researchers like Fishman have interpreted their findings based on a model that sees the prime reason for variation between the language use of each gender as being to do with the historically **patriarchal** structure of society. This is the dominance model, also supported by Dale

Key terms

Patriarchal: this term describes ways of thinking or doing that are male-centred or male-dominated.

Spender, the author of *Man Made Language*. The difference model takes the view that males and females, either biologically, or by socialisation, are inherently different – although it does not imply that one is superior to the other. Tannen's work, discussed earlier, is seen by some as an example of this difference model.

Finally, the 'deficit' model states that men and women are not only different, and that one dominates the other (men dominating women), but that this exists because of inferior female attributes, in terms of their language use. Such models set up a 'male norm' as the form of language that is standard, and attributes prestige, and see women's language as deviating from this because of its deficiencies. Lakoff's work, mentioned earlier, is often seen as adopting this position, for example in her book, *Language and Woman's Place*, by implying that women must modify their language use, in order to meet this expectation of a male-structured language.

Open and closed networks and Network Strength

Lesley Milroy carried out research in Belfast, Northern Ireland in 1977 and 1980, into the ways in which separate communities spoke, and how language represented the way that they integrated into their community. She gathered data through an **ethnographic study** of communities in three working-class areas: Ballymacarrett (a Protestant area in East Belfast); Hammer (a Protestant area in West Belfast); and Clonard (a Catholic area in West Belfast).

Milroy assessed the individuals in each community and gave them a Network Strength Score, rated from one to five, which reflected that person's knowledge of others in his or her community, with five representing close, strong ties with others in the community. She then tested the use of several linguistic variables, including the pronunciation of the /th/ sound in a word like 'mother' and the backing of the /a/ phoneme in words like 'hat', as they were evident in both standard and non-standard forms.

The approach adopted by Milroy is interesting to contrast with the social stratification approach described earlier in the work of Trudgill. 'Social stratification' means that Trudgill structured his results set based on a socio-economic 'ranking' of the respondents that he researched. This had the effect of presenting social class as the dominant way of interpreting his findings. Milroy's approach sought to 'describe' the way that language was used by groups to form and maintain relationships, and so presented a different form of analysis – the idea of a variety having a language community, rather than being directly linked to social status, or another social variable.

Milroy's findings showed that a high Network Strength Score correlated with use of non-standard pronunciation and therefore with a broader use of the vernacular, local accent forms. She observed that gender had an impact on these forms. Men more commonly exhibited a high usage of vernacular and belonged to close-knit social networks, and women tended to use less vernacular forms and be part of less dense social networks. Where this gender trend was reversed, in the younger women of the Clonard, it was because the social context (high male unemployment and women working together) created a closely knit community amongst themselves.

Milroy's conclusions put forward the idea of open and closed networks: an open network being one in which members tend not to know each other well or at all; a closed network being a community in which all members know each other, and Network Strength is high.

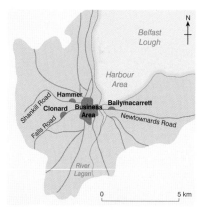

Fig. 30 *The areas of Belfast in Milroy's study: geographical location and the roles within working communities combine to shape language variation*

Regional and contact variation theory

Koineisation

The concept of koine (pronounced /coy-nay/ or /coy-nee/) languages is related to the phenomenon of language contact. The process of **koineisation** is one in which a new, standard variety of language is formed by the contact of two existing dialect forms of a language. The new koine form that emerges exists separately from the source dialects and does not interfere with their use, and all three forms remain as mutually intelligible language options for the speakers involved.

Paul Kerswill, some of whose other research is described elsewhere, identified a regional koine in existence in Milton Keynes, as a result of speakers from the south of England relocating there in the mid-20th century. Milton Keynes represents a special focus for linguistic research as it was 'created' as a city during the second half of the 20th century, with the population of the area more than quadrupling from the 1950s to the 1990s, when it then exceeded 200,000 people. Milton Keynes saw a large number of speakers come into it with existing regional dialect forms different from that spoken by the natives of the Milton Keynes area.

In terms of koineisation, Kerswill identified the emergence of a Milton Keynes dialect that was a shared, standard form in the area, representing the combination of accent forms of the native and incoming communities – whilst the distinct accent forms were retained by the communities in their own language use.

Dialect levelling

The concept of dialect levelling has been mentioned in the previous case studies, and particularly in relation to Estuary English. Dialect levelling is the gradual eradication of the marked differences between local dialect, or sociolect forms. It has most commonly been applied to the change in accent features of regional forms in recent decades.

Kerswill's research in Milton Keynes and Reading in the 1990s is one example of study that has unearthed some evidence of dialect levelling, and that has seen Estuary English as a variety wielding particularly strong influence over localised, regional dialects. The features emerging in the Milton Keynes dialect included the fronting of vowel sounds, in a similar fashion to that described in the Estuary English accent patterns earlier – north of the originating areas of Estuary English. Similar patterns were found in Reading, to the south-west margin of the original Estuary English heartlands.

Some researchers have identified some individual Cockney and Estuary English features even further afield, for example the work of Jane Stuart-Smith and a Glasgow University study into accent changes in Glasgow. Her findings did not conclude that Estuary English was supplanting the existing Glaswegian dialect, but features like **th-fronting** (found in Cockney where 'think' may shift to /fink/), and the glottal stop did appear in her findings.

Extension activity

If you have a friend or relative with a non-southern accent, record his or her speech and assess it for Estuary English features (see page 61). Do you see any evidence that he or she is using Estuary English features? Ask if he or she is conscious of being exposed to Estuary English at work, home, on television, or by other ways.

Code-switching

Code-switching is a term used to describe the ability of a speaker to 'switch' between different language varieties in his or her language use, often with other individuals that are able to do this, and have shared experience of several different language forms.

London Jamaican (page 54) is an ideal example of code-switching in use: the speakers in Sebba's research are able to incorporate Standard English, RP, Jamaican Creole and Cockney forms in their use of language. Code-switching can result in complex new linguistic combinations and exists in other English-speaking communities where there is significant language contact with another language. For example, the term 'Wenglish' is coined in Wales to refer to the combination of English and Welsh language forms, and code-switched language forms are in evidence in the strong Asian communities in several British towns and cities, where Asian languages like Urdu or Punjabi may be mixed with local dialect and Standard English forms, in a similar way to that seen in London Jamaican.

The environment in which code-switching takes place means that some speakers, usually young speakers, will have to adapt to a world in which they encounter many language forms. For example, a member of Sebba's 'Catford Girls' Possee' might encounter Jamaican Creole in their family and at home; perhaps it is the only language form used by older family members. Their schooling is likely to expose them to Standard English and RP forms and may even expect them to use and reproduce these forms themselves. Also, their social lives at school and outside will bring them into contact with local, Cockney speakers, in shops and in their friendships. In this context, it is easy to see how a variety like London Jamaican, or Fox's MLE emerges, and how a skill like code-switching enables such speakers to deal with the complexities of their language community.

Code-switching can take place across the whole range of accent and dialect forms. Therefore, a speaker may end up merging different layers of varieties: for example, using a Cockney dialect word but pronouncing it with a Jamaican Creole accent pattern – and maybe even placing it in a Standard English sentence, in terms of grammatical construction. Adopting this perspective shows why researchers like Sebba are keen to point out the sophistication of such language use, and the highly-skilled manipulation of language involved – in opposition to the criticisms sometimes levelled at new forms as being 'dumbed down', or inferior.

Other variation-related theory

Status and solidarity

The research of Ellen Ryan and others proposed two different approaches to assessing the attitudes people have towards different speakers. She proposed two sets of value systems, summed up as 'status' and 'solidarity'. A similar theory by Robert Hopper and Christopher Zahn extended these values to include assessments of an individual's superiority, attractiveness and dynamism. These were then used to judge the perception people had of different speakers through their speech forms – look at Table 18 to see an amalgamation of the values proposed by Ryan, Zahn and Hopper.

Link

Look back at Mark Sebba's London Jamaican work on pages 54–5.

Table 18

Status		Solidarity	
Low	High	Low	High
Uneducated	Educated	Untrustworthy	Trustworthy
Poor	Wealthy	Unfriendly	Friendly
Unintelligent	Intelligent	Unkind	Kind
Illiterate	Literate	Awful	Nice
Lower class	Upper class	Hostile	Good-natured

Extension activity

Use the characteristics listed in Table 18 to carry out your own research into Ryan, Zahn and Hopper's concepts of status and solidarity. Design a way of asking people to select from these characteristics to describe different accents – perhaps playing them audio clips from the internet.

In the 1980s, Ryan, along with other researchers, tested these out with male American and British English speakers, presenting lower class and middle class speakers to a panel of undergraduates, to assess against the values in Table 18. They found that British and middle class speakers were given high 'status' ratings, exceeding the significantly lower 'status' ratings of the American and lower class speakers.

These values have become part of a wider debate about accent forms, with the relationships between different regional accents and sociolects being understood to operate on status and solidarity grounds. A typical view from this perspective has been of the standard prestige form RP being associated with high status values, but not necessarily high solidarity values. In contrast, specific regional forms tend to attract lower status ratings and offer a mixed pattern of solidarity values, depending on the cultural status of that variety at the time. Generally, however, regional forms report higher solidarity scores – no doubt being one of the reasons behind the increased use of regional-accented telephone call centre workers mentioned on page 72.

Link

Look back at the findings of Howard Giles on page 75 for more information on attitudes towards different accents.

Fig. 31 *Call centres are often located where the local population uses a particular regional dialect*

Sociolinguistic maturation

The concept of sociolinguistic maturation refers to the age at which a speaker becomes far less susceptible to the influence of different varieties of language on their own usage. There is no set age for this, although researchers have often found results in their work that suggest that it 'sets in' around the late teens to early twenties, after which adult speakers are much less likely to significantly alter their accent or dialect patterns because of any new, strong sociolinguistic factor – like moving to another part of the UK, for example.

Conversely, children, before reaching sociolinguistic maturation, are much more likely to modify and vary their own usage. Sebba's findings of the 'Catford Girls' Possee' can be understood in these terms, with the older family members not merging with London and English speech forms to anywhere near the same level as the girls themselves. So, in turn, these younger speakers are able to employ techniques like code-switching and form new varieties like London Jamaican, by becoming the main promoters of change.

Kerswill's Milton Keynes study returned similar results. In his study, the older caregivers and parents of children had not had their speech modified by the features of the new Milton Keynes dialect emerging. Even more telling though was the pattern emerging from the language use of the children themselves. The youngest children exhibited similar speech patterns to the caregivers, perhaps showing that most of the language forms they experienced were from within the home, and from the caregivers themselves. The older girls surveyed, who were in their mid-teens, showed the strongest incidence of the emerging Milton Keynes dialect – they were being shaped by their exposure to the koineisation described on page 78, and were shaping the new speech community and form. You might speculate that their speech would in turn 'harden' over the next 5 to 10 years, as they too entered into sociolinguistic maturation, and the new form was established. Fox and Kerswill's research into MEYD varieties also hypothesises about the future for such youth dialects, and whether they will be carried into adulthood by their speakers.

> ### Study tip
>
> Sociolinguistic maturation is a good example of a theory you can apply to many areas of the language variation debate. Evaluate different theories to identify the most versatile ones when answering a language variation question.

Language around you 5

Do you think you have begun the process of sociolinguistic maturation? Think about the source of different aspects of your own language usage – turns of phrase and idioms, the accent (or accents!) you use, and whether you think they will be something you will keep, or are just a passing phase.

Topic revision exercise

1. Name three of the aspects of anti-language set out by Halliday.
2. How is Estuary English related to the concept of dialect levelling?
3. Why do some English speakers make use of the ability to code-switch?

Further reading

Lancaster University has a language variation and linguistic theory research group. Visit their homepage on the Lancaster University website (http://www.lancs.ac.uk/fass/groups/LVLT/index.htm) and read some of the documents in their 'News' and 'Publications' sections.

Exam preparation

In this topic you will:

- learn how to approach the comparative format of the exam

- apply what you have learned about language change and variation so far to help analyse and evaluate texts and data.

The exam

In the exam you must choose to complete a task on either language change or language variation. Both tasks consist of an essay question based on the comparison of two pieces of data (which may take the form of a spoken or written text, or a presentation of research findings of some kind). In the essay you are required to draw on the understanding and knowledge you have gained during the English Language A course to evaluate ideas and issues about language change or variation.

The language change and language variation tasks are each worth the same number of marks (45) and have the same breakdown of three AOs: AO1; AO2; and AO3.

Assessment objectives

- AO1: Select and apply a range of linguistic methods, to communicate relevant knowledge using appropriate terminology and coherent, accurate written expression: *10 marks.*

- AO2: Demonstrate critical understanding of a range of concepts and issues related to the construction and analysis of meanings in spoken and written language, using knowledge of linguistic approaches: *20 marks.*

- AO3: Analyse and evaluate the influence of contextual factors on the production and reception of spoken and written language, showing knowledge of the key constituents of language: *15 marks.*

You are probably familiar with the idea of AOs from your AS study – and with these three in particular. For AO1, you will need to make good use of linguistic terminology, from the main linguistic concepts that you learned at AS level, through to the new, specific terms involved with language change and variation. AO2 will assess your ability to apply and evaluate the details of concepts, debates and research in Section A of this book to the texts you analyse. AO3 asks you to consider the contextual factors described in these sections, but also to engage with what the texts are actually about. How is the subject matter of each text being represented by the speaker, writer or narrator?

Exam strategy

There are three main ways you should handle the texts or data you are given in the exam questions: planning how you will break them down, the process of writing up your analysis, and finally proofreading your work briefly.

For planning, it is a good idea to annotate the texts well before you write. You probably have time in the exam to make points about four or five main aspects of each text or piece of data in your essay.

Usually, tackling them chronologically in the text is fine, but it is also acceptable to jump between texts, or change the order, if you see a particular reason to do so – you are looking to generate an overall argument of some kind across your essay. Begin your writing with a brief introduction and end with a definite conclusion.

Try to leave a little time at the end of each response to proofread it. Look for any spelling mistakes you tend to make, and check your phrasing is clear.

Study tip

Your own practice written essays in response to paired texts like these should make full use of quotation within your points, and extend to 1,000 words as a rough guide, given the 75 minutes available to read the texts, plan and write an answer.

Language change

Below is an example of a Section A exam question on Language change. It is followed by a sample response, and comments on that response.

If you choose to answer the first of the two questions in Section A, you will need to feel comfortable reading and understanding texts taken from any time in the past 400 years. You will need to combine the linguistic, historical and social insights that you gain, to construct a well-rounded idea of the development of the English language across the modern era.

Practice question 1

This paired data and task question focuses on language change. As you compare the texts, try to include reflections on some of the relevant research and issues that you have studied in this unit.

Text A contains the beginnings and endings of two letters written by men anticipating their deaths; the first letter, written in 1603, is from Sir Walter Raleigh to his wife Elizabeth, after he has been sentenced to death, and the 1943 letter is written by Jack Yeoman, an RAF officer who was later killed on a raid over Germany in the Second World War.

Text B is taken from an article entitled 'Age of informality' from the website of a digital agency specialising in web design and marketing.

Fig. 32 *Sir Walter Raleigh*

- Analyse how the writers of Text A use language to express their thoughts and feelings, and to present the situation they find themselves in.
- Referring to Text A and Text B and your own studies, evaluate the extent to which language used in private communication has changed between these two eras.

Text A

When I am gonne, no doubt you shal be sought unto by many, for the world thinks that I was very ritch; but take heed of the pretences of men and of their affections; for they laste but in honest and worthy men. And no greater misery cann befall you in this life then to become a pray, and after to be despised. I speak it (God knowes) not to disswad you from marriage – for that will be best for you – both in respect of God and the world. As for me, I am no more your's, nor you myne. Death hath cutt us asunder; and God hath devided me from the world, and you from me …

The everlasting, infinite powerfull, and inscrutable God, that Almightie God that is goodnes itself, mercy itself, the true lief and light, keep thee and thine, and have mercy on me, and teach me to forgeve my persecutors and false accusers; and send us to meete in His glorious kingdome. My true wief, farewell. Blesse my poore boye; pray for me. My true God hold you both in His armes.

Written with the dyeing hand of sometyme thy husband, but now (alasse!) overthrowne.

Your's that was; but nowe not my owne,

W. Ralegh.

J. E. Lewis, (ed.) The Mammoth Book of Private Lives, *1999*

Fig. 33 *RAF bombers during the Second World War*

RAF April 1943

Stella Darling,

This is a letter written despite our decision not to write again – it is a letter I hope you will never receive because it will only be sent to you if I am killed, posted as missing or something equally final.

This, especially put as such a bold statement, will probably be a most unpleasant shock to you. I am very sorry about that, but there are one or two things I want to tell you which will hardly be breaking our agreement as I shall have ceased to be the Jack you knew and loved …

So this is my final goodbye. Thank you once more, my darling, for your love and may God bless you and grant you the success and peace in your life to come which you so richly deserve.

My love goes with you always.

Jack

R. Hamilton and N. Soames (eds), Intimate Letters, *1994*

Text B

Age of informality

Dear Sir or Madam,

Is there really any need to be so formal?

Obviously, the need to be formal is entirely dependent on context. However, the way in which we define and differentiate contexts is changing. This change is not simply with whom we are communicating or when we do so, but the major catalyst has been the method by which we communicate.

Email was initially considered as an electronic form of "snail mail" and much like other areas of early digital, old print rules applied. The amount of time it takes to send or receive, and even format a letter is considerably longer than an email. As a faster way of formatting emerged with email, separate paragraphs were left hanging on for dear life.

As more people adopted mobile phones, very few had access to their emails via their handset. This created a need to communicate quickly without speaking and gave rise to Short Messaging Services (SMS) or Texting.

By placing a limit on the number of characters that could be sent in one message SMS has been responsible for the growth of a new language. Textese. This has evolved from the necessity to convey a message in as few characters as possible in order to save time and money.

Having identified an evolution of language there is also a militant minority that refuses to abbreviate anything from 'etcetera' to 'great' and who continue to punctuate correctly. There have been many sticklers who despite the growth of a new written form of language have stayed true to the "rules" of the written word. They abbreviate nothing, even if it does take an eon to type and a small fortune to send.

The large uptake in smartphones has enabled users to access email, SMS, Instant Messaging and Social Networks from one handset. Whereas before each platform had its own purpose, the boundaries have blurred and a new style has transcended across all of these avenues of communication.

Culturally, there has been a paradigm shift in the way that context and technology affect the style we adopt when interacting with one another. This shift is somewhat comparable to the 1650s phasing out of the use of "Thou" and "Thy". The use of these words was once a relevant way of denoting status and respect. The beauty is that language, form and style are constantly evolving.

Ttyl.

http://www.electricdialogue.com/age-of-informality/

A sample response

Texts A and B represent a neat overview of the change that private messages have undergone over the Modern English period, from personal letters through to SMS texts and emails. The archaic and non-standard features in Text A, and the abbreviated forms of 'textese' described in Text B suggest that language has always contained non-standard forms, even if the technology we use to produce it changes over time.

Apart from the dates of writing, the two extracts in Text A seem to share remarkably similar contexts. The genre of both is a letter – even more specifically, a personal and private letter. Both are written by male writers in a situation where they are contemplating their death. The audience is very similar, with both writers writing to a loved one and partner. The purposes of the texts share some common ground as both try to comfort the receiver to an extent and both writers are trying to express their final thoughts and wishes. However, the two letters do contrast in the times in which they were written, between the Early Modern and later Modern English texts, spanning nearly 350 years.

Raleigh's text employs a direct opening through the subordinate clause 'When I am gonne', making the immediate assertion that he is going to die. The compound-complex sentence that follows, as well as being typical of the 'suspended' sentences found in Early Modern English writing, might well reflect the disorganisation of the writer's mind in the face of the psychological pressure his situation exposes him to. This is also shown in the way bracketed phrases are used in the clause '(God knowes)' and the exclamation '(alasse!)'.

Jack's letter opens with a good deal of qualification owing to the uncertainty of his position, for example in the triad list of possible fates he offers in the conditional clause at the end of the first paragraph: the past-participle phrases 'killed' and 'posted as missing' and the noun phrase 'something equally final'. It is also a multi-clause sentence, but the tone and delivery are different from Raleigh's letter; Jack's feels more definite and seemingly more planned.

Study tip

Aim to give as much depth and detail as you can in your linguistic description. For example, if you quote a clause, aim to define its type (conditional and main clauses are quoted in this essay).

There is frequent use of lexical items from the field of religious belief in Raleigh's text, which reflects not only his own faith, but also the mainstream position of the Christian faith at the time, shown in proper nouns like 'God', as well as extended, highly modified noun phrases like 'The everlasting, infinite powerfull, and inscrutable God' that may even be taken from the words to some kind of church service at the time. This is probably also part of the reason for the archaic and formal terms like the adverb 'asunder', suggesting perhaps that Raleigh takes some comfort in liturgical language and finds it easier to express himself that way when faced with death.

Jack's letter becomes more personal, emotional and affectionate as it continues – and more informal – with the main clause 'I am very sorry about that' beginning this trend. The final paragraph includes a term of endearment in the noun phrase 'my darling', although it is interesting that the writer also uses religious language in the compound verb phrase 'may God bless you and grant you' to help him bid his final farewell to his wife.

Text B raises many contemporary technological issues that have changed the way language is used to create personal messages. However, it also discusses the idea of changes in formality and the attitudes people hold towards standard and non-standard forms.

The examples of language provided by Text A suggest a change in formality, although neither use a formal salutation like the 'Dear Sir or Madam' reference contained in Text B. The religious language, like the capitalisation of the noun 'God' and the possessive determiner 'His', are treated with a formal reverence by Raleigh, and similarly, Jack's letter does not use a formal salutation or signing off, just the simple sentence 'My love goes with you always', and its only real formality is in the references to 'God'. However, Text B suggests that the technological change and speedier ability to send and reply in an email have produced even more informal modes of writing, involving heavily abbreviated forms, for example.

However, formality is not necessarily the same as how standard or non-standard language is, and Raleigh's extract in Text A provides an insight into language written before standardisation had fully taken hold. For example, there are common non-standard orthographical patterns common to the Early Modern English period, like the use of the final 'e' in the present tense verb 'laste', and the consonant doubling seen in the modal verb 'cann' and the adjective 'powerfull'. These sometimes reflect older origins of particular words, but also the pronunciation of the writer. The idea of 'Textese' in Text B is another example, this time of modern non-standard forms, like the use of phonetic spelling in the abbreviated conjunction 'coz', and forms that also use non-alphabetic characters such as in the adjective 'gr8'. It is ironic perhaps that prescriptivists might be more likely to view textese in a negative light, like the 'sticklers' mentioned in Text B, and see it as a symptom of Aitchison's 'crumbling castle' metaphor – ruining a once-beautiful language – whereas Raleigh's text also shows that such experimentation with the rules of English has been a continual process in the language.

Both texts are good examples of functional theory in practice. Jack makes use of features like punctuation dashes to help him express his train of thought, and Raleigh does the same, with communicating their ideas being more important than observing more formal conventions. Functional theory is identifiable in many contemporary and electronic language forms, for example in the rise of initialisms like the 'TTYL' used at the end of Text B and acronyms like 'LOL' (when pronounced to rhyme with 'loll').

These lead to issues of identity, particularly in personal written language. David Crystal detailed some of the language forms common in electronic communication, for example in the creation of emoticons using rebus constructions of many different forms of character, including numerals and punctuation marks. This appears to be a novel change in private communication: the blurring of spoken and written modes in texts, as well as their brevity, leading to ways of reproducing tone and paralinguistic features such as facial expression through pictures like :-) to represent a smiling face or happiness.

In conclusion, because private writing has a much smaller audience, it is often a rich place for non-standard language forms to change and flourish over time, as it is not subject to the normal tests of standardisation. People might also feel freer to express themselves in this context, and these texts show how writers have always taken that opportunity in personal letters, texts and emails.

Comment

This is a good example of the sort of essay you should practise producing. Look back carefully at the following features of it.

- The first paragraph is an overall introduction followed by a clear 'audience, purpose, context' paragraph for Text A (AO3). These 'APC' paragraphs are a good way to get started as they help you to understand exactly what sort of texts you are working with. These help as the analytical examples you then go on to give can refer back to a point of audience, purpose or context to help explain the reason for the meaning or effect involved (AO2).

- The essay is approximately 1,100 words long (AO1). Answers of around 1,000 words long would be a good guide length to work towards producing, given the amount of time (approximately 75 minutes) you will have to prepare your answer and write it.

- The essay tackles the two bullet points in the question, one by one, the first half of the essay working mostly to explore the meaning and effect of the language in the letters (AO3) and the second half of the essay concentrating on discussing theoretical points (AO2).

- A number of references to the student's own study have been brought in to the answer, including Aitchison's crumbling castle metaphor, functional theory, Early Modern English, orthographical change, functional theory, and David Crystal's computer-mediated communication research (AO2).

Language variation

The following is an example of a Section A exam question on Language variation. It is followed by a sample response, and comments on that response.

If you choose to answer the second of the two questions in Section A, you will need to have a good understanding of the features of a range of social and regional varieties of English. You will also need to be able to refer to examples of research and theory put forward by linguists about language variation.

Practice question 2

This paired data and task question focuses on language variation. As you compare the texts, try to include reflections on some of the relevant research and issues that you have studied in this unit.

Text C is an example of character dialogue taken from Chapter One of D.H. Lawrence's novel *Sons and Lovers,* published in 1913.

Text D is an extract from a book by John Honey entitled *Does Accent Matter?*

- Analyse the way in which the language of Text C portrays the life of a coal miner in the north east of England.
- Referring to Text C and Text D and your own studies, evaluate the way spoken language varieties are related to regional and social identity.

Text C

Her smile was very beautiful. It moved the man so that he forgot everything.

"No, I won't dance," she said softly. Her words came clean and ringing.

Not knowing what he was doing—he often did the right thing by instinct—he sat beside her, inclining reverentially.

"But you mustn't miss your dance," she reproved.

"Nay, I don't want to dance that—it's not one as I care about."

"Yet you invited me to it."

He laughed very heartily at this.

"I never thought o' that. Tha'rt not long in taking the curl out of me."

It was her turn to laugh quickly.

"You don't look as if you'd come much uncurled," she said.

"I'm like a pig's tail, I curl because I canna help it," he laughed, rather boisterously.

"And you are a miner!" she exclaimed in surprise.

"Yes. I went down when I was ten."

She looked at him in wondering dismay.

"When you were ten! And wasn't it very hard?" she asked.

"You soon get used to it. You live like th' mice, an' you pop out at night to see what's going on."

"It makes me feel blind," she frowned.

"Like a moudiwarp!" he laughed. "Yi, an' there's some chaps as does go round like moudiwarps." He thrust his face forward in the blind, snout-like way of a mole, seeming to sniff and peer for direction.

Extension activity

Use the internet to research the north-east dialect of Pitmatic, which flourished in and around mining towns like Ashington between the 18th and 20th centuries.

Fig. 34 *Industries like mining once dominated the towns they operated in, including the dialect of the region*

"They dun though!" he protested naively. "Tha niver seed such a way they get in. But tha mun let me ta'e thee down some time, an' tha can see for thysen."

She looked at him, startled. This was a new tract of life suddenly opened before her. She realised the life of the miners, hundreds of them toiling below earth and coming up at evening. He seemed to her noble. He risked his life daily, and with gaiety. She looked at him, with a touch of appeal in her pure humility.

"Shouldn't ter like it?" he asked tenderly. " 'Appen not, it 'ud dirty thee."

She had never been "thee'd" and "thou'd" before.

Text D

Standardization can provide benefits, but it also involves loss. The richly diverse linguistic forms of the historic dialects and 'basilectal' accents are a precious part of our heritage – like the blacksmith, the village stocks and the ducking-stool, and a thousand other historic artefacts and customs from our past. Their loss is part of the price we pay for modernization. Sentimentalists like me mourn their passing with a special grief because unusual linguistic phenomena are as fascinating to a student of language as butterflies to a collector, or exotic fertility rites to an anthropologist.

A practical disadvantage attending the reduction of accent differences over the next fifty years will be a decreasing reliance on accent features to identify wrongdoers. At present, police descriptions of wanted criminals often mention a specific local accent (or, in other cases, 'well-spokenness' which, not surprisingly, is frequently an attribute of confidence tricksters) which can sometimes be a readier means of identification than height, build, or hair colour. Many police forces throughout Britain retain the services of specialists in accent and dialect who can give important information on the recorded voices of, say, people who make hoax telephone calls to fire brigades. Occasionally such procedures misfire, as when the hunt for the Yorkshire Ripper was unduly extended – and more lives were lost – because attention was diverted away from the real culprit after a cruel hoaxer with a north-eastern accent made a number of telephone calls to the police claiming to be the Ripper.

So from one point of view the English-speaking world is set to become a duller place. Though I will not be alive to witness the new, grey world in which the old regional and social accents are reduced to mere traces of their former richness, the ones I would miss most would be those which have become my favourites, usually because of happy memories of living and working, in my formative years, in places where they are spoken: Cockney, Scouse, Lancashire, Edinburgh Scottish, and – sweetest of all upon my ear – Newcastle Geordie, with its distinctive grammar and vocabulary as well as the music of its spoken form.

What reconciles me to the gradual and eventual passing of accent varieties in Britain is my awareness that accent differences are one of the greatest obstacles to genuine social equality in this country. So long as accents persist, they will be made the excuse for some people to discriminate against others and belittle them. It is no accident that the USA, where a much larger proportion of the population speak with a standard accent (General American) than is the case with RP in Britain, is plausibly regarded as a much more open and genuinely democratic society than our own. A similar judgement has been made on Australia, where nearly everybody speaks with the same accent, though in a varying degree of breadth.

There is a simplistic argument which says that rather than requiring the child to adapt to society, we should change society to accommodate the characteristics of the child. Those who use this argument to deny children access to any awareness of the implications of speaking with one accent rather than another are doing them an obvious disservice, if they cannot also guarantee that society's attitudes will have changed in time for that generation of children to benefit. Sadly, such a guarantee is impossible, if only because, as I have repeatedly stressed, accent involves a more complex set of judgements than mere social snobbery.

A sample response

Both the example of language in Text C and the comments of John Honey in Text D appear to celebrate regional variation in English, although Honey's text also raises other issues about attitudes towards different accents.

In being an extract from a novel, Text C consists largely of character dialogue and vividly presents a variety of English used by a male miner. In this case, it is a fictional and literary representation and is the author's, Lawrence's, own version of the character's speech, which may not be entirely authentic, but it is direct speech and is intended to reproduce actual conversation, although the purpose of the text is partly to entertain.

The body language of the miner reported by Lawrence in Text C is revealing in the way he presents a man of that social class and region, especially in relation to the woman at the dance. The verb phrase 'inclining reverentially' suggests he at least subconsciously sees the woman as being of a superior status to himself, in terms of social class. This is reinforced by the 'surprise' with which the woman delivers the exclamative 'And you are a miner!', and the pity with which she then appears to view him, for example in the prepositional phrase 'in wondering dismay'.

However, Lawrence also makes the miner a strong character, stating in a matter-of-fact way, through a subordinate clause, that he began working in the mine 'when I was ten'. The woman's reaction to him develops across the extract and she begins to admire in him 'a new tract of life', the noun phrase revealing how her initial prejudices are changing, leading to the adjective 'noble' to describe him a little later on, although Lawrence presents the miner's life as physically hard.

The figurative language the man uses to describe his life as a miner likens him to 'mice' and moles. Lawrence uses this to generate humour, through the image in the complex sentence 'He thrust his face forward in the blind, snout-like way of a mole, seeming to sniff and peer for direction.' Earlier, the simple sentence 'He laughed very heartily at this' is similarly light-hearted in tone and, although Lawrence portrays the life of a miner through the dynamic verb, present participle 'toiling', the portrait he paints is perhaps sentimental and unrealistic.

Lawrence uses phonetic spelling to represent pronunciation patterns. These reveal regional accent features that broadly belong to a northern variety of English. For example, the contraction of 'o'' (for 'of'), the

Study tip

Use the annotations you make on the exam texts to help you plan your answer.

final consonant dropping in 'an'' (for 'and'), and the clipping of 'th'' (for 'the'). However, underlying these is a tendency towards archaic forms, described in the narrative as being '"thee'd" and "thou'd"'. These include variations on the pronoun system like the contracted 'Tha'rt' for 'Thou art', which also includes an archaic present tense form of the verb 'to be' – even though the publication of the novel, in 1913, is long after such archaic features would have been a part of the standard language. It is difficult to position these features specifically as being part of a particular region, although it appears to represent a form of north-east accent, similar to the Newcastle Geordie mentioned positively by Honey in Text D as 'sweetest of all upon my ear'. Honey's reference, however, seems to contradict his usual position, as I have come across him as a prescriptivist in my own study.

Honey refers to the '"basilectal" accents' he lists as being both regional and social. Research in several areas of the UK has made links between the strength of the accent of an area and the social variables of class, age and gender. For example, evidence of final consonant dropping is common in many different regional accents, and is seen in Lawrence's reproduction in Text C. It was one of the main variables that Trudgill focused on in his work on pronunciation in Norwich, and he found it occurred more frequently in lower social classes, and in males. In Text C the closest link is of the use of the word ''appen', not just as an instance of H-dropping, but as an adverb, like that found in the Yorkshire dialect, appearing in research by Petyt. Honey's use of 'basilectal' suggests the lowest prestige forms of a language in an area, reinforcing the idea that there are strong attitudes to the social values different accents hold.

In addition to phonological non-standard elements and the appearance of archaic lexis, Lawrence's language in Text B also presents distinctive dialect terms, like 'moudiwarp' (which, interestingly, shares the same opening syllable as its standard counterpart, 'mole'), the use of 'curl' in the idiom 'taking the curl out of me', and of 'mun' as a kind of modal verb in place of a word like 'must', 'may' or 'might'. There are also non-standard grammatical elements like the verb phrase 'as does go round', with its periphrastic use of 'do', linking with some of the other archaic elements of the text. Honey's point, however, in the last paragraph of Text D is that non-standard varieties like this are regarded negatively in society, and so children should be discouraged from using them. This is much more akin to Aitchison's 'infectious disease' metaphor, that non-standard forms are in some way inferior and dangerous to people, and the more usual point of view of John Honey, although it seems to contradict the celebratory tone with which he initially spoke of regional forms. Honey laments 'the new, grey world' that seems to allude to the concept of dialect levelling identified by several linguists, including Trudgill and Kerswill, often connected to the spread of Estuary English, as identified by David Rosewarne in 1984.

Howard Giles found evidence of similar prejudices towards accents in his matched-guise research, with varieties like Brummie scoring lower for attributes such as intelligence and industriousness against **acrolect** forms like RP.

In conclusion, both texts show evidence of the English language being shaped by regional and social forces. Lawrence's characterisation in Text C makes use of a representation of working class speech being regionalised. It is interesting to note that, in the age of Estuary English and dialect levelling, perhaps these represent dying varieties, with a diminishing number of speakers and features that are no longer as strongly different from more widespread forms of the language.

Key terms

Acrolect: the form of speech in a region or a country that is regarded as the standard and prestige version of the language.

Study tip

Remember, your analysis should show that you are engaged and interested in the language issue or debate being discussed. Don't be afraid to offer your own opinions, but be prepared to support them with linguistic or research-based detail and evidence.

Study tip

Assessment objectives can be useful in helping you prepare for the exam. Work on 'translating' them into the terminology, content and skills that your answers should exhibit. Examiner's reports are available online that can help you pinpoint specific material that has appeared in successful work in the past.

Comment

This essay follows the guideline of approximately 1,000 words in discussing language variation. Read through it again and look at the following aspects of it.

- The essay recognises the non-standard features (AO3) provided in the data and aims to place them in the context of the regional varieties spoken in Britain (AO2) when tackling the second half of the essay. This includes general points about northern English accents and dialects, and links to specific, named research (AO2).

- Some of the specific features from the texts are selected and described with a good level of linguistic detail (AO3), making use of specific terminology (AO1). The essay quotes well and ensures that all language used as evidence for the points made is treated linguistically, whether it is a word, phrase, clause or sentence.

- The material in the two pieces of data suggests ideas about wider concepts to do with variation, which are brought into the discussion in the essay. For example, dialect levelling, Trudgill's Norwich study, Estuary English and Petyt are all referenced, as well as evidence of the student's own study being brought in about the attitude of John Honey.

Topic revision exercise

1. What advice have you been given about the time/length of your Section A answer?

2. What particular skills does the Section A question demand?

Further reading

General

Crystal, D. *The Cambridge Encyclopedia of the English Language*, Cambridge University Press, 1995

Crystal, D. *Making Sense of Grammar*, Longman, 2004

Crystal, D. *The Stories of English*, Penguin, 2005

McArthur, T. *The Oxford Companion to the English Language*, Oxford University Press, 1992

Else, D. *British Language and Culture second edition*, Lonely Planet Publications Ltd, 2007

AQA English podcasts website: http://www.theenglishfaculty.org/

Language change

Barber, C. *Early Modern English*, Edinburgh University Press, 1997

Boardman, M. *The Language of Websites*, Routledge, 2004

Crystal, D. *Txting: The Gr8 Db8*, Oxford University Press, 2009

Shortis, T. *The Language of ICT*, Routledge, 2000

Trousdale, T. 'Language Change' in Clayton, D. (ed.) *Language: A Student Handbook on Key Topics and Theories*, English and Media Centre, 2013

Oxford English Dictionary Online 'English in time' page: http://public. oed.com/aspects-of-english/english-in-time/

Oxford English Dictionary Online 'What's new' page: http://public.oed. com/whats-new/

Wikipedia has pages on 'History of the English language', 'Early Modern English', and 'Modern English': http://en.wikipedia.org/

Language variation

Cameron, D. 'Language and Gender' in Clayton, D. (ed.) *Language: A Student Handbook on Key Topics and Theories*, English and Media Centre, 2013

Cameron, D. *The Myth of Mars and Venus: Do Men and Women Really Speak Different Languages?*, Oxford University Press, 2008

Foulkes, P., Docherty, G. *Urban Voices: Accent Studies in the British Isles*, Hodder Education, 1999

Hughes, A., Trudgill, P., Watt, D. *English Accents and Dialects: An Introduction to Social and Regional Varieties of English in the British Isles*, Hodder Education, 2012

Przedlacka, J. *Estuary English?*, Peter Lang, 2003

Sebba, M. *London Jamaican*, Longman, 1993

Talbot, M. *Language and Gender second edition*, Polity Press, 2010

Upton, C., Widdowson JDA. *An Atlas of English Dialects: Region and Dialect*, Routledge, 2006

British Library website, 'Accents and dialects' page: http://sounds.bl.uk/ accents-and-dialects

Looking ahead

Developing a habit of reading widely in a subject is excellent practice for higher education and university courses, where the more focused and independent nature of study will mean this is essential.

Feedback

This part of the book provides all the feedback for the Classroom activities and Data response exercises in Unit 3, Section A. For the answers to the Topic revision exercises, please go to pages 208–11.

How does language change?

Classroom activity 1

You should find that the majority of these short words come from Old English and the related Dutch, German, Scandinavian or Celtic languages that influenced this period. Make notes like this.

- **Ship**: from Old English 'scip' and related to Dutch 'schip' and German 'Schiff'.
- **Wood**: from Old English 'wudu', from a Germanic word related to the Welsh 'gwydd'.
- **The**: from Old English 'se', 'seo' and 'thaet', of Germanic origin that is related to Dutch 'de', 'dat' and German 'der', 'die' and 'das'.

Early Modern English

Classroom activity 2

Printing meant that many copies could be made of one text quite easily, quickly and cheaply. This in turn made it possible for many people to read the exact same words and version of the language, complete with its spellings and phrasing, across a wide area of the country. As printing technology developed and printers used the same letter shapes, texts and letters started to appear more similar.

Classroom activity 3

Language from the Bible would be read aloud to church congregations by ministers – at a time when church-going was a relatively common practice across a wide cross-section of society. Because ministers read from a printed text, a form of standardisation was taking place – even if they could not read it, people throughout the country heard the same grammatical constructions, idioms and phrasing. The fact that these have entered into common use in the language is evidence of the widespread influence of the King James Bible.

Data response exercise 1

1 The first example, together with line numbers, is given for each of the orthographical features listed.

Feature	Example 1	Example 2	Example 3	Example 4
u for v	haue (line 3)			
v for u	Svch (line 1)			
long s	especially (line 2)			
capitalisation	Preachers (line 2)			
ligature	admonished (line 5)			
y for i	neyther (line 9)			
final e	inkhorne (line 6)			

2 The switching of u and v seems to happen without a clear pattern; however, the long s is not used where s is the final letter in a word. The two non-standard capitalisations are of nouns, and particularly nouns naming people of a particular profession. Ligatures are used to join commonly paired consonants like st. The use of y for i is not common in this text and the non-standard use of a final e is not common, but does not have a particular pattern as it is used in an adjective, noun and a verb.

3 The variations, and lack of patterns in some cases, show that standardisation had not yet completely taken hold of the language. This is especially evident as there are inconsistencies in the text and instances of contradictory 'rules' in place. Ligatures might seem to be a throw-back to written, joined-up writing, being kept for particularly closely linked letters as printing finds its own conventions.

Data response exercise 2

1
- Fagot/faggot – concrete noun.
- Faggots – plural noun.
- To faggot – transitive verb.

2 The expansion of lexis and meaning within English is evident here – with five distinctive uses becoming attached to the one lexical item. Notice the way that the function of a word can develop across different word classes – in this case, a noun becomes a verb.

Data response exercise 3

Dekker's written style makes use of suspended sentences and this is one of the ways he generates humour, for example, by using bracketed clauses '(hauing first torne foure or fiue of them)' and clause elements to add asides to his reader, as in 'theres none such fooles as dare take exceptions at them'.

This is added to by the use of wordplay that makes use of various semantic devices, like the pun on the hyponymy of 'musick' and 'frets', as well as the phonological joke of this latter word being similar to 'threats'.

There is a good deal of non-standard orthography, with letter substitutions, such as the use of 'u' for 'v' in both medial positions in 'behaue' and 'fiue', and 'v' for 'u' initially in 'vp'. There are also inconsistencies within the spelling patterns that Dekker uses, as shown in 'cardes' and 'cards'.

In the punctuation of the text, the apostrophe is not used to mark the omission of letters, for example 'theres'.

Dekker's lexis is expanded by use of borrowed words ('a loofe' from Dutch), and use of the specific lexis of the theatre ('Comedy, Morall or Tragedie'), which itself was a highly formative influence on the language of the time.

Data response exercise 4

Harley reveals the personal nature of the letter in her use of lexis drawn from a positive register, creating a loving and reassuring manner, in words like 'deare', 'longe', 'hope' and 'affectinate'.

The non-standard orthography is perhaps made more inconsistent by the private nature of the text and audience, showing idiosyncrasies of Harley's own usage, like the double 'll' used in standard ('will') and non-standard ('blles') positions. Part of this idiolect may show the features of the accent that Harley spoke being translated into her spellings, for example in the emphasis of elongated vowel sounds in 'goo' and 'Londoun'.

Grammatically, the imperative mood is constructed at times, and the intimate nature of the text means that it retains many features common to speech. These include the reliance on the first person, and on the use of coordinating conjunctions to extend sentences and develop detail and information.

Data response exercise 5

Writing after Rochester's death, Aubrey presents his account solely in the past tense and makes Rochester the subject of nearly every clause – so much so that a fairly repetitive syntax, reliant on the anaphoric referencing of the third-person pronouns 'he' and 'his', runs throughout the text.

The language used is largely standardised, although there are some phrases that reveal Early Modern English features. The periphrastic use of 'do', repeated in the distinctive syntax of 'fortune did sometimes make him do', and some archaic terms like 'wont', and perhaps even a now redundant term in 'pigherd' are examples of this.

Complex punctuation features (including colon and semi-colon) allow the sentence structures to be varied. Simple sentences are used, rather than the reliance solely on suspended, complex forms, often found in the period.

Modern English

Data response exercise 6

Some of the more distinctive features that you might have recognised are as follows.

- A formal manner is apparent in Austen's constructions of politeness, like 'I have the pleasure', and, although almost entirely standardised and recognisable to a modern reader, some of her words, like 'civil', 'soothed', 'estimation' and 'felicity' appear dated and archaic.
- Grammatically, there are some non-standard constructions: the use of the preposition 'to' differs from modern usage in 'shall you put it to your chintz' and 'an evening spoilt to Fanny and me'.
- A full, standard range of punctuation is evident, including question and exclamation marks, and subordinating forms like bracketing, dashes, colons and semi-colons, throughout.
- There is a variety of sentence moods and types, some of which reflect the nature of correspondence – interrogatives to elicit information or opinion in the audience's reply, or imperatives requesting them to carry out some service.

Data response exercise 7

This text makes considerable use of the lexical field of illness and symptoms, through archaic forms like 'costiveness', 'a weak stomach', or 'the human machine'. 'Druggist' has become largely obsolete in UK English use.

The absence of firm scientific knowledge is perhaps revealed in the way that the nouns 'magic' and 'facts' are held in quotation marks.

The extensive use of positive lexis, and the use of the third person throughout, represent the method and manner adopted to persuade the reader.

Standardised forms are evident throughout.

There is evidence of newly emerging words like 'patent'.

Data response exercise 8

The non-standard features that appear in this text are not as a result of using pre-standardisation forms but represent the informality and spoken language features adopted by the writer in this personal letter.

The widespread use of positive lexis can be understood in the context of the war, with the daughter wanting to present a positive picture to her parents about the conditions she was living under.

Punctuation marks are used expressively, rather than to follow prescriptive conventions, with repeated exclamation mark strings and dashing used to mark some sentence boundaries, achieve parenthesis, or to signal or replace conjunctions. The non-standard punctuation signals the informality, familiarity and personal nature of the relationship with the reader.

Other spoken mode features include the use of contracted forms like 'isn't', and colloquialisms like 'jolly good', 'mucks in' and 'the local', and 'grand', which is possibly derived from the writer's regional dialect.

New lexical items are used that entered the language during the Second World War, like 'Waafs', and there is evidence of the change caused by military language in English: 'A.T.S.' and others.

Contemporary language change

Classroom activity 4

It is likely that the part of the country that you live in will have its own unique colloquial forms. Some possible examples, with etymology, are given below.

- **Skanger**: Used in Ireland, with a similar meaning to 'chav'. It is thought to be a corruption of the word 'scavenger', and linked to a West Indian word for an untrustworthy person, 'skanker'.
- **Ned**: Scotland's 'chav' equivalent. It has been suggested the word is a backronym (see Glossary) attached to 'non-educated delinquent', or that it dates back to the 1950s, when Teddy Boys were called 'neds' in Glasgow. A variant form, 'nid', is used to refer to the Niddrie housing estate in Edinburgh.

Classroom activity 5

- **Metrosexual**: An urban man concerned with fashion, personal grooming and appearance. Used as a noun or an adjective, the word is formed using the prefix 'metro-', linked to the word 'metropolitan' to make a word that plays on the phonology of the word 'heterosexual'.
- **Smirt**: As a noun, describes a person who flirts while smoking with others outside office buildings. The verb form represents this activity. The word is formed from a blend of 'smoker/ing' and 'flirt'.
- **Brand Nazi**: An individual who shows extreme loyalty to particular clothing, or other brands. This noun phrase is formed by compounding the idea of a 'brand' with the connotations of the extremism of a 'Nazi'.

Classroom activity 6

'Unusual symbol combinations' may be related to alternative spellings by placing different emphasis on the stress patterns of words through capitalisation, or by replacing phonemes altogether with a non-standard character, like a '4' for the sound /for/. They can be seen as a definite way of representing individuality, particularly if used to represent a person's name, or username within a group. Unusual symbol forms may create emphasis, for example, the widely accepted convention of representing 'shouting' in emails by capital letters, and expression can be represented in the construction of emoticons. Communication may be made more speedy, especially where combinations make use of contractions, as in 'txt speak' – which is certainly an example of a growing trend in the language, spreading beyond usage in just SMS messages.

Data response exercise 9

A wide range of non-standard features have been used by the writer, John Mullan – in fact, the way that he is able to coin new usages with them reveals the flexible nature of 'txt speak' and related forms.

- Contractions are dominated by vowel removal, but also include reducing consonant clusters. This is sometimes purely to shorten the lexical item and to speed up the process of writing. It places spoken pronunciation forms over spelling rules, e.g. removing the silent 'w' in 'rote', altering the vowel representation in 'wot', and representing double letter forms with capitals in 'aTractive' and 'btwEn'.

Similarly, where syllables are subject to elision, the spelling has reflected this, as in 'bleve'.

- Grammatically, conventions of paragraphing have been retained. Syntax, however, is often fragmented with minor sentences like '2 tru', and heavily contracted noun phrases, like the subject '13yr grl' for 'The 13-year-old girl', omitting the determiner and full modification phrasing.
- Other coinages include acronyms and initialisms, often to replace idiomatic or clichéd phrases that are easily recognisable. Non-alphabetic characters are used to replace phonemes and even create emoticons, e.g. in the symbolic representation of 'surprised' as ':-o'.
- Even though the tone is tongue in cheek, Mullan takes a more positive approach than some other writers in the media. He does not adopt the overt prescriptivist attitude towards language use, which often leads on to criticism of teenagers in general.

Data response exercise 10

- Perhaps the first striking feature regarding the cohesion of this text is the way that each paragraph succeeds one that is below it, rather than above it, in the sequence of the text. This is due to the live context of the way that the text is put together to form a webpage – it is a form of news and means that visitors to the page will be presented with the latest news, rather than the oldest news first.
- The authorship of the text creates a complex form of cohesion – there are many contributors, although a central thread is maintained by the 'commentator'.
- The structure of the text is evidently partly automated, with a range of graphological elements such as icons, thumbnail photos, embedded video, font variations, etc., used to organise the text and integrate its various sources and media.
- A lexical field of popular music and culture runs throughout the text, but the informality that is characteristic of many online communication forms is evident in abbreviated forms and colloquial language, as well as other spoken language conventions.

Data response exercise 11

- There are several textual segments, with hyperlinked text underlined in blue or red text and linking to other pages, creating exophoric references in the text. A unique feature of this is the 'tag cloud', acting as a kind of index to other articles, largely by presenting noun phrases that have been taken from the text of other pages.
- There is a range of examples of different language change processes in the lexical items present: initialism, acronym, compounding, clipping, coinage, contraction, derivation.
- Punctuation is varied, often to incorporate detail and to support multi-clause structures. This includes the use of colons, dashes, brackets, quotation marks, bullet points, as well as graphemes present in URLs.
- Additional interactive and multimedia elements include a date-stamped digital photograph, a text-input box, a clickable button and rolling Twitter feed updates.

Attitudes towards language change

Classroom activity 7

Non-standard usage	Prescriptivist attitude	Descriptivist attitude
Using 'txt' spellings such as 'gr8' (great), or 'c u ltr' (see you later).	'txt' style spellings cause a lot of problems. They make it harder for children in particular to learn the correct, standard English spellings of words. This is especially the case with words that have an irregular spelling pattern. People will start to use these spellings in particularly inappropriate contexts like exams, job applications, or in business communication.	'txt' style spellings are a creative and innovative part of modern English. They should not be used in every context (for example, in formal written texts) but are very convenient in other situations, making language easier, quicker and simpler. They are also an example of the language making use of new technological inventions to shape it, like the mixed-mode forms of text messaging and emails.
Using 'Americanisms' such as spellings like 'color' (colour), or words like 'pants' (trousers).	Americanisms entering British English usage contradict the rules of standard English. These American words and spellings can be quickly picked up by British English users who may forget or never learn the standard British English equivalent, and replace it with American forms. The overall effect is to corrupt standard English over time and ruin its heritage and history.	Americanisms represent an inevitable change to English. Fashions, trends and culture are commonly shared and swapped between America and Britain, and these are often accompanied by related terms and language. The difference between spelling 'colour' or 'color' (and other Americanisms) is very minor and only there for unintended historical reasons. As new technology and increased travel bring the American and British forms of English into closer contact, it should be expected that such minor differences are reconciled by the language.
Blending languages to form new varieties like London Jamaican, or MLE (explored on pages 54–6).	Blending other languages with English corrupts the language and produces inferior varieties that cannot be considered languages in their own right. This also has a negative effect on the standard form of the language as borrowed words, pronunciations, or grammatical forms often find their way into mainstream usage. New speakers of such a blended variety are disadvantaged as they are restricted to using an informal, low-status form of language.	Language contact is an essential and healthy part of human communication and exchange, crossing national, religious or ethnic boundaries. The English language itself is historically formed by a series of prolonged passages of contact with other languages and the heavy blending that took place during those times. New varieties spring up to meet the needs of new communities and populations and require just as much linguistic skill as English does. In addition, speakers with this linguistic background are often able to use several languages and varieties fluently, including Standard English.

Language change theory

Classroom activity 8

Examples might include:

- immigrants intermingling with native speakers
- workplaces, especially of national and international companies
- regional borders
- the imposition of foreign power, for example in a military occupation
- tourism and travel
- international culture and multinational events
- the translation of written texts from other source languages.

What is language variation?

Classroom activity 9

Further examples could be drawn from a wide variety of sources, but some of the mainstream ones might include the following.

Aspect of social variation	Examples of language and their usage or origin
Age	The terms 'emo', 'townie' and 'goth' are almost exclusively used by teenagers and youths
Sexuality	'Camp' ways of speaking among homosexual men
Gender	Use by male children and teenagers of colloquial terms like 'mush', 'mate', 'mater' and others
Social class	The use of the pronoun 'one' in upper-class speakers
Ethnicity	English speakers using an accent pattern from another language, such as an Indian language
Deviance	Terms like 'spliff', 'gear' and 'weed' surrounding the deviant subculture of soft drugs
Occupation	Technical terms in the British Army to refer to ranks like 'private', 'corporal' and 'sergeant'
Region	The basic differences in pronunciation between a 'northern' and 'southern' English speaker
Hobbies	Subject-specific lexis based around an interest like off-road cycling with phrases and terms like 'getting some air', 'wheelies' and 'bunny hops'

Social variation

Classroom activity 10

You could come up with any number of examples – such as:

- lawyers and the courts – bail, tort, sub judice
- filmmaking – boom, dolly, grip
- football – slide tackle, bicycle kick, sweeper.

Classroom activity 11

You will notice that the emoticons you use are related to Leet forms. Although you might use a pretty full range of alphabetic characters, you probably won't make use of the range given in the list of Leet forms shown in Table 8 on page 49. Your use of characters for non-standard spelling will be guided by speed, and therefore much shorter than Leet forms which, in many cases, are produced to be deliberately cryptic.

Classroom activity 12

- LMC male in 'casual' task: perhaps this result is related to the idea of covert and overt prestige, with male speakers using non-standard forms in formal situations like the workplace, as a part of their own code.

- The results across the LMC male row have a different pattern as they do not have the 'drop off' between the reading and conversation tasks. Reasons for this might be to do with social mobility – perhaps the LMC males have moved from a WC group and modified their non-standard use. This might mean that their use is more evenly spread, as they do not 'relax' their speech between the different tasks, and they have already reduced it to the lower level of non-standard use that they are capable of.

- The word list task would buck this trend by being such a contrived task, and not eliciting any extended utterances. Alternatively, the result may be flawed, perhaps being affected by the issue of the observer's paradox, discussed later.

Data response exercise 12

Officer A could be interpreted as exhibiting a mixture of traits under Tannen's model, with a majority of female ones, although he is in fact a male speaker. For example, the first sentence suggests an emphasis on connection, although this may also be about status. The comments on personal feelings are perhaps more private in nature – a female attribute – which is extended to seek a kind of rapport in the tag question that follows (a feature reported as female by other researchers).

Officer B reports experience of the training as well as the status it seemed to confer, both male attributes. The realisation that others might be 'jealous' could be seen as a competitive awareness, perhaps aligned with Tannen's oppositional trait. However, the last sentence appears to value the connection and supportive nature of the environment and team. So, a mixed picture emerges, although this officer was female.

Overall, this suggests that, although Tannen's styles of male and female speech can be helpful in identifying particular characteristics in speakers, the link to gender may not be as strong or definite as she asserts. For example, in a profession like bomb disposal, perhaps the personal characteristics of the sort of individuals that would follow that route are a stronger influence on speech than gender, which is closer to the view taken by Cameron.

Data response exercise 13

There are a variety of non-standard elements in these extracts for you to find and describe. Two main examples from each follow.

1 In Extract 1, there is a series of non-standard verb uses, ranging from the lack of concord between the singular pronoun 'he' and the plural present tense forms of 'tell' and 'get'. There is omission of auxiliary verbs, particularly those which serve a copula, linking function. In the verb phrases constructed it is possible to interpret potential missing modal use in 'he will tell me', and missing the particle in the infinitive form 'okay to marry'. Lexically, there is a non-standard Hawaiian Pidgin item in the word 'haole', meaning 'foreigner'.

2 Extract 2 from Karen King-Aribisala's novel is in fact the result of language contact between at least three language sources as she was born in Guyana, moved to Nigeria, and makes use of English as the source language in the novel. It shows a non-standard construction of the superlative adjectival form in 'most worstest'. There is a non-standard use of the verb 'do' periphrastically to construct the past tense in an unorthodox way in the verb phrase 'did fall'.

3 Extract 3 reveals Caribbean-derived pronunciation patterns being used. There is substitution of /d/ for /th/ in 'dis', and the elongation and modification of the vowel sound /o/ for a spelling that would probably be reproduced in speech as /ah/ in the words 'salim' and 'pramis'. There is evidence of creole grammatical constructions with the use of 'fi' as a particle in the verb phrases 'fi tell' and 'fi tek care', to serve a similar function to the infinitive construction of 'to tell' and 'to take' in each case.

Data response exercise 14

Here is a commentary on some of the features, where a definite shift in the sort of language being used is evident – you may well have found some more, too.

C begins to talk using Standard English, perhaps moving into London English with the choice of 'this' rather than 'a' as the determiner preceding 'party'. Interestingly, the first use of 'party' has the medial /t/ sound produced, in line with the standard pronunciation of RP, whereas, by the second use, a glottal stop is used – a clear feature of Cockney and London English. Creole pronunciation forms become evident, in the substitution of the initial consonant sound /d/ for /th/ in 'de'.

Grammatically, too, the Standard English construction of 'Jane and I' is used, but contrasts with the London English use of 'well' as an adverbial intensifier in 'well rude', and 'you know' as a hedge. Creole forms are to be seen in the use of the particle 'a' as part of the verb phrase 'a seh', in this case to mark the progressive aspect (see pages 69–70 where Jamaican Creole is discussed in more detail), and the non-standard first-person pronoun use with 'mi' for 'I'.

What Sebba shows in his research is the ability of London Jamaican speakers to switch between several varieties to express themselves. This ability to code-switch is detailed in his work as a complex skill, discussed further in the Language variation theory topic on page 79. Look at the following extract, again from the Catford Girls' data, with the switch from Jamaican Creole to Cockney to Jamaican Creole shown by italics, within a conversation.

'*she never invite me neither* … she just told 'er she's 'avin' a christenin' … *me no know if me a go*'.

Again, in the creole form, the particle 'a' is used, this time to mark the present participle, which would be 'going' in Standard English. Note the use of multiple negation, another prominent feature of creole language.

When you bear in mind the different levels that each variety works on: phonological, lexical and grammatical, it is possible to see how complex the mix of London Jamaican can become, and how, as it develops over time, it may well move towards becoming a fully blended language in its own right. For example, it would be possible for an item of Jamaican Creole vocabulary to be pronounced with a Cockney accent pattern, as part of a Standard English grammatical construction. Sebba discusses this in his research and suggests unique London Jamaican variants already appearing, like /bava boot/ for the Cockney term /bovuh boots/ ('bovver boots'). This phrase uses the Jamaican vowel sound of /a/ in /bava/ (and the omission of /s/ inflection for a plural), but not the medial consonant form, which would be /d/, as in /bada/ – leading to the creation of a genuinely unique blend.

Classroom activity 13

- **Bevvy**: Abbreviation of 'beverage' (itself borrowed from French) to a diminutive form
- **Bitch**: Has undergone semantic change, from a denotative term (noun) for a female dog, to a Polari word – and then has entered mainstream usage as a derogatory word. It has also undergone conversion into a verb 'to bitch'
- **Bona**: A borrowing from Latin, meaning 'good'
- **Camp**: Possibly an altered acronym of 'Known As Male Prostitute', although this may be an example of folk etymology
- **Ecaf/eek**: Backslang from 'face', with 'eek' being a first syllable clipping
- **Fantabulosa**: A complex blending of 'fantastic' and 'fabulous', with the addition of a mock-Hispanic language word ending in 'osa'
- **Mangarie**: A borrowed derivation from the French word for 'to eat', *manger*
- **Scarper**: A borrowing from the Italian verb meaning 'to escape', *scappare*

Regional variation

Classroom activity 14

This utterance offers pronunciation patterns that would potentially make use of:

- l-vocalisation in 'Alr-'
- glottalling in '-ight'
- yod-coalescence in 'Du-'
- vowel fronting in each of the 'a', 'i' and 'u' vowel positions.

This results in a possible Estuary English pronunciation of: /awr-eye jook/.

The utterance may also make use of high-rising intonation which, although not a specific Estuary English feature, occurs frequently in colloquial English usage.

English as a world language

Classroom activity 15

There are many non-standard features represented here – one from each of the areas could be as follows.

- **Phonological**: The alteration of the standard /th/ sound in 'think' and 'de'. Although this extract only provides two examples, a pattern does emerge of the unvoiced /th/ becoming /t/, as in 'tink', and the voiced /th/ sound becoming /d/, in 'da'.
- **Lexical**: Use of the word 'Shoots' as an exclamatory.

Grammatical: Tense and aspect are constructed using additional marker words. The past tense includes 'wen' as an addition to the main verb, in 'wen go', and 'wen tell'. The marker 'steh' is similarly used as part of the verb phrase to construct the present progressive aspect in 'steh going deaf' for 'is going deaf'.

Classroom activity 16

Standard English	Kowaiti Bay cartoon	Jamaican Creole
my father	mi father	mi faada
car	car	kyar
knocked down	lik down	lik doun

The Kowaiti Bay cartoon chooses to keep a Jamaican Creole dialect form in terms of lexis and grammar, but appears to represent the Jamaican accent in only some sounds, spelling the others in a way that represents a standard British English pronunciation. For example, creole constructions like 'wey him deh now' are retained in the cartoon but seem to differ from the authentic Jamaican pronunciation, with slightly elongated and different sounding vowels which are closer to Standard English forms.

Classroom activity 17

Indian language source: accha, chuddies, haina, kati.

English translation source: badmash, buck, filmi, timepass.

Classroom activity 18

- **friend-friend**: A best or close friend (from Singlish)
- **hom-reon**: Home run (from Konglish)
- **inner clothes**: Underwear (from Chinglish)
- **ryukkusakku**: Rucksack (from Japlish)
- **siyampu**: Shampoo (from Taglish)

Attitudes towards language variation

Classroom activity 19

Both Mr Houston and the caller exhibit negative attitudes towards non-standard features: in Extract 1 this is directed at a specific accent feature, and the caller in Extract 2 picks on an element of pronunciation common in Black English Vernacular in America. Mr Houston objects to 'James' using a glottal stop as part of his Scots English, Dundee accent. The caller to the radio talk show believes in a set pattern between orthography and pronunciation, and suggests that altering the consonant cluster sound of /sk/ to /x/ or /ks/ is an indicator of ignorance. Both perspectives are prescriptivist at best, in regarding a deviation from the standard pronunciation form, in Standard English and General American respectively, as inherently inferior – although, at worst, both display prejudice and bigotry and see alternative language forms as indicative of lower cognitive ability and status.

B Language discourses

Introduction

In this section you will:

- explore the different approaches to studying language variation and change

- apply the material that you have studied on language variation and change to popular and academic debates.

Section B of the exam draws on the full range of your knowledge of language change and variation, which means that the range of language issues and skills that you need to cover is potentially very wide. Although it makes use of all of the information that you have studied in Section A, it develops this by asking you to evaluate the topics themselves, and place yourself within the debate. No doubt, you have formed your own opinions about some of the issues discussed so far and have found yourself thinking about the various attitudes and theories that have been applied to language over time.

Carrying out your own research into change and variation is a good way of preparing for Section B, and the first part of this section of the book is about how you can do just that, before we look at some examples of Section B-style tasks and feedback.

Extension activity

The topics you have studied in language variation and change are often ideal stimulus for your language investigation coursework. Think about whether any of the researchers, varieties or texts that you have encountered give you an idea to try to research further in your investigation.

Fig. 1 *The language discourses unit is a great excuse to 'follow your nose' and read up on a wide variety of language topics*

Studying language variation and change

Starter activity

With a study partner, think back over the language change and variation topics you have been introduced to and make a list of the most significant debates that have emerged. For example, you might write down, 'whether creoles are "proper" languages' or 'Do men and women speak differently?' Decide on a way you could get some data for each and note a few ideas on what language features you would look for if you studied it: recording male and female friends chatting at college and analysing the way they interrupt each other, for example. Once you have at least half a dozen, discuss which you think would make the most fruitful investigation and rank the top three from 1 to 3.

Approaching the study of a changing and varied language

As well as working on the texts and materials in this book and in your classes, it is a good idea to set up your own study and research into language change and variation. This will lead to a greater understanding of the subject and give you more confidence as you approach the exam. One of the best ways is to involve yourself with texts from different times, and regional and social dialects first hand. Below are tips to help you to get hold of data, and to explore the methodologies and approaches that researchers have used – and which you could have a go at.

Synchronic and diachronic approaches

Swiss linguist Ferdinand de Saussure in his collected notes, published in 1916, put forward two main approaches to studying language: synchronic and diachronic.

Synchronic study suggested focusing on the range of variation in a language at one point in time. For example, rather than identifying particular periods of English, a synchronic approach would look at all the evidence available for language used by speakers in London in the early 17th century and describe the variety of features that characterised that form of the language. In Unit 3 of this book, the topics dealing with language variation mostly adopt a synchronic approach.

De Saussure's other approach represented what had been the traditional approach of linguists in the time up to the 20th century. Diachronic study charted the changes in language across time and marked the features of change, or apparent 'periods' of usage. In this unit, the topics on language change take a diachronic approach in introducing you to the evolution of English from its early roots to contemporary usage.

Etymology

Etymology, the study of the history of words, seems to deserve a separate mention as an approach to studying language, as it can be such a useful tool for understanding language change. Using etymology (for example, by researching words in an etymological dictionary) is fundamentally a diachronic approach, allowing you to see when and how a word appeared in the language and what different uses of it have been recorded over time.

Psycholinguistics

Psycholinguistic causes of change are those rooted within the minds of language users, or in the language system itself, as opposed to any external influences. Such factors are most clearly seen in phonological changes, where sounds can be dropped, merged or simplified in pronunciation owing to speakers tending towards easier forms of articulation, and these becoming a norm over time. For example, many English speakers would not fully pronounce the verb in this utterance: 'He banged the drum', with the final 'ed' sound being lost, and similarly, and now very commonly, in 'I texted you'. These changes are often understood to be psycholinguistic as the main factor of influence seems to be an internal, possibly subconscious, decision on the part of the speaker to alter his or her language because of the easier articulation involved, rather than any external social pressure – although, of course, in real life, both psycho- and sociolinguistic causes tend to be in operation.

Other areas of the language can be altered in this way, with syntactical structures moving from subject–object–verb to subject–verb–object over time (as in the transition from Old English to Modern English structures) – and, of course, changes like this to one part of the language system can then have consequences for other parts.

Sociolinguistics

The wide range of external influences on a language are all collected under the umbrella of **sociolinguistics**. Sociolinguistics is concerned with the way that social issues affect language change, principally those of gender, age, occupation, social class and ethnicity.

Methodologies

One of the prime considerations, when linguists are working with different accent and pronunciation forms, is how to represent accurately the different sounds they use. This text has simplified the different examples of accent forms it gives by using a basic form of phonetic spelling, using only the standard alphabetic characters. There exist many different ways of writing down the sounds of words in a reliable way, used by dictionaries, encyclopedias and researchers.

Perhaps the most developed form, used in most university-level linguistic research, is that of the **International Phonetic Alphabet (IPA)**, which has a highly complex system of special characters and accent markings to aim to express all sounds made by the human voice in different language forms across the world. It is principally broken down into vowel and consonant forms, although there are many other markings used to show more unusual or specific sounds, like vocal clicks or particular kinds of voice quality, like breathiness. Some examples of IPA appear below.

- ŋ – for the /ng/ sound in 'running'
- ð – for the /th/ sound in 'the'
- æ – for the /a/ sound in 'cat'

The following link from Wikipedia shows more detail about some of the main IPA symbols and sounds – and some of the other phonetic respelling forms that have been used: http://en.wikipedia.org/Pronunciation. Search for 'respelling' then for 'English'. This text has mostly used a system similar to the World Book Online phonetic spellings.

When researchers work with linguistic data, they select particular linguistic variables to test the difference between that dialect and the

Key terms

Psycholinguistics: the study of the way 'internal' factors like thought and speech production affect language use.

Sociolinguistics: the study of the way 'external' factors like culture and social status affect language use.

International Phonetic Alphabet (IPA): a detailed system containing over 160 symbols to represent the sounds of spoken language (including things like lisping and teeth grinding!).

Link

The ENGA4 Language investigation topics in Section A explain in more detail the sort of considerations involved in conducting language study, including data gathering and handling methods.

Looking ahead

Learning about, and carrying out, different research methods is an excellent preparation for higher education. The methodologies behind many of the research examples in Unit 3, and the chance to practise these yourself in your language investigation, will give you a taste of the sort of thing you could take further – not just in linguistics, but in many areas of social science.

Link

For an example of research involving the Queen's speech over several decades, see pages 107–8.

Study tip

Having an understanding of the methodology used by a particular researcher can be useful. Aim to be able to reflect on and evaluate methodological ideas on how data was collected.

Key terms

Qualitative: an approach to language study that involves analysing examples of language use in detail and context.

Quantitative: an approach to language study that makes use of statistical analysis of data that has been gathered.

standard language. These need to be specific and easily measurable. In accent terms, this might involve isolating a particular phonological pattern like the way that /t/ sounds are pronounced – for example, if looking for evidence of the glottal stop being used. Linguistic variables might also be grammatical: for example, the way in which the past tense is constructed, as explored in the difference between some pidgin and creole forms. Similarly, linguists also use lexical or semantic variables.

If you need to ask people to contribute particular data (for example, recording a person's accent while they answer some questions), it is difficult to avoid the concept of the observer's paradox. One way around this is to try to use data that has been naturally generated in context – for example, comparing the Queen's speech over several decades. It is important to remember that data must be gathered ethically – it is not ethical to just record speakers without their explicit consent, which means the observer's paradox is always something to come to terms with.

There are several different ways that you could investigate social and regional variation yourself, and some of the main methodologies are corpus analysis; ethnographic study; experiments; interviews; and surveys. In brief, corpus analysis involves making use of a significant (often very large) collection of examples of real language use – there are some examples of corpus datasets you can use in the next topic. Ethnographic study involves fieldwork, gathering language in use in the context that you would like to investigate. Experiments, interviews and surveys are probably more familiar forms of gathering data and involve collecting **qualitative** or **quantitative** data outside of its natural context. Sometimes you might need to use a combination of these to gather your data, or for different parts of your research.

Resources

If you have enjoyed studying language change so far, the good news is that there are a number of excellent resources available nowadays, usually entirely free, through using the internet. Here is a selection of some of the best resources available.

The most up-to-date form of the *Oxford English Dictionary* is no longer available in a printed format, but through the OED Online. Although this is quite an expensive subscription service, you may find that it is accessible for free through your local library or your school or college, and it also has a wide range of non-subscription pages. The *OED* provides comprehensive information on the pronunciation, usage, history and etymology of words in the English language.

The *OED* works by adding words to the language once they have appeared with a certain frequency in the wide range of print and spoken media that its team constantly scans: newspapers, websites, transcriptions of radio and television, speeches, published books or e-books, etc. Because of this, many words that are in contemporary use, especially informal, colloquial forms, may not enter the *OED* for several years, if they register in it at all.

There are many excellent sources of written texts available online, stretching across many centuries, and even offering high-quality facsimile images of original manuscripts. If you are looking for a particular text, then you may need to use an internet search engine to find some of the more specific websites. The following are excellent online collections.

- OED Online, 'Previous updates' section
- British Library online
- Project Gutenberg

There are plenty of good examples of existing corpus collections of spoken variation data. Some of these are available online, with two main sites being the BBC Voices project (http://www.bbc.co.uk/voices/) and the British Library accents and dialects archive.

BBC Voices is a diverse and growing project, making use of reader contributions to an online database, as well as providing examples of audio material. It provides UK data of the usage and frequency of particular dialect terms, in its Word Map. It has recordings of recent examples of accents across the UK. Finally, it brings these collections together with online articles and discussion forums of the issues arising from the data.

The Collect Britain website has a particular section dedicated to accessing over 650 recordings. These are drawn from two sources – an archive of the Survey of English Dialects recordings, stretching back over many decades, and more modern recordings made as part of the Millennium Memory Bank. By using either source, you are likely to be able to listen to examples of speakers from the research examples presented in the variation section, as well as in your own local area.

Classroom activity 1

The following examinations of language variation and change are examples of the methodologies listed in the table below. Copy the table and match each examination to its corresponding methodology (the first one has been done for you).

- Mark Sebba's London Jamaican research (see page 54)
- Janet Hyde's gender similarities hypothesis (see page 46)
- BBC Voices project (see page 105)
- Peter Trudgill's Norwich study (see page 51)
- Lesley Milroy's Belfast study (see page 77)
- *Oxford English Dictionary* (see page 15)

Methodology	Research
Survey	BBC Voices project
Meta-analysis	
Ethnographic study	
Experiment	
Interview	
Corpus analysis	

Topic revision exercise

1 What are the features of the diachronic and synchronic approaches to language study?

2 What is etymology?

3 Why might psycholinguistics be understood as the 'internal' and sociolinguistics the 'external' aspects of language?

Further reading

The Open University 'English Language' webpages have some good materials in their 'Study' section that explain different approaches to research in linguistics: http://www.open.edu/openlearn/history-the-arts/culture/english-language.

Exam preparation

☑

In this topic you will:

- read and analyse a range of paired texts concerned with language change and variation
- engage with and evaluate each of the four language debate areas
- apply your knowledge and understanding of language change and variation.

Study tip

You need to be prepared for any of the four focus areas – do not be tempted to try to 'guess' the paper and revise only selected topics.

Link

Look back at page 82 to read the suggested approach to an exam question in this paper. Although the emphasis is slightly different in Section B, the same overall procedure is a good place to start your essay practice.

Study tip

Make sure you are aware of key researchers, theories and case studies as it is important to have a good range of relevant wider knowledge to draw upon.

The exam

In Section B of the exam, you are presented with texts that are explicitly about language variation and change topics. You are required to develop the debate about a particular issue – using the texts to help you to reflect on the way that it has been represented in society. The four major areas of variation and change that you need to study for Section B are:

- international, regional and social accents and dialects
- language change
- gender and interaction
- political correctness.

In the exam, the question will be about only one of these topics – but you must be prepared to tackle any of them!

Assessment objectives

- AO1: Select and apply a range of linguistic methods, to communicate relevant knowledge using appropriate terminology and coherent, accurate written expression: *10 marks.*
- AO2: Demonstrate critical understanding of a range of concepts and issues related to the construction and analysis of meanings in spoken and written language, using knowledge of linguistic approaches: *20 marks.*
- AO3: Analyse and evaluate the influence of contextual factors on the production and reception of spoken and written language, showing knowledge of the key constituents of language: *15 marks.*

The balance of the AOs shows that it is important to both analyse the style of the texts and engage with the wider debate that they present.

Writing a successful essay

The remainder of this topic will help you to develop your ability to evaluate how language issues are debated and represented in society. This will focus on the four language discourse areas listed above. You will look at a pair of texts for each area of debate, and an essay question to evaluate the sociolinguistic topic they cover. Use these sample tasks to revise and evaluate relevant material from elsewhere in this unit, and in AS Units 1 and 2. Then look at the 'Essay guidelines' to check the main areas that a successful essay would address, and how these relate to the AOs.

Discourse 1: Accent and dialect

If you are presented with a pair of accent and dialect texts, the range of topics that they cover could be anything from the regional variation topic, the ethnic and the class-based social variation material seen in Texts A and B that follow. You will need to be familiar with the ways in which language variation occurs, and the theories that surround it, so that you can apply these to the particular varieties described on the day. As the main focus of Section B is to engage with linguistic debate, make sure that you are familiar with the main attitudes and debates surrounding accent and dialect.

For example, you might get a pair of texts that set out the dialect levelling debate by presenting an article on the rise of Estuary English and some contrasting data on the distinctive features of a strong northern English dialect, like Scouse, for example. In this instance, you would need to be ready to apply the concept of dialect levelling to the two issues, and would aim to bring some new ideas to the discussion you generate in your essay.

Task 1

Read Text E and Text F below. Both are about Received Pronunciation and the voices we hear on broadcast media. Text E is a newspaper article discussing the way the Queen's own speech has changed over several decades. Text F is a blog entry by the voiceover artist, Emma Clarke.

- Analyse and evaluate how these two texts use language to present their ideas about RP and the value of different accent forms.
- Evaluate these ideas about the nature of RP and regional accents in modern Britain, drawing on your knowledge and study of language.

Text E

How Queen's English has grown more like ours

By Neil Tweedie

As the common tongue continues its inexorable slide towards a new dark age of glottal stops and 'innits', news comes that even the Queen is drifting slowly down river towards Estuary English.

A scientific study of Christmas broadcasts to the Commonwealth since 1952 suggests the royal vowel sounds have undergone a subtle evolution since the days when coal was routinely delivered to Buckingham Palace *in sex*.

The Queen in 1998 had become 'definitely less upper class'.

Her Majesty may not be quite ready to engage in fully-fledged Bermondsey banter with Jade Goody, but her speech has nevertheless followed the general trend from cut-glass URP (Upper Received Pronunciation) towards the more democratic Standard Received Pronunciation and its close relative, Standard Southern British English.

The findings are contained in the *Journal of Phonetics*, which, in addition to the Queen, addresses such topics as, 'The temporal domains of accent in Finnish' and 'Perceptual correlates of Cantonese tones'.

Jonathan Harrington, Professor of Phonetics at the University of Munich, and author of the study on the Queen, said his team had conducted a thorough acoustic analysis of all the Christmas broadcasts during her reign.

'We chose the broadcasts because it is very rare indeed to find high-quality recordings of a person's voice stretching back over such a long period,' he said. 'The changes in the Queen's speech have been very, very slow, but they are there nevertheless.

'In 1952 she would have been heard referring to "thet men in the bleck het". Now it would be "that man in the black hat".

Fig. 2 *Queen Elizabeth II: do you speak like her?*

'Similarly, she would have spoken of the citay and dutay, rather than citee and dutee, and hame rather than home. In the 1950s she would have been lorst, but by the 1970s lost.'

And indeed, the Queen's first Christmas broadcast was pure Dartington Crystal.

She began: 'As he (King George VI) used to do, I em speaking to you from my own hame, where I em spending Christmas with my femly.'

Prof Harrington said he did not believe the changes in the royal delivery were a conscious attempt to lower social barriers.

'Half a century ago the social classes were much more demarcated.

'That changed with the social revolution of the 1960s and 1970s and the much greater blurring of boundaries,' he said.

'I don't think the Queen changed consciously at all. What the study suggests is that we all participate in sound changes, whether we like it or not. The Queen has merely altered her way of speaking in line with her host community in south-east England.'

But did that mean that she would soon be mixing it with Jade darn the Dog 'n' Duck?

'She may be drifting slowly downstream towards Estuary, but she has a very, very long way to go before she gets anywhere near the open sea.'

The historian and royal biographer Kenneth Rose said the Queen's accent had undoubtedly changed during her reign.

'She has become definitely less upper class – dropping an octave and coming nearer to her own "Queen's English", by which I mean nearer to standard English,' he said.

'There have always been variations in royal speech. The Queen Mother was the embodiment of the upper class lady in the first class compartment, while George V was more like a hoarse country gentleman.

Edward VIII adopted a kind of upper class cockney, talking of 'moi house', but after his marriage began to sound more American.

'About two or three years ago I was sitting next to the Queen at tea and she remarked that some of her grandchildren talked Estuary. I think she was talking about the Phillips children – but then Princess Anne always sounded a little suburban.

'And then there's Prince Edward, who sounds a bit Estuary – whereas the Dukes of Kent and Gloucester are proper country gents.'

And was Her Majesty happy about the Estuarisation of the Royal Family?

'She was absolutely neutral on the subject.'

Is one bovvered? Does one look bovvered? One thinks not. 'A merry Christmas and a happay New Yeah.'

www.telegraph.co.uk, 5 December 2006

Text F

The power and prejudices of received pronunciation

FRIDAY, NOV 2 2007

"It is impossible for an Englishman to open his mouth without making some other Englishman despise him." (George Bernard Shaw, Preface to *Pygmalion*, 1910)

In advertising and broadcast media, speaking in RP is essential. The attitudes generally held about RP suggest we feel that RP speakers are well-educated, authoritative, persuasive, intelligent and professional. Indeed, these words often constitute the direction at the top of the script for the voiceover to follow. In the world of voicing, these qualities so often reflect the brand values of the product being spoken about and the voiceover's job is to embody the characteristics of credibility, quality, reliability and prestige in order to successfully sell that product. It's generally believed that only RP can achieve all that. Interestingly, regional accents are often perceived to convey qualities such as friendliness, generosity, honesty, integrity and sense of humour. For most British people, how a person speaks is a social symbol. These attitudes (prejudices?) have been confirmed by socio-linguistic research, and suggest that accents are judged by the stereotypes listeners already hold about their speakers.

The British Broadcasting Corporation (BBC) was founded in 1922. From the start, the nature and characteristics of the voices heard on the airwaves was a matter of hot contention. John Reith, the first Director General said: "One hears the most appalling travesties of vowel pronunciation. This is a matter in which broadcasting can be of immense assistance … We have made a special effort to secure in our various stations men who … can be relied upon to employ the correct pronunciation of the English tongue." The BBC cast itself as the guardian of Received Pronunciation and had a policy of only employing RP speakers as announcers and news-readers. In 1926 the BBC Advisory Committee on Spoken English was established.

Regional voices were used, but were only really heard in comedy and light entertainment shows, making jokes that reinforced social and cultural stereotypes. RP was regarded as the voice of authority, used for all 'serious' broadcasting and the national news. And in a move that reflected the spirit of the age and its deference to status and status-consciousness, news announcers were required, from 1925, to wear dinner jackets while broadcasting.

In 1941 the BBC hired Wilfred Pickles – a Yorkshireman with a broad Halifax accent – to read the news. There was a flurry of complaints. Listeners claimed they didn't believe what he was telling them; they thought he was untrustworthy. The BBC's motive for using Pickles as a London announcer in the middle of the Second World War also gives an insight into the prejudices and assumptions made about regional accent speakers; the BBC thought the Germans would have greater difficulty in understanding and imitating a Yorkshireman. As Pickles noted in his autobiography: "The BBC's standard English had become a firmly rooted national institution like cricket and the pub and, Hitler or no Hitler, it meant something when there was a threat of departure from the habit."

Study tip

Don't forget that the first bullet point of the Section B question is targeted at both texts. Try to use material from the second text as well as the first when discussing how the writers present their ideas.

Today, RP is giving way to a new kind of generic southern accent; Estuary English. But the stereotypes and assumptions continue. Estuary English admits people to the inner circle and acts as a 'class barrier'. It's interesting to note that Margaret Thatcher adopted RP to appear more educated, powerful and authoritative to the electorate, while Tony Blair has swapped RP for Estuary English in an attempt to identify more closely with the people he represents. For advertising media though, Estuary English probably wouldn't cut it. It wouldn't be 'posh' enough, credible enough. For advertising, although voiceovers are often asked to be 'classless' the accent required is almost always reflective of upper-middle class values and ideals.

Of course there are regional accents used in advertising – Dervla Kirwan's Marks and Spencer campaign has been hugely successful with her light Irish burr, as has Sean Bean's Yorkshire-accented O2 work – but these are relatively recent departures from RP. In Britain today, RP is still generally regarded as the voice of authority, the voice we trust, the voice we most want to be like, and certainly the voice we usually choose to endorse our marketing.

For me, I love hearing regional accents. I love the diversity of English speakers, how they communicate and the feelings they engender in their listeners. I hope the trend to use regional accents in advertising continues. I think if it does, it indicates a more accepting, less class-conscious society. As Wilfred Pickles said in 1949, "May it be forbidden that we should ever speak like BBC announcers, for our rich contrast of voices is a local tapestry of great beauty and incalculable value, handed down to us by our forefathers." I couldn't have put it better myself.

http://www.emmaclarke.com/blogs/2007/october/received-pronunciation

Essay guidelines

AO3 points on the style of the texts.

'How Queen's English has grown more like ours', by Neil Tweedie (Text E)	'The power and prejudices of received pronunciation' by Emma Clarke (Text F)
Tweedie makes use of an extended metaphor throughout the article. He draws upon collocations related to the idea of the Thames estuary by using imagery of 'drifting slowly down river' and 'near the open sea' to describe the Queen's accent.	Clarke's style is not figurative, although it does use terms like the noun phrase 'the inner circle' and the idiom of 'a class barrier' to represent the structures of social status in the UK. However, the quotation from Wilfred Pickles does use the metaphor of a highly modified noun phrase, 'a local tapestry of great beauty and incalculable value' with its connotations of a priceless and historical treasure, not possible to reproduce if lost.

The use of the alliterative 'fully-fledged Bermondsey banter' contributes to the entertainment purposes of Tweedie's article. He makes use of phonetic respellings of words to connect them with the two extremes of language debated in the article: Estuary/Cockney English forms and Upper RP. These range from reproducing the clipped vowel sounds of 'sex' for 'sacks', through to the Cockney patterns of 'darn' with its fronted medial vowel.	There is a wide collection of phrases used to describe and define the qualities of RP throughout the text. For example, it is an accent seen in the adjectival phrases as '"posh" enough, credible enough', which Estuary English has not yet achieved. Clarke uses anaphora to repeat the noun phrase structure of 'the voice of authority', replacing the prepositional phrase here for a clause in 'the voice we trust'. This is also seen in the alliteration of the title of the text, with the two abstract nouns 'power' and 'prejudices' showing the different possible interpretations of RP.
To support his article, Tweedie makes a lot of use of exophoric referencing, for example to the *Journal of Phonetics* and its topics, and quotes interview sources throughout.	In presenting historical detail, Clarke makes use of paragraphing to produce a chronology of RP and accent forms in broadcasting. These are often led by topic sentences like the simple sentence 'The British Broadcasting Corporation (BBC) was founded in 1922', and the complex sentence 'In 1941 the BBC hired Wilfred Pickles – a Yorkshireman with a broad Halifax accent – to read the news.' These help Clarke to chart the evolution of attitudes towards different accents, and the subtle changes over the 20th and 21st centuries.
As part of the popularisation of the debate, Tweedie coins the phrase 'Estuarisation' to explain an exaggerated view of the changes to the speech of the Queen and Royal Family.	Clarke makes use of the coined adjective 'classless' to describe the irony in the way that term is often used; in fact having connotations of higher class forms. The hyphenated compound adjective 'class-conscious' is given as a kind of antonym of 'classless', to describe the sort of attitude that leads to accent prejudices taking hold, although Clarke suggests this is now lessening.
A complex sentence is employed by Tweedie in the opening paragraph of the article to contextualise the piece by opening the sentence with a subordinate, comparative clause, 'As the common tongue …'. The tiny main clause of the sentence, 'news comes', is placed in between the first subordinate clause and a further subordinate clause, 'that even the Queen …', to begin a clear attitude towards the story.	Coordinate clauses, especially ones begun by the coordinating conjunction 'but', are used on several occasions to qualify the points Clarke makes about RP. For example, after the main clause 'Regional voices were used', Clarke continues with the coordinate clause 'but were only really heard in comedy and light entertainment shows' to show the lowly status of accents at that time, compared to RP. At the other end of the chronology, Clarke uses the same device to place in context the rise of regional accents as an alternative to RP in 'but these are relatively recent departures from RP'.

AO2 points on the related accent and dialect debate.

'How Queen's English has grown more like ours', by Neil Tweedie (Text E)	'The power and prejudices of received pronunciation' by Emma Clarke (Text F)
There seems to be a prescriptivist attitude in Tweedie's article when referring to 'a new dark age of glottal stops' and the depiction of the Queen's accent shift as a 'slide'.	Clarke represents both prescriptivist and descriptivist positions in her article. She celebrates regional accent forms, their rise, and those who use them, and upholds Wilfred Pickles as a pioneer in her field. However, she is also pragmatic in stating the reality of the role of RP in modern marketing. The assertions she makes (that RP speakers are deemed 'well-educated', 'authoritative', 'persuasive', etc.) echo Howard Giles's matched-guise research of some 25 years previously, where respondents rated RP favourably in this way. However, Giles's work with Ellen Ryan also identified the positive attributes people attached to regional forms, developed further in the 'solidarity' model of Zahn and Hopper, describing the perception of 'friendliness, generosity', etc. that Clarke described herself.
Kerswill's research, and that of others, has found evidence of the spread of Estuary English features across regional and social borders in Britain. The typical features of Estuary and Cockney, like 'glottal stops' and the th-fronting shown in 'bovvered' are portrayed in the article.	The significance of Estuary English is raised by Clarke, which links well with Rosewarne's 'RP replacement' theory. Clarke acknowledges the way that Estuary English appears to be taking over the territory once held by RP, for example in politics and its influence on the idiolect of prime ministers.
The use of the Queen's Christmas broadcast is a particularly good methodology to follow, given that it removes problems of the observer's paradox and presents authentic data of language in use.	Broadcast voices, and the different sorts of programme or advertisement particular varieties are used for, are an interesting way of examining attitudes towards accents. The Aziz Corporation carried out their own research into the perception of regional accent forms and reported similar findings to Giles, Ryan, Zahn and Hopper in the way RP was ascribed a high status form of prestige, but some regional forms were seen positively in terms of more social attributes.

Discourse 2: Language change

Language change is another wide-ranging topic that you need to be familiar with. Perhaps most important is to be comfortable with texts of a range of genres and time periods from 1600 onwards. Also, it will be important to understand the different processes and concepts of change, as well as the attitudes towards change that linguists have voiced.

For example, you may be presented with an example of a particularly new form of emerging English usage, like those connected with mobile phones or email use. This might compare with an older debate in the language, related to the way in which new forms of English appear. In this instance, you would need to be able to describe some of the features of examples of language change presented in the texts, like acronym formation, as well as discussing other examples, like the orthographical changes of emoticons. Prescriptivist and descriptivist debates, together with some named linguists, would be an important way of opening the debate, together with ideas about the concepts attached to change, like lexical change and obsolescence.

Task 2

Read Text E and Text F below. Text E is a discussion from the 17th century on the sort of language used by members of The Royal Society. Text F is a newspaper article presenting a humorous summary of some of the jargon and slang of the modern office workplace.

- Analyse and evaluate how these writers use language to express their ideas and opinions on language and occupation, jargon and slang.
- Evaluate the views given about the language used by particular groups of people, drawing on your knowledge and study of language.

Text E

Note: The Royal Society is an organisation of scientists who discuss, advise on and publish material on the range of the sciences. Sprat's book was a commentary on the role of the society and this extract sets out standards for the use of English in scientific writing.

There is one thing more about which the Society has been most solicitous; and that is, the manner of their discourse: which unless they had been very watchful to keep in due temper, the whole spirit and vigour of their design had been soon eaten out by the luxury and redundance of speech. The ill effects of this superfluity of talking have already overwhelmed most other arts and professions; inasmuch, that when I consider the means of happy living, and the causes of their corruption, I can hardly forbear recanting what I said before, and concluding that eloquence alight to be banished out of all civil societies, as a thing fatal to peace and good manners. To this opinion I should wholly incline; if I did not find that it is a weapon which may be as easily procured by bad men as good: and that, if these should only cast it away, and those retain it; the naked innocence of virtue would be upon all occasions exposed to the armed malice of the wicked. This is the chief reason that should now keep up the ornaments of speaking in any request; since they are so much degenerated from their original usefulness. They were at first, no doubt, an admirable instrument in the hands of wise men; when they were only employed to describe goodness, honesty, obedience, in larger, fairer, and more moving images: to represent truth, clothed with bodies; and to bring knowledge back again to our very senses, from whence it was at first derived to our understandings. But now they are generally changed to worse uses: they make the fancy disgust the best things, if they come sound and unadorned; they are in open defiance against reason, professing not to hold much correspondence with that; but with its slaves, the passions: they give the mind a motion too changeable and bewitching to consist with right practice. Who can behold without

THE
ROYAL SOCIETY

Fig. 3 *The Royal Society has been presenting discussion on scientific issues for several hundred years*

indignation how many mists and uncertainties these specious tropes and figures have brought on our knowledge? How many rewards, which are due to more profitable and difficult arts, have been still snatched away by the easy vanity of fine speaking? For, now I am warmed with this just anger, I cannot withhold myself from betraying the shallowness of all these seeming mysteries, upon which we writers, and speakers, look so big. And, in few words, I dare say that of all the studies of men, nothing may be sooner obtained than this vicious abundance of phrase, this trick of metaphors, this volubility of tongue, which makes so great a noise in the world. But I spend words in vain; for the evil is now so inveterate, that it is hard to know whom to blame, or where to begin to reform. We all value one another so much upon this beautiful deceit, and labour so long after it in the years of our education, that we cannot but ever after think kinder of it than it deserves. And indeed, in most other parts of learning, I look upon it as a thing almost utterly desperate in its cure: and I think it may be placed among those general mischiefs, such as the dissension of Christian princes, the want of practice in religion, and the like, which have been so long spoken against that men are become insensible about them; every one shifting off the fault from himself to others; and so they are only made bare common-places of complaint. It will suffice my present purpose to point out what has been done by the Royal Society towards the correcting of its excesses in natural philosophy; to which it is, of all others, a most professed enemy.

They have therefore been most rigorous in putting in execution the only remedy that can be found for this extravagance, and that has been, a constant resolution to reject all the amplifications, digressions, and swellings of style; to return back to the primitive purity, and shortness, when men delivered so many things, almost in an equal number of words. They have exacted from all their members a close, naked, natural way of speaking; positive expressions; clear senses; a native easiness: bringing all things as near the mathematical plainness as they can; and preferring the language of artizans, countrymen, and merchants, before that of wits or scholars.

Thomas Sprat, The History of the Royal Society, *1667*

Text F

Talking improper

Office talk can be a mystery to outsiders. We sent our aphid, **Tim Hitchcock**, *to avoid the Lombards, KISS in the adminisphere, and report back*

Don't eat at your desk in the office this lunchtime: show your independence and call it "dining al desco in the Cube Farm". From christening bad managers "seagulls" to labelling training days "AFLOs", using workplace slang is a little rebellion that lets you say what you really think of the boss, ridiculous management-speak or the public without being handed a P45. Expressing yourself frankly but safely on the office intranet requires a covert language. No wonder slang's popularity is growing.

Further reading

Take a look at the Office Life website and its comprehensive business jargon dictionary for more examples of the kind of office slang discussed in Tim Hitchcock's article: http://www.theofficelife.com/business-jargon-dictionary-A.html.

"It's how workers retaliate," explains Laurie Taylor, a former professor of sociology who now presents the BBC Radio 4 programme 'Thinking Allowed'. "Slang excludes internal authority and the public because neither can understand it." Taylor says workplace slang has always existed but is much more prevalent now for a simple reason: "It's a revolt against the rise of bullshit management-speak."

Fig. 4 *A little bit of 'percussive maintenance' – office talk for hitting the computer when it stops working*

Subversive variations of the business acronyms loved by disciples of management-speak are particularly popular. Alan Chapman, an expert in personal and organisational development, defends some workplace acronyms. "Ones such as KISS [Keep it simple, stupid] and AIDA [Attention, Interest, Desire, Action] are useful ways to teach important things by a mnemonic," he says. However, he does concede that when corporate talk gets incomprehensibly complex or daft, as often happens in the public sector, subordinates mock it. Chapman runs a website (www.businessballs.com) listing proper business terms and acronyms together with ones invented by employees. "One I like is 'AFLO', standing for 'Another F ... Learning Opportunity'," he says.

Proper acronyms too are frequently subverted. When Paula Clarkson worked for a chain of department stores going through hard times, part of her job was to prepare a weekly cash report or WCR. But she and her colleagues chose to pronounce it phonetically. "We called it the Wuh-cu-rur because the figures got worser-er and worser-er," she explains.

Other slang mocks management-speak by sounding as if it might just be real. "Adminisphere", for example; it could be something invented by middle-management to inspire their employees but actually refers to the faceless tier of bureaucracy that churns out memos stating the obvious or the irritating. Or how about the impressively polysyllabic "percussive maintenance"? It means whacking an obstinate computer, photocopier or other electronic device until the damn thing works.

Study tip

Quote examples from the texts exactly as they appear, including full-stops and capital letters if quoting a whole sentence, and other punctuation like quotation marks.

Nicknaming bosses is another popular pastime. "Seagull manager" is an Americanism gaining ground here. This boss flies in, squawks noisily as he messes everything up and then flaps off again. No doubt their promotion was due to "assmosis"; the process of becoming successful by sucking up to the powerful rather than by being any good. The responsibility for their cock-ups will tend to be dumped on others after a blamestorming session.

Traditional slang titles like "Napoleon" and "Daddy on the Board" are holding their own while "Lombard", which started as an acronym for Loads Of Money But A Real [expletive deleted], is so popular in City back offices it has become a word in its own right.

Another category of office slang bonds management and staff together in a way no team-building exercise can. What do you call the members of the public who habitually foul up the smooth running of the working day? Nowadays the approved term is almost always "customers" but the whingers, time-wasters and prize idiots amongst them are called all manner of nasty things when management is out of earshot.

The mildly discourteous "punters" is ubiquitous but less restrained terms frequently crop up. "Pond life", for example, is used by workers everywhere, from the financial services to the police. The former use it to describe small investors, the latter employ it to define persistent but unsuccessful petty criminals. It is also a popular term in technical support centres, where it refers to people who cause inexplicable computer failures (probably by conducting percussive maintenance).

Medics are the masters of the hidden slang insult. The caring facade of the NHS's angelic nurses and saintly doctors has been dented by the revelation that those official-looking scribbles on your notes are an unexpected form of professional shorthand: FLK means Funny Looking Kid, BUNDY is used to describe someone who is on their way out But Unfortunately Not Dead Yet, and HIVI means Husband Is Village Idiot.

Even academics use office slang. After some cajoling, Laurie Taylor admits that university lecturers refer to lazy students as "re-sit material" and downright thick ones as CDs, short for the euphemism "culturally-deprived". Another piece of faux political correctness is "sobriety-challenged", used by the legal profession to describe particularly thirsty clients. But the kings of office slang are, perhaps inevitably, those most in need of an escape valve – the poor souls who man complaints lines. Understandably, they have a lot of simple insults to hand, but they also use their own true slang. "People who act like sulky toddlers get called Nappy Heads and pensioners who stay on the phone because they haven't spoken to anyone for days are Lineblockers," reveals Catherine, who used to handle customer complaints for an electrical goods manufacturer. "There's one more you should know," she adds. "We used to call journalists who rang up investigating people's gripes 'aphids'." Is that a snappy acronym? "No, it's because they were a pest for 24 hours then buzzed off and died for all we cared." Sometimes office slang can be cruel.

The Guardian, 19 January 2004

Essay guidelines

AO3 points on the style of the texts.

The History of the Royal Society by Thomas Sprat (Text E)	'Talking improper' by Tim Hitchcock (Text F)
Sprat makes use of metaphorical imagery to portray his concerns about the use of borrowings and new words, which he accuses of bringing 'mists', which draws upon connotations of a lack of clarity and inability to see clearly.	Hitchcock constructs metaphors to form a part of the subversive attitude his article takes towards authority in business, as with the image of a 'faceless tier of bureaucracy that churns ...'
There are a wide range of lexical items used by Sprat to refer to the lexical items and phrases that his text is aimed at critiquing: 'ornaments', 'tropes', and 'figures'. These are mostly synonyms, and the use of pronoun cohesion makes the terms themselves the third-person object of the piece, as 'them' and 'they'.	Hitchcock makes deliberate use of office slang and jargon terms within his own narrative for humorous effect, for example in labelling himself an 'aphid' and later defining this term in the final paragraph.
Highly complex, suspended sentence structures are used by Sprat that are representative of other Early Modern English writing.	Hitchcock begins his article with an imperative to apply immediately some of the office jargon that is the subject of his article, to his reader. Hitchcock constructs a fast-paced style that employs spoken-language features like the fronting of connective forms like 'Even...', 'Another...' and 'Other...' to open paragraphs.

AO2 points on the related language change debate.

The History of the Royal Society by Thomas Sprat (Text E)	'Talking improper' by Tim Hitchcock (Text F)
Sprat's argument is related to the inkhorn controversy of the Early Modern English period, with the attitude he adopts being similar to the attitude of those who opposed the use of borrowed classical terms (inkhorn terms) in their writing.	There are many processes of change exhibited in the examples provided by Hitchcock, including acronyms, initialisms and Americanisms.
The causes of Sprat's concern for changes to the language are common with any new, expanding field, like technology and science, entering into the language.	Many of the examples of use raise the debate of political correctness, either by being politically incorrect, or examples of alternatives, or satirical alternatives to perceived language inequalities.
Sprat presents a kind of prescriptivism, similar to the 'crumbling castle' model presented by Aitchison to describe such approaches to language.	The fertility of colloquial language as an area of rapid language change is foregrounded.

🔍 Discourse 3: Gender and interaction

Gender and interaction is a specific part of language variation, and you may be presented with the findings of a particular researcher into language and gender, alongside an academic or a popular text. The ability to relate your answer to the work of one or two of the named researchers, and others that you may have researched, will be important, as will adding some detail of their findings.

Task 3

Read Text E and Text F below. They both discuss views of the way the communicative styles of men and women can differ. Text E is a newspaper article by Anita Chaudhuri that responds to research suggesting women are genetically more avid speakers than men. Text F is a more recent newspaper article by Bryony Gordon that examines evidence that men are the more dominant speakers in mixed-sex conversation.

- Analyse and evaluate the ways these two texts use language to present their ideas about men and women and the way they interact.

- Evaluate these ideas about the differences between male and female communication, drawing on your knowledge and study of language.

Text E

Vocal discord

Scientists are trying to prove the existence of a "chatterbox" gene. Anita Chaudhuri asks, are we born to blab?

When I grow up, I want to be a genetic scientist. No, really. What a brilliant life they must lead, lounging around all day isolating chromosomes to explain away our irritating personality traits. Out-of-control drinking, eating, sex and shopping have all been attributed to compulsive behaviour genes. Now researchers at the Institute of Psychiatry are attempting to prove the existence of a "chatterbox" gene which – surprise, surprise – they expect to be more dominant in females.

"The research shows there are sex-specific influences on early language development. It seems the ways genes work is different in boys and girls. It could be that this trigger is hormonal," says Michael Galsworthy, one of the researchers. Although psychologists have previously suggested that sex differences in verbal ability occur because parents talk to girls more than boys, Galsworthy and his team believe that it has more to do with differences in genetic make-up.

Another theory might be that in evolutionary terms, women were the ones setting up camp and nurturing communities while the men were off in the woods killing dangerous beasts and lugging them home. However, one thing is clear: despite the fact that ours is an increasingly talk-driven culture, chatting is not a highly valued talent.

The Collins dictionary definition of the word chatterbox sums it up nicely: "A person who talks constantly about trivial matters". Note, it doesn't say "a woman" but it might as well, for when did anyone ever hear of a male being referred to as a chatterbox? Popular culture thrives on the notion of girl talk – the apotheosis of female bonding through chat.

Whatever the context, there is this lingering idea that women talk about inconsequential things, therefore it's a facility that goes unrewarded. Nowhere is this more marked than in the arena of broadcasting. Inexplicably, in the very medium where chat is king, women fail to shine. Men do the talking and women are forever doomed to aimless chit-chat.

Patsy Rodenburg, director of voice at the National Theatre, believes that women have been discriminated against because of their voices and she has written an essay on the issue for *Well-Tuned Women*, an anthology about women's voices.

"It seems that after the initial intellectual awareness of the feminist movement, the physical manifestations surfaced in the mid-70s. Women seeking my help either felt that their voices were denied, not heard or, if they had good strong voices, they were mocked or called unfeminine, their vocal power deemed inappropriate."

Rodenburg has been called in to provide voice coaching for a number of corporations and observes how difficult it is for women to express opinions in arenas of power. "Gossiping, giggling and flirting, yes, but an intelligent woman speaking with freedom, clarity and power was too much and these women were constantly punished. No wonder voice specialists are sought by professional women."

Linguistic theorists have long suspected that men and women spend half their lives talking at cross-purposes. In her best-selling book *You Just Don't Understand*, Deborah Tannen examined the differences in the way we talk. She concluded that men see conversations as a forum for male power games with domination as their goal and noted that where women use language to seek confirmation, make connections and reinforce intimacies, men use it to protect their independence and negotiate status.

It will be interesting to see what the gene team at the Institute of Psychiatry come up with after they've analysed the DNA samples of all the participants.

http://www.theguardian.com/world/2000/jul/18/gender.uk1

Text F

Women must rip off the gag and speak up

A new report suggests that in mixed company, men do most of the talking. Why should that be?

There is a very funny Harry Enfield sketch that I suggest you all go and look up on YouTube now. The sketch, which claims to be a public service announcement, is filmed in flickering black and white, and is narrated by a man with the diction of a Fifties BBC radio announcer. "An ordinary dinner party," he says, opening the scene. "The sort of occasion we all enjoy. The men are exchanging witty stories, and look at the women. Aren't they pretty? Look at the way they laugh. Aren't they delightful?"

The men at the party discuss the gold standard; the women look on adoringly. Then one of the females pipes up with her economic theory, and the whole dinner party is thrown into disarray.

Viewers are shown evidence of how over-education in women "leads to ugliness, premature ageing and beard growth", before the narrator concludes the so-called public service announcement with the following withering words: "Women, know your limits. In thought be plain and simple and let your natural sweetness shine through."

Funny, because many decades ago that used to be true. Not today, of course. No, no, no. Now we can all have a laugh at the little woman role that our grandmothers and great-grandmothers were cast in. At dinner parties and other gatherings of both sexes, women are just as vocal as their male counterparts – if not more so. We have opinions, not all of them are particularly nice, and we are not afraid to use them.

Right? Wrong!

A study published in the *American Political Science Review* has found that women speak "substantially less" when outnumbered by men in group discussions. In fact, when observing 94 groups of at least five people, the political scientist Chris Karpowitz found that "the time that women spoke was significantly less than their proportional representation – amounting to less than 75 per cent of the time that men spoke."

Researching this piece, I spoke to the only female in an eight-strong team of professionals, and asked her how she dealt with all the testosterone. "I keep quiet," she responded over email, "because I have found that in meetings it is just easier. You let them speak. Afterwards, you flatter the ones you happened to agree with and ignore the ones you didn't."

Fay Weldon told me that she now turns down invitations to appear on television shows with lots of men. "They are so busy making their points that you are forced to butt in, and I don't enjoy that any more. There is a degree of aggression to it that many women don't have."

The wonderful Emily Maitlis says she has been cross about this for years, "but possibly in a squeaky voice at the back of the room without piping up, so no one has heard. Women are much more loath to state their point of view loudly in a crowded auditorium. I've noticed that when they do, even if they're a Nobel Prize-winning neuroscientist unique in their field, they will often phrase it like a question, so that it seems less offensive than a statement.

"My very brilliant American Harvard Law School mate Sharon used to point it out when we were [studying] at Cambridge – in lectures, the men would go first, then the women, ie me, would timidly say 'perhaps I misheard, but could I just ask possibly whether …?' which is RIDICULOUS and COWARDLY and APPALLING."

Weldon thinks that more than anything, our reticence is down to manners. "It's not that one is frightened – it's more that one just can't get a word in edgeways without being rude. I don't like to interrupt, but the same cannot be said for men, I'm afraid.

"Nowadays I just think, 'Oh, I'll give up and let them get on with it.' And you know, what they are saying is not necessarily all that interesting anyway. Often they are simply behaving like boys in a school playground. So in that respect, we can feel oddly superior."

http://www.telegraph.co.uk/women/mother-tongue/9562830/
Women-must-rip-off-the-gag-and-speak-up.html

Essay guidelines

AO3 points on the style of the texts.

'Vocal Discord' by Anita Chaudhuri (Text E)	'Women must rip off the gag and speak up' by Bryony Gordon (Text F)
Chaudhuri begins with an anecdote, which opens with the fronted adverbial clause 'When I grow up', which then provides a light-hearted way of establishing the heavier, scientific basis for the research the article discusses. This is then carried in technical verb phrases like 'isolating chromosomes' in the complex sentence that follows.	Gordon begins with an exphoric reference to another text, in this case a television excerpt described in the noun phrase 'a very funny Harry Enfield sketch', to simultaneously set an informal tone and set out a prevailing stereotype in the world of gender politics.
There is a repeated pattern of negative adjectives used to describe characteristics of female 'chat', including negated forms like the adjectives 'inconsequential' and 'aimless'. This also extends into a range of hyponyms for female talk, such as the diminutive 'chit-chat', 'gossiping' and 'blab', which can have derogatory connotations.	The minor sentences 'Right? Wrong!' are paired as an interrogative and exclamative adjacency pair. This is a more spoken mode feature and relates well to the nature of the topic, as well as enabling Gordon to challenge past and current perceptions of female conversational roles.
At the heart of the text is an articulate and serious-minded exploration of ideas related to female conversation, communicated through highly modified noun phrases such as 'sex-specific influences on early language development', 'the apotheosis of female bonding through chat' and 'the initial intellectual awareness of the feminist movement.	Gordon uses quoted speech as part of the interview material in her article, and, in one example, emphasises the adjectival forms Maitlis uses to criticise her own acceptance of a subordinate role in conversation. The capitalisation of 'ridiculous' and 'cowardly' and the present participle adjective 'appalling', match the emotive tone of the article's title and attack the perceived inequality in male and female interaction.

AO2 points on the related gender and interaction debate.

'Vocal Discord' by Anita Chaudhuri (Text E)	'Women must rip off the gag and speak up' by Bryony Gordon (Text F)
Far from being genetically hard-wired, the research of Janet Hyde and work of Deborah Cameron have recorded verbal and language differences between men and women as small. Furthermore, Cameron suggests that differences we do find between male or female speakers are based on individual personality.	The work of Zimmerman and West recorded men as producing the vast majority of interruptions when speaking in mixed-sex company. In their research, 96 per cent of interruptions in mixed interactions were male, showing men to be adopting a dominant and domineering role.
Robin Lakoff's description of 'empty adjectives' and the language of women's work, as part of a 'women's language' connects well with the idea of 'this lingering idea that women talk about inconsequential things'. Here, female conversation is marginalised, and occupies a similarly subordinate role to the one detailed by Lakoff.	Maitlis's comments about her own intimidation in meetings, and the way she found herself speaking, suggest some of Lakoff's 'women's language' forms in use. For example, hedges, superpolite and indirect forms match Maitlis's own example of 'perhaps I misheard, but could I just ask possibly whether …?'
Generally, the 'difference' model of gender and interaction is supported by the text, matching the stance of John Gray's 'Mars and Venus' assertion of innate gender differences, as well as others that followed in this vein.	A different emphasis in the way men and women use language is evident in Janet Holmes's research into different tag question forms. She found overall that men used tags for more factual, 'referential' reasons, while women were more facilitative and collaborative in their usage.
The work of Deborah Tannen is referenced directly, so expanding into discussion of male 'report' and female 'rapport' traits would be a good idea, to identify the different conversational roles she saw the sexes adopting.	Pamela Fishman's critique of the 'conversational division of labour' – that women do the hard work in conversation but that conversations serve men's purposes, is reflected in the status quo the article challenges.

Discourse 4: Political correctness

If your paired texts are centred around this debate, you are open to make use of more recent language change material with specific reference to the influence of political correctness. This will encompass understanding the objections levelled at specific examples of language use, with the linguistic detail required to explain the problems language poses, and possible solutions.

For example, you might be presented with an extract from a feminist text setting out an objection to a particular feature in the language like the use of the generic masculine, alongside an article criticising the effects of the political correctness debate and putting forward some of the satirical forms that have emerged. In this instance, theories of linguistic determinism and reflectionism would be an important part of the debate, together with the use of appropriate linguistic terminology concerning generic language and the inclusion of relevant research to provide evidence of deeper knowledge in the discussion.

Task 4

Read Text E and Text F below. They set out differing approaches to the language of political correctness. Text E is a parody of a traditional fairy tale. Text F is an article from *The Guardian* newspaper.

- Analyse and evaluate how these two writers use language to present different views on the political correctness debate.
- Evaluate these ideas about the nature and value of political correctness, drawing on your knowledge and study of language.

Text E

Fig. 5 *Little Red Riding Hood – harmless children's story, or hornet's nest of social prejudice?*

Little Red Riding Hood

There once was a young person named Red Riding Hood who lived with her mother on the edge of a large wood. One day her mother asked her to take a basket of fresh fruit and mineral water to her grandmother's house – not because this was womyn's work, mind you, but because the deed was generous and helped engender a feeling of community. Furthermore, her grandmother was not sick, but rather was in full physical and mental health and was fully capable of taking care of herself as a mature adult.

So Red Riding Hood set off with her basket through the woods. Many people believed that the forest was a foreboding and dangerous place and never set foot in it. Red Riding Hood, however, was confident enough in her own budding sexuality that such obvious Freudian imagery did not intimidate her.

On the way to Grandma's house, Red Riding Hood was accosted by a wolf, who asked her what was in her basket. She replied, 'Some healthful snacks for my grandmother, who is certainly capable of taking care of herself as a mature adult.'

The wolf said, 'You know, my dear, it isn't safe for a little girl to walk through these woods alone.'

Red Riding Hood said, 'I find your sexist remark offensive in the extreme, but I will ignore it because of your traditional status as an outcast from society, the stress of which has caused you to develop your own, entirely valid, worldview. Now, if you'll excuse me, I must be on my way.'

Red Riding Hood walked on along the main path. But, because his status outside society had freed him from slavish adherence to linear, Western-style thought, the wolf knew a quicker route to Grandma's house. He burst into the house and ate Grandma, an entirely valid course of action for a carnivore such as himself. Then, unhampered by rigid, traditionalist notions of what was masculine or feminine, he put on Grandma's nightclothes and crawled into bed.

Red Riding Hood entered the cottage and said, 'Grandma, I have brought you some fat-free, sodium-free snacks to salute you in your role of a wise and nurturing matriarch.'

From the bed, the wolf said softly, 'Come closer, child, so that I might see you.'

Red Riding Hood said, 'Oh, I forgot you are as optically challenged as a bat. Grandma, what big eyes you have!'

'They have seen much, and forgiven much, my dear. '

'Grandma, what a big nose you have – only relatively, of course, and certainly attractive in its own way.'

'It has smelled much, and forgiven much, my dear.'

'Grandma, what big teeth you have!'

The wolf said, 'I am happy with who I am and what I am,' and leaped out of bed. He grabbed Red Riding Hood in his claws, intent on devouring her. Red Riding Hood screamed, not out of alarm at the wolf's apparent tendency towards cross-dressing, but because of his wilful invasion of her personal space.

Her screams were heard by a passing woodcutter-person (or log-fuel technician, as he preferred to be called). When he burst into the cottage, he saw the melee and tried to intervene. But as he raised his axe, Red Riding Hood and the wolf both stopped.

'And just what do you think you're doing?' asked Red Riding Hood.

The woodcutter-person blinked and tried to answer, but no words came to him.

'Bursting in here like a Neanderthal, trusting your weapon to do your thinking for you!' she exclaimed. 'Sexist! Speciesist! How dare you assume that womyn and wolves can't solve their own problems without a man's help!'

When she heard Red Riding Hood's impassioned speech, Grandma jumped out of the wolf's mouth, seized the woodcutter-person's axe, and cut his head off. After this ordeal, Red Riding Hood, Grandma and the wolf felt a certain commonality of purpose. They decided to set up an alternative household based on mutual respect and cooperation, and they lived together in the woods happily ever after.

J. F. Garner, Politically Correct Bedtime Stories, *1994*

Study tip

You don't have to agree with the opinion of a text to still be able to make effective points about it. It is equally valid to challenge a text and make your linguistic points that way, although you should still show awareness of the wider debate.

Text F

Mind your language – and know what it means

We should be teaching political correctness in schools, says Philip Beadle

Society has changed greatly since the 80s. Shoulder pads are now viewed as a sign of inadequacy and woe betide the man who rolls the sleeves of his jacket up to the elbows. If you had written in defence of being free with the many contrived moralities of language

Fig. 6 *Some linguists have been critical of the role of Standard English in suppressing language varieties that don't fit a perceived white, male, middle class orthodoxy in the UK*

in those days, you would first have had to nail your PC colours to the mast: 'Some of my best friends are black/gay/disabled, but...'

Today, it's the opposite, and this article is written in defence of teaching children about political correctness. Not teaching them that it is right or wrong – it's not a teacher's job to draw the conclusions – but that it exists.

As anyone who has stared unflinchingly into the vacant eyes of 'PC gone mad' will tell you, it's as terrifying and as totalitarian as its supposed antithesis. Servicing the needs of social workers in a now infamous social services department of a north London council was a bleak period for me. Once, on a training day, I made the mortal error of being bashful when someone had complimented my handwriting. Blushing, unused to being the recipient of anything like praise in that environment, I said: 'Oh, thanks. I think I've got the handwriting of a 17-year-old girl.' My colleague found just enough time to turn purple, before rushing gleefully to submit a written complaint about the many unacceptable 'isms' in my innocent expression.

In practice, political correctness became the thing it set out to combat. Its heart, though, may well have been in the right place at some point before it became jealousy with a halo. It sought to protect people, mainly minorities, from the impact of words, be they thoughtless or mindful. Sadly, in doing so, it punished others.

Most dialect versions of English, and often standard English itself, are intrinsically racist. We have a thousand unpleasant slang terms for black people, with just the innocuous 'honky' kicking its legs blithely in the air at the other end of the see-saw. The phrase 'honest injun', for instance, has been part of my own argot since childhood. I never thought to question its morality. It was just something people from London said to emphasise that they were telling the truth. But in the realms of the politically correct, such dialect forms are outlawed. This leaves us in the paradoxical position of upholding immigrant children's right to use their own language, at the same time as banning indigenous children from using theirs.

Why, then, would anyone be prepared to speak up for teaching political correctness in the classroom? As a small child, I remember being in receipt of another form of idiocy, the brain dead, sing-song naivety of 'sticks and stones may break my bones, but names will never hurt me'. Given the choice between a whack round the leg with a twig or a mean-spirited comment about my appearance or family, I'd argue that the callous word causes more lasting damage. Words can hurt like hell.

My council colleagues would refer to a thing called 'the language of equality'. And if you ignore its somewhat clumsy title, I think there's still a place for the ideas behind this outmoded expression. It's useful for kids – day-to-day practitioners of language – to know such a system exists.

Take, for instance, the phrase 'Aids victim'. During the early 90s, there was a drive to tag people as 'living with HIV', as opposed to being 'victims' of it. There are few, outside the most militant political group, who would argue with this drive. The word 'victim' implies defencelessness and defeat, whereas 'living with' suggests the fat lady hasn't even begun tuning up yet, and that the person in question is vital, active, getting on with the task of living, and not the passive recipient of an immediate death sentence.

I think children should be given the opportunity to experiment with these ideas; to think about whether being considerate in their expression is a good thing. And it is possible to teach the existence of a more considerate version of expression in a disinterested manner, raising it as a possibility to consider, at the same time as satirising its extremities. Kids love being asked to define their own politically correct expressions, and respond with glee to describing a baldy as being follically challenged and a porker as calorifically enhanced.

Study of this subject causes them to investigate the intrinsic morality of their own language, and to see how this may have changed over the years. It also politicises. A black girl who comes to the realisation that standard English is the language of a white male orthodoxy is a girl who may well be motivated to do something about this in her own life.

So, yes, I admit it. I am in favour of political correctness being taught in schools. But, then I would be. I am a Guardian-reading schoolteacher who has lived in Stoke Newington, had a bottle of extra virgin olive oil out on display next to the cooker and, I am utterly ashamed to say, have not just eaten couscous, but thoroughly enjoyed it.

The Guardian, 16 May 2006

Essay guidelines

AO3 points on the style of the texts.

Politically Correct Bedtime Stories by J. F. Garner (Text E)	'Mind your language – and know what it means' by Philip Beadle (Text F)
In the tale of 'Little Red Riding Hood', Garner makes use of standard narrative development phrases to open his sentences. This provides a traditional contrast with the satirical content, in examples like 'There once was a …' and 'One day …'	Beadle uses spoken mode forms to structure his argument, with use of anecdote: 'I made the mortal error …' and '… part of my own argot …'
Garner makes use of lexical items taken directly from the field of the political correctness debate to create humour, with the feminist respelling of 'womyn', and adjectives representing ideologies, such as 'sexist' and 'traditionalist'.	Beadle adds to this lexicon with some serious ('living with HIV', 'honky') phrases involved with the politically correct debate, and some of the satirical forms ('follically challenged', 'calorifically enhanced').
There is a high level of noun pre-modification in Garner's story, often to create the effect of satirising political correctness, for example in 'linear, Western-style thought' and 'a wise and nurturing matriarch'.	Beadle employs alliteration to link related concepts in his discussion, like 'defencelessness and defeat' and 'terrifying and totalitarian'.

Grammatically, Garner's text makes use of several subordinating clauses to add the detail to sentences that creates the humour he is aiming for, as in '... because of your traditional ...' and '... because his status ...'	Beadle makes use of a number of short sentences to create effects, for example in 'Words can hurt like hell' and 'It also politicises'.
Semantically, the Garner text presents extremes of negative and positive language in generating a 'moral' aspect to the story: 'slavish' and 'wilful' as compared with 'nurturing' and 'respect'.	Beadle employs imagery to represent metaphorically the inequality of racial language in his childhood, with '"honky" kicking its legs blithely in the air at the other end of the see-saw'.

AO2 points on the related political correctness debate.

Politically Correct Bedtime Stories by J. F. Garner (Text E)	'Mind your language – and know what it means' by Philip Beadle (Text F)
The context of the political correctness debate involves its origin in US feminist and liberal movements towards the end of the 20th century.	Beadle's text puts forward some examples of politically correct and incorrect language use – 'honest injun' for example – which can be analysed further to explain their offence.
The Sapir-Whorf hypothesis of linguistic determinism is related to models of language that would support political correctness as a valid tool for changing attitudes and thought.	Political correctness discussion gives the opportunity to detail some of the ways that the English language can be seen to be inherently biased, for example through over-representation or asymmetry issues, as alluded to in Beadle's 'see-saw' metaphor.
There is a distinction to be drawn between the genuine proposals of the political correctness movement and the satirical, parodied forms that arose in the 1990s especially.	The precise etymology and social context of terms like 'nigger' can be brought into the debate.

And finally ...

You have now come to the end of your tour of English and the ENGA3 exam. The topics covered here may well encourage you to look into studying language further and there is a wide range of courses, pursuits and careers available.

Looking back over Unit 3, check that you have understood the different ideas represented. They are many and various, which means that you need to consider them with your eyes and mind wide open. If you complete the tasks set, you will have covered the sorts of question that you may encounter in the exams – and your teacher will, no doubt, supply you with even more!

Topic revision exercise

1 What are the four major areas of language variation and change you need to study for Section B of the exam?

2 Which AO is worth the most marks and what does it cover?

3 What form does the Section B question take?

Further reading

General

Crystal, D. *The Cambridge Encyclopedia of the English Language*, Cambridge University Press, 1995

Crystal, D. *Making Sense of Grammar*, Longman, 2004

McArthur, T. *The Oxford Companion to the English Language*, Oxford University Press, 1992

Language change

Baugh, A. and Cable, T. *A History of the English Language*, Routledge, 2002

Crystal, D. *A Glossary of Netspeak and Textspeak*, Edinburgh University Press, 2004

Crystal, D. *The Stories of English*, Penguin Books, 2005

McCrum, R., MacNeil, R. and Cran, W. *The Story of English*, Faber & Faber, 2002

British Library, Turning the Pages website: www.bl.uk (search for 'Online Gallery' and 'Turning the Pages')

Language variation

Chirrey, D. *Urban Voices: Accent Studies in the British Isles*, Hodder Arnold, 1999

Sebba, M. *Contact Languages*, Palgrave Macmillan, 1997

Talbot, M. M. *Language and Gender*, Blackwell, 1998

Wells, J. *Accents of English 2: The British Isles*, Cambridge University Press, 1982

Barrie Rhodes on the BBC Voices website: http://www.bbc.co.uk/northyorkshire/voices2005/glossary/barrie_rhodes.shtml

BBC Voices website: www.bbc.co.uk/voices

Feedback

This part of the book provides the feedback for the Classroom activity in Unit 3, Section B. For the answers to the Topic revision exercises, please go to pages 208–11.

Studying language variation and change

Classroom activity 1

Methodology	Research
Survey	BBC Voices project
Meta-analysis	Janet Hyde's gender similarities hypothesis
Ethnographic study	Lesley Milroy's Belfast study
Experiment	Peter Trudgill's Norwich study
Interview	Mark Sebba's London Jamaican research
Corpus analysis	*Oxford English Dictionary*

Language investigations and interventions

Assessment objectives:

- **AO1** Select and apply a range of linguistic methods, to communicate relevant knowledge using appropriate terminology and coherent, accurate written expression.

- **AO2** Demonstrate critical understanding of a range of concepts and issues related to the construction and analysis of meanings in spoken and written language, using knowledge of linguistic approaches.

- **AO3** Analyse and evaluate the influence of contextual factors on the production and reception of spoken and written language, showing knowledge of the key constituents of language.

- **AO4** Demonstrate expertise and creativity in the use of English in a range of different contexts, informed by linguistic study.

General introduction

Unit 4 can be seen as having two purposes: first, to allow you to demonstrate the skills and knowledge that you have been developing throughout your English Language course, and second, to build on these through more challenging coursework tasks.

During this unit you will be working more independently than in any other part of the course. This is not to say that your teachers won't be supporting and helping you through the module, but that you will have the opportunity to come up with your own ideas for projects, and to plan and produce assignments that are very much your own work.

This coursework represents 40 per cent of the marks of your A2 course, 20 per cent of the whole A Level; the marks are evenly split between the two tasks.

Section A: Language investigation

In Section A you will carry out an original piece of language research into spoken language, building on the techniques you used in Unit 2 Representation and language. This task gives you the opportunity to look in more detail at an aspect of the course that has interested you the most: for example language development or language change. Alternatively, you could focus on an outside area of interest – a hobby or pastime, for instance – and perform a language-based study into one aspect of it. The investigation will require you to collect your own language data, perform a detailed analysis of it and come to conclusions about its implications and relevance. In addition to these core elements, you will learn how to plan an effective research project, to formulate aims and hypotheses, and to produce your finished submission using academic standards of presentation, such as bibliographies and appendices.

Section B: Language intervention

In Section B you will produce one or two texts discussing one or more of the language issues that you studied in Unit 3 Language explorations. Again this means you can look back at an area that you found interesting and develop it further, writing a text that comments upon and maybe adds to the debate. There is a wide variety of text types that you might produce – a newspaper article, short story, or textbook page, for example – but whichever you choose will need to conform to the expected conventions of that type of text. This means you will need a good knowledge of the particular features of language and layout associated with a range of styles of writing. The work you did in Unit 1, Section A Language and mode – looking at the conventions of various text types – will act as a starting point for this.

Language investigation

Introduction

In this section you will:

- develop an understanding of the requirements of this part of the coursework

- look at a range of ideas on how to choose your investigation topic

- learn what is needed in a successful investigation

- learn how to collect data and consider issues surrounding its collection

- develop your analysis skills and look at how to apply them to the task

- learn how to present your work using academic research standards.

Link

Look back over your coursework project in AS Unit 2 Representation and language. Many of the skills you learned and used in that activity will be needed in your Unit 4 investigation.

Key terms

Question: a key question that the investigation sets out to answer.

Aims: a statement or set of statements detailing what the investigation is attempting to find out.

This section will take you through the requirements for the investigation part of the coursework. You will look at possible topics for your project, what needs to be included in it, methods of collecting and analysing data, and how to organise and present your final submission. You will have already completed a mini-investigation – back in Unit 2 of the AS course. In this section of Unit 4 you will build on that work, but here we will take a more rigorous and academic approach to the investigation. Many of the skills and ideas that you will look at are 'generic' research methods – in other words, methods that you can apply to any type of investigative project. In this way, the section will also help you to understand what is expected in research projects in the business world or in higher education.

Basic requirements for the investigation task

To start off with, you need to know some important things about the investigation. These are the basic requirements, and you need to be clear on them before you begin thinking about your investigation in more detail.

- Your investigation must be an original piece of work – your own ideas and data (examples of language that you have collected).

- Your investigation must be based on primary language data; this means language data that you have collected yourself.

- Your investigation must focus on spoken language so an investigation based on written texts is not an option unless the texts involve language that is spoken or intended to be spoken.

- Your investigation should consist of 1,750–2,500 words (excluding data). Often students worry about writing too little in coursework tasks but you will probably find one of the difficulties here is writing too much.

What needs to be in my investigation?

Your final coursework submission should contain eight different sections. The assignments and exams you have already done contain similar 'sections', just not as clearly separated or headlined. The role of each section is outlined below.

1 **Introduction, hypotheses and questions:** The introduction will explain what your investigation is about, what kind of language it will explore and may also discuss your reasons for choosing it and some background information on how it fits into the whole language system. It should also state what hypothesis the investigation tests or what **question** it explores.

2 **Aims:** Your **aims** will outline exactly what you are trying to find out, breaking down the hypothesis you wish to test or the questions you seek to explore into separate strands or approaches. A good investigation always has precise and well-focused aims. If they are too broad or 'woolly' you may have problems later on.

3 **Methodology:** This is a technical word meaning the method you will use to carry out your investigation. Methodologies answer questions like how, where and when you will collect your data and explain the reasons for your decisions. Methodologies should be in the future tense, explaining what you intend to do rather than what you have done.

Your methodology must also contain a **linguistic framework** which will identify and discuss the features you are intending to investigate. By now, you should be quite at home with frameworks but, to recap, look back at your work at AS. For your investigation task you will choose the ones that are relevant to your data. They must be sufficiently wide (to look at a range of different features) and deep (to look at these features in detail).

4 **Analysis:** This is the key part of any investigation, and the one that will go a long way to determining your final mark. It is the bit where you actually discuss your data, and all of the other sections of the investigation lead to, or away from, this. You may also bring in **secondary sources** here (such as surveys, other people's research, books, websites and articles), perhaps to consider your **primary language data** in the light of the theories or research of others.

5 **Conclusion:** In the conclusion you will explain what you have (or haven't) found out. Your conclusion will summarise the findings from your analysis and will link back to the aims you laid down at the beginning.

6 **Evaluation:** This is often confused with the conclusion, but whereas the conclusion states what has been found out, the evaluation discusses how useful these findings are and how successful you think your investigation has been. This is where you write about how the project went, its strengths and weaknesses, and the significance of its findings. You may also include ideas that you have for further possible research into your topic.

7 **Bibliography:** This is a list of all the sources you have used. You may have referred to books, websites or other places for information, and the details of all of these must be included. Your bibliography may well be the last thing you do in your investigation but it is important, even at this early stage, that you make a note of any books, magazines, periodicals or websites you have used so that you have this information for when you complete your bibliography later on. If you don't, you will end up spending lots of time trawling back through your investigation to find the details that you need. It is a good idea to start a research log now where you can write down all the sources you have used as your investigation progresses. Note, also, that when recording webpages in the bibliography, you must include the date that you accessed the page, so remember to make a note of these as you go along.

8 **Data and appendices:** Data is the 'stuff' you will be investigating. Some will appear in the main part of your submission: some will appear in the **appendices**, along with anything else you think you should include, such as letters, permissions slips and questionnaires.

Fig. 1 *Your investigation must focus on spoken language*

Key terms

Linguistic framework: a list of the particular language features that will be explored in the investigation with commentary on reasons for their use.

Secondary source: work done by others, e.g. surveys, other people's research, books, websites and articles.

Primary language data: examples of original spoken language collected by the researcher.

Appendices: (singular appendix) a collection of supplementary material at the end of the submission.

Looking ahead

Knowing how to put together an investigative research project is a key skill in many areas of study at A Level, degree level and beyond. Understanding how to engage in research and how to present a set of results is important in subjects as diverse as linguistics, psychology and physics, and in a range of career areas including law, science, journalism and economics.

Choosing an area to investigate

In this topic you will:

- examine what areas of language are acceptable for an investigation
- look at some key questions that can be asked in an investigation.

What is spoken language?

The first thing you need to decide is the area of language you are going to look at. As already mentioned, there are a few restrictions on what you can choose, so let's look at these in a bit more detail.

One of the requirements is that you must look at spoken language, but what exactly does that mean? For the purpose of this investigation task, spoken language refers to any language which is spoken or is intended to be spoken. So the first category would include, for example, conversations between people at work, a radio DJ presenting a programme, a child answering a teacher's questions, or a teacher answering a child's questions. If you choose to look at a topic from this category, you will need to collect actual spoken data.

The second category, language intended to be spoken, is slightly different and increases the number of possible areas you could look at. Into this category would fall a politician's pre-planned speech, the script from an episode of *EastEnders* or the planned questions an employer may have prepared for an interview with a prospective employee. In these cases, some of your data may consist of written material.

Types of spoken language data

You are required to base your investigation on original data, i.e. examples of spoken language that you have collected yourself. This is also known as primary language data and will include spoken language, written language and maybe word lists (e.g. lists of new words, slang terms, etc. and pronunciation features). Bear this in mind when doing Coursework activity 1.

Link

For a more detailed explanation of data types, see page 147.

Coursework activity 1

Think about the following suggestions for projects and whether they would meet the requirement of basing the investigation on primary spoken language data.

1. An investigation into a five-year-old child's spoken language development
2. An investigation into attitudes towards Chris Moyles's use of language on his radio show
3. An investigation into the teletext subtitles used for an episode of *Coronation Street*
4. An investigation into Jonathan Ross's interview technique on his TV show
5. An investigation into the representation of speech in the *Harry Potter* novels
6. An investigation into the comments of witnesses to a crime as reported in a daily newspaper
7. An investigation into the differences between two newspaper reports of a football match
8. An investigation into people's attitudes to politically incorrect language
9. An investigation into a judge's summing up at the end of a court case
10. An investigation into Seamus Heaney's use of imagery in five poems.

Questions to explore

An important stage in thinking about your investigation topic is to consider the type of investigation you want to carry out and the questions you might explore. You have a choice of four broad types.

- A **features**-based investigation, which answers the question *What features are used in the type of spoken language being studied?*
  For example, do politicians' speeches share the same language features?

- A **function-** or **use**-based investigation, which answers the question: *What is the language being used to do?*
  For example, what techniques does a teacher use in a lesson and for what purposes?

- An **attitudes**-based investigation, which answers the question *How do people feel about the language use of a group or individual?*
  For example, what do people think about a particular dialect?
  If you choose this type of investigation, your data will probably consist of the results of questionnaires and/or interviews, but you will still need to include and discuss the spoken language respondents are commenting on. Investigations using questionnaires often result in data consisting of random views and prejudices. In considering the use of the questionnaire you will have to think carefully about the selection and monitoring of respondents to ensure you get useful and valid data.

- A **user**-based investigation, which answers the question *Who uses a particular type of language?*
  For example, in informal conversations, do males use a different type of language to females?

A good way of ensuring that your project is on the right track is to make sure you are answering one of these questions. If it is not focusing on any of these questions, it is probably asking the wrong thing, and, if it is trying to answer more than one, it is probably trying to answer too much. Try to be clear about the differences between these questions and then consider how they might apply to areas you want to look at.

Fig. 2 *Does the language of business exclude women?*

■ Making your decision

Don't rush into making a final decision on your topic. Spend some time thinking about different options. A good way to begin doing this is to come up with three or four possible areas and then to do some preparatory work that may help you to decide whether they look promising or, indeed, whether they are realistically possible as topics (read through the next topic, Narrowing it down, to get a better idea of how to do this). Get hold of some sample data and think about whether it would be interesting to discuss, and what questions you could ask about it. Think back over the areas you have already covered during your English Language course (e.g. language development, change or variation). If you particularly enjoyed studying a past topic, you may think about using it as the focus of your coursework. Alternatively, you may have interests or hobbies of your own that would make good topics for an investigation. Consult your teachers throughout the process. They will be able to help you refine or rework a broad idea into a more detailed task and will be able to suggest approaches and methods. In the end, the best investigations are usually those in which the student has a strong and active role in the decision making.

Narrowing it down

Choosing a topic

As well as deciding on a language area on which to focus your investigation, you also need to decide what particular aspects you are going to look at. This decision will dictate what your aims are going to be. If the topic you have chosen is an area that you have already covered on the course, go back and look at your notes on the topic. Think about the types of question you might want to ask. If your topic is a more general one or an interest or hobby, think about what spoken language questions could be asked about it. We will look at these two types of approach below.

As you try to narrow it down, you may find that the area you have chosen is not as good as you thought it might be. This is a good thing because it shows you are now thinking about your investigation like a language researcher. It also means you have time to go back and modify your topic, or even choose something entirely different, rather than realise the problem in a month or two when it's too late. This is why planning is so important.

Basing your coursework on a topic you have already covered

If you have chosen an area for study that you have studied on the course, you should already have some ideas about the kinds of debate involved with it. In many areas of the course, you have studied research and theories that attempt to explain the reasons behind language use or the processes involved within it. Below is a summary of four such areas, together with some of the important questions each is concerned with.

Language development

- Do some children learn more quickly than others?
- How do children learn to speak?
- In what order do children acquire features of language?

Language and representation

- How are groups, ideas, events or institutions represented by spoken language?
- How does spoken language affect the way we see the world?
- How are our ideas of people and things affected by the spoken language we use to describe them?

Language change

- How does spoken language change over time?
- What are the attitudes to changes in spoken language?
- Why does spoken language change over time?

Language variation

- Do men and women differ in their speech, and if so, how?
- What opinions do people have of regional dialects?
- How does a person's age affect his or her language use?

Link

Remind yourself of the key questions posed in these language areas that you have already studied.

- Language development – Unit 1
- Representation and language – Unit 2
- Language change and variation – Unit 3

Fig. 3 *Children's language development can be an interesting topic to investigate*

Condensing a broad question into a tightly focused investigation

You might choose one of these questions as a broad topic for investigation. It will then need narrowing down further to make it manageable as a coursework project.

There are a number of benefits to this kind of approach: for a start, you have already looked at these topics so should have a good insight into what's involved. Second, as A Level topics, there should be a lot of further information you can research on each. Third, the research and theory involved can be used as a starting point to 'hang' your investigation from. For instance, you can take a theorist's idea about language use and perform your own research to find out whether it seems to work or not.

Below is a list of suggestions as to how the first question from each area might be approached in a language investigation and the types of investigation that might consequently emerge.

Language development

Do some children learn to speak more quickly than others?

This is a big question but does attempt to answer *Who uses a particular type of language?* The fact that it matches one of our key questions means that this has possibilities.

One possibility would be to look at whether particular factors seem to influence language development, and this is certainly something you could investigate on a small scale. Possible investigations would include:

■ an analysis of male and female children of the same age investigating whether one gender uses more developed speech than the other

■ an analysis of children from different geographical areas (rural and urban, for example) investigating whether this seems to affect language development.

You could find useful research on both of these questions that could be used as a foundation for your assignment.

Language and representation

How are groups, ideas, events or institutions represented by spoken language?

This question looks at *What is the language being used to do?* Remembering that the focus must be on language that is spoken or intended to be spoken, you could look at how language shapes our ideas and views of something or someone. Possibilities might be:

■ an investigation into how the language of party political broadcasts attempts to represent the ideologies and beliefs of political parties

■ an investigation into how youth culture is represented in television soap operas.

Language change

How does spoken language change over time?

This matches the *What features are used in the type of spoken language being studied?* question. With some refining it could have potential. Possible approaches would include:

Fig. 4 *How is youth culture represented in television soap operas?*

- an investigation into language change using recordings of the Queen's speeches from 1958 to 2008
- an investigation into language change using examples of television or radio advertisements from 1978 and 2008.

Language variation

Do men and women differ in their speech, and if so, how?

The 'do' part of the question could match the *Who uses a particular type of language?* and the 'how' part would address *What is the language being used to do?* A good investigation could emerge from either part.

You could choose a variety of participants and situations to narrow down the question.

- An analysis of males and females in a problem-solving situation (planning a holiday, for instance) to investigate their different roles (*What is the language being used to do?*)
- An analysis of the language of male and female chat show hosts to see whether they use similar techniques in their interviews. (*Who uses a particular type of language?*)

Fig. 5 *Jonathan Ross's unique interviewing style*

As with the children's language topics, you could hang your investigation from either a theory or a piece of research. For example, you might take a theory on gender and language use and see whether it seems to work with your data.

Basing your coursework on a topic from another area

An alternative to choosing an area you have already studied on the course is to pick something that you have a particular interest in, e.g. a sport, films or music. The beauty of this A Level is that most aspects of life involve language use and are, therefore, perfectly acceptable to use as investigation topics. You will, after all, be asking the same 'kinds' of question and using the same language frameworks to investigate it.

The advantages of choosing this route are numerous: you will be studying something you are enthusiastic about, and this almost always leads to better assignments; you will probably be fairly knowledgeable on the topic, which will give you a head start in thinking about your coursework; you will probably produce an investigation that is interesting, original and unusual – three words that send a tingle down the spines of teachers and examiners!

There are pitfalls though. You must be careful that your project is actually focusing on language. Sometimes students' enthusiasm for a particular topic results in them attempting to squeeze non-linguistic projects into a language straitjacket, and this almost always ends in disaster. Think about what it is you actually want to look at. If it's not spoken language, forget it and choose something else.

However don't let the pitfalls put you off considering this type of project. As long as you get your planning right and get advice and guidance from your teachers in the early stages, these types of investigation can be fruitful. Also, they are actually often concerned with many of the ideas already mentioned – like language change, variation, representation and development – although this might not be obvious at first.

Narrowing down your ideas for this kind of project may take longer than for one based on previous study and you may have to think more laterally when deciding a particular question or focus. Let's think about how we might go about this.

When you have completed Coursework activity 2 and checked the feedback on page 172, look at the following suggestions as to how some of these ideas could be further refined into possible investigations.

The language of sport

The language of sports commentaries – examples include an analysis of the techniques used for two different types of sport or of the different features employed for the same sport in TV and radio commentaries. Do they share similar features?

The language of sportsmen/sportswomen – an analysis of the techniques used by Premier League football managers in post-match press conferences would be an example, or the techniques used by male/female sports stars in post-match interviews. Is there a marked similarity or difference in these techniques?

Fig. 6 *The use of cliché in the language of sport*

The language of comedy

The techniques used by a comedian over time – examples include an analysis of Billy Connolly's stand-up routines from 1975 and 2005. Or it could be an investigation into different comedians' use of language (the

■ **Coursework activity 2**

Look at the following broad areas of interest. Make a list of some possible aspects you could look at for each. Remember, you must focus on language that is spoken or intended to be spoken, and your investigation needs to be answering a question.

1 The language of sport

2 The language of comedy

3 The language of film

selection of two or three from Simon Amstell, Josie Long, Russell Brand, Ricky Gervais, Catherine Tate or Frankie Boyle for example). Is language being used in the same way or for the same purposes? How does the use of language establish a relationship with the audience?

The different techniques used by comedians – examples would be an analysis of the language use of a male and female comedian on *Have I Got News for You*. Does the use of language support theories on language and gender?

The language of film

The spoken techniques used by film reviewers – this could be an analysis of Jonathan Ross's and Mark Kermode's language in their respective TV and radio film reviews. How do their techniques compare and contrast?

The language of film trailers – examples include an analysis of the voiceovers from a variety of trailers from a particular film genre (horror, thriller, romance, etc.), or a comparison between genres or types (British v. American films). What features do they share, or how do their techniques differ?

Again, these are only examples but they illustrate how a broad interest can be thinned down to a manageable and focused investigation. Notice, also, how many of the examples are concerned with language topics you have covered (change, gender, variation and representation).

Summary of key points in choosing a topic

Let's briefly round up the important things you must consider in deciding on your investigation topic. If you bear these in mind when choosing your topic, you will end up with a task that has **PURPOSE** – we can use that word as an acronym to summarise the key points.

- **Promising:** Choose something that will allow you to analyse language with range and depth – an investigation into orders given by a sergeant to troops in a parade (Attention! Stand at ease!) would end up with data that would be simple and not particularly interesting or fruitful to analyse (even if you could get the data in the first place).
- **Useful:** Choose a question to which the answer is not clear – an investigation into whether an eight-year-old child uses more developed language than a four-year-old is going to produce obvious conclusions.
- **Relevant:** Choose something that focuses on language – an investigation into the varying representations of Batman through films could easily drift away from a language investigation into a media studies or film studies project unless you rigidly stick to how the character is represented through his speech alone.
- **Precise:** Choose something that has clear focus – an investigation into how age affects language use is far too broad. Looking at the differences between specific groups – 16- to 25-year-olds, say, compared with 40- to 60-year-olds – would be much better.
- **Obtainable:** Choose something realistic and achievable – an investigation into the changing phonological features of a dialect over 200 years would be interesting, but how and from where will you get the data? Also, check to see whether it matches one of the key question types we looked at earlier.

Fig. 7 *How does Josie Long establish a relationship with her audience?*

If you paid to see Norbit, *look deep inside yourself and take the same amount of money you paid to see that movie and give it to a good cause because, believe me, you're karmically unbalanced if you paid to see that film.*

Fig. 8 *Mark Kermode demonstrates the language of the film critic*

■ **Speech-related:** Choose something that focuses on language which is spoken or intended to be spoken – it doesn't matter how much you like a particular band or how brilliant you think they are: a study of their album reviews is not focusing on spoken language.

■ **Enjoyable:** Choose something you find interesting – if you found language development the least stimulating subject of the course, don't choose it as a topic for your investigation.

Coursework activity 3

As a final exercise, have a look at the following narrowed-down suggestions for investigations. In each case, decide whether you feel the proposal would lead to a successful project. What exactly are the strengths and weaknesses of the proposal?

1 An investigation into turn-taking strategies used by males and females in an episode of *Dragons' Den*

2 An investigation into the spoken language development of a monolingual and a bilingual child

3 An investigation into the regional dialect of North Yorkshire looking at three generations of the same family

4 An investigation into the representation of Willy Wonka through his language use in the 1971 and 2005 films, *Willy Wonka & the Chocolate Factory* and *Charlie and the Chocolate Factory*

5 An investigation into the use of metaphorical language in political speeches using the party leaders' conference speeches as data

6 An investigation into different politeness strategies used by males and females when talking to a customer service representative in a supermarket

7 An investigation into evasion techniques used by politicians in political interviews

8 An investigation into spoken strategies used by a teacher in classes of students from different age groups

9 An investigation into the attitudes to Estuary English of different age groups

10 An investigation into the news language used on *Newsround* and by ITN to address different age groups

Topic revision summary

■ A subject for investigation can be drawn from an area you have studied on your course, or from another area of interest.

■ Looking back over the language issues you have covered on your course is a useful way of generating ideas for a coursework project.

■ If you choose something from your own area of interest, make sure you are focusing on a spoken language issue and are not trying to 'create' a linguistic study from non-linguistic material.

■ Narrowing down your investigation so that it has a specific focus will always lead to a better investigation.

■ Remember the key word PURPOSE. Make sure your planned investigation meets its criteria.

Introduction, hypotheses and questions

▨ Introduction – what to include

Your introduction has a number of different roles.

▨ It should outline the topic you intend to study.

▨ It should justify why this topic is relevant to the study of spoken language.

▨ It should state what hypothesis the investigation tests or what question it explores.

▨ It should place the investigation within a particular level of language study.

Outlining the topic

A good way to begin your introduction is to discuss broadly the area you are going to investigate and to explain the reasons behind your choice. For an area previously studied on the course (language development or variation for example) you will need to explain what particular aspect or perspective you intend to look at (the language development of five-year-old boys, or attitudes to Estuary English). For this type of investigation, you could explain why you have chosen it: perhaps it was your favourite part of the course, or a particular aspect of it looked to have potential in terms of further research. For areas not studied previously, you might explain why they are hobbies or interests – your interest in science fiction may have urged you towards a study of the language of sci-fi film trailers. This is also a good time to introduce a brief discussion of any secondary sources you have looked at – a survey's findings of a drop in dialect use, or a theory on language codes and social class would form a good introduction to an investigation of these areas. Use the work you did in the previous topic, Narrowing it down, to help you here.

Justifying the topic

The justification for the study of an area previously studied should be fairly self-evident from its inclusion on the course. Referring to your previous work, explain why this is an important issue in discussions about language – a comparative study on politeness strategies and gender, for instance, could give useful insights into the changing roles of men and women in modern society. For areas selected from your own interests, this part of the introduction is especially important as it is here that you need to be clear about why your choice is relevant to the study of language – an investigation of the main characters in soap operas is a media studies project, but an examination of how the language of these characters compares with authentic models of conversation is a study of language. Again secondary sources, such as surveys or theories, could be used to show that your topic is especially relevant today because, perhaps, previously held views on language have shifted.

▨ Hypotheses and questions – what to include

A hypothesis, predicting your findings, or a question, summarising your aims, is another requirement of this section of your coursework. Which one you will choose will depend on the nature of your investigation.

▨ **Link**

▨ Look back at pages 45–6 for an example and explanation of a research hypothesis.

141

■ Key terms

Secondary data: data previously collected by others and used by the researcher.

Fig. 9 *A hypothesis is not a random guess at the investigation's outcome, but should be based on considered judgement of available information*

Study tip

As you begin analysing your data later on in the investigation process, don't worry if your findings are going against what your hypothesis predicts. It is how you discuss and explain your findings that matter.

■ Link

See the linguistic frameworks on page 156.

Hypotheses are useful if you are testing or challenging research or theory and will summarise what you expect to find. You will need to have some grounds for justifying your hypothesis; it is not a random guess at the expected outcome of the investigation, but a considered judgement based, perhaps, on secondary sources that you may have discussed in your outline of the topic. Using secondary sources as part of a hypothesis is a good way to give your investigation a solid linguistic foundation. Using **secondary data** or the theories of others in this way will also help you to meet AO2, part of which is concerned with the knowledge and understanding of language issues and concepts. The hypothesis should be short and succinct, usually only one sentence in length. Below is an example of how a language theory can be integrated into a hypothesis.

■ I predict that the politeness strategies of females will have converged towards those of males, reflecting changes in gender roles and society and challenging Robin Lakoff's theory in *Language and Woman's Place* (1975).

At times, though, researchers find that useful hypotheses are difficult to generate. This may be because they are investigating an area in which not much research has previously been done. In this case, a more open question may be appropriate. Unlike the hypothesis, this will not attempt to predict an outcome but rather clarify what it is exactly that the research is attempting to find out. The question will summarise the key focus. Using this option may be more suited to an investigation topic drawn from an area of your own interest. In investigating the language of football press conferences, for example, it is unlikely that you will find much theory or research to support a hypothesis so a broader question may be better suited. Below is an example.

■ Are there any significant differences in the language strategies of the BBC and Channel 4 News, and do these reflect differing news values?

One drawback with using the open question is that the investigation can lack a clear focus. One way around this is to use a two-pronged approach to the project where some preliminary research may suggest a hypothesis that can be tested by a second more substantial piece of investigation work. Using the example above, a preliminary questionnaire gauging people's attitudes towards the news programmes could result in data that might suggest that the programmes employ differing techniques. This information could then form the basis of a hypothesis that could be tested in an investigation into the actual language used on the programmes.

■ The language level

This is where you specify in even more detail the aspects of language that you will be investigating. For example, a broad area of study would be language development; the particular area of study might be the language development of five-year-old boys; but the language level will explain what specifically you will be analysing, for instance phonological development. These levels are the same as the categories used in the linguistic frameworks toolkit you have worked with in the AS and A2 texts, and your choice will influence your selection of the particular features which will make up the framework part of your methodology. To recap, they are:

■ speech

■ lexical-semantic

■ grammatical and morphological

■ interactional

- rhetorical
- phonological
- syntactical.

The graphological feature is omitted because here you are focusing on spoken language only.

Investigations may focus on just one of these levels, or two or three, but you need to be definite about which ones you are using. The number of these selected will dictate the **range** of the investigation's **framework**, and the extent to which each is explored will affect its **depth**. Avoid trying to cover too many of these levels, and make sure that you are clear about which you are using. These considerations will be examined in more detail in the Methodologies topic.

Coursework activity 4

Look again at the following three coursework titles that we examined in Coursework activity 3 on page 140. What language level(s) might we choose to apply to each? Are some more straightforward than others in terms of choosing a level?

1. An investigation into turn-taking strategies used by males and females in an episode of *Dragons' Den*.

2. An investigation into the spoken language development of a monolingual and a bilingual child.

3. An investigation into the use of metaphorical language in political speeches using the party leaders' conference speeches as data.

Don't go overboard with your introduction. It should introduce and contextualise your investigation but the real marks are to be had in the later sections. Don't ramble or include pieces of irrelevant information, and keep it relatively short – 500 words should be enough to cover everything.

Topic revision summary

- Your introduction should outline and justify your area of study.
- It should state what level(s) of language you intend to investigate.
- You will need a hypothesis (a prediction of your findings) or a question (a simplification of your aims).
- Using secondary data or linguistic theory can help you to build a hypothesis.
- Hypotheses are good for investigations which test the findings of secondary data or the perspectives of theoretical positions, while questions are suited to more exploratory approaches.
- Limit the whole introduction section to about 500 words.

Study tip

Just because the introduction is the first section of your coursework doesn't mean it should be the first thing you write. The introduction needs to feed into and make connections with your aims and methodology sections so it is often useful to think about and draft these parts of the coursework together, amending and updating each where necessary. This will give your submission cohesion.

Key terms

Framework range: the number of language levels or features within a level to be investigated.

Framework depth: the extent to which a particular level or feature is explored.

Fig. 10 *Metaphor is a powerful tool in political language*

Aims

Looking ahead

If you go on to study at university, you will find one of the key differences in most subject areas will be the length and complexity of the assignments that you will be asked to produce. With these types of assignment, planning in advance is vitally important. Time spent in careful planning at the aims and methodology stages of your language investigation will help you to develop this skill as well as ensuring a well-structured and effective piece of coursework.

Link

For more information on variables, see pages 154–5.

Definition and roles

Having looked at narrowing down big ideas into realistic and manageable topics, and having formulated a hypothesis or question, you now need to think about the particular aims that lead on from this. Your aims should break down your hypothesis or question into separate strands or approaches.

Together with your hypothesis or question, this section will give your coursework a sense of direction and purpose. Just as when travelling in a car, if you don't know where your destination is how can you possibly start to decide on how to get there? You should spend time thinking about precisely how to word your aims so that you understand exactly what it is you are trying to find out.

Looking back at the acronym, PURPOSE, you should concentrate on whether aims are **Promising**, **Useful**, **Precise** and will lead to **Obtainable** goals.

- **Promising:** You need to make sure your aims will lead to data that can be analysed with range and/or depth. Ask yourself whether your aims are ambitious enough to lead to an interesting discussion of language. Will they allow you to explore language in enough breadth or detail?

- **Useful:** Obvious aims lead to dull investigations – avoid aims that are self-evident or widely accepted as fact in language debates. For example, the aim below is not a useful one:

  To investigate whether the language used by a teacher differs according to the age of the students.

  > The fact that the language will differ is obvious; it is how it will differ that will prove an interesting focus for investigation.

- **Precise:** The number of aims chosen for an investigation will vary from topic to topic. You may decide that just one aim is enough if it has potential to produce interesting results. On the other hand, you may decide that what you are attempting to investigate is best expressed in two or three separate but distinct aims.

  You need to be careful that you are not trying to find out too much. Investigating gender and age variables in conversational techniques, for example, is actually two investigations rolled into one. This could lead to your project becoming confused and muddled as it attempts to deal with too many issues and questions. Focus on a particular issue and be clear about what it is you are trying to find out. If you use more than one aim make sure they are pointing towards the same 'destination'.

  On the other hand, don't be too detailed in your aims; leave the selection and discussion of methods of research and particular features to be examined to your methodology section.

- **Obtainable:** Aims need to be realistic and restricted to what can be conceivably achieved in a 2,500-word investigation. Don't set out to attempt to answer 'big' language questions – an analysis of a teacher's questioning strategies might result in your being able to come to some interesting conclusions, but it won't lead to your being able to make sweeping generalisations about the language of education.

Selecting aims

Taking a couple of the example topics discussed earlier together with their hypotheses and questions, look at how you might draw out some useful and purposeful aims, and how they fit together to give the investigation purpose. As a final test as to whether the focus is a clear one, see if they match with one of the key question types discussed on page 133 in Choosing an area to investigate.

1 An investigation into different politeness strategies used by males and females when leaving answerphone messages

Hypothesis: I predict that the politeness strategies of females will have converged towards those of males, reflecting changes in gender roles and society and challenging Robin Lakoff's theory in *Language and Woman's Place* (1975).

Here, the focus of the investigation is quite specific already, with the hypothesis employing a theory that will be tested in the investigation. The aims need only to break down the task into its three distinct strands.

Aim 1: To examine distinctive patterns and features in the use of interactive politeness strategies by males and females. (This specifies more clearly the language we will be focusing on.)

Aim 2: To highlight any differences in the use of these strategies by the different groups. (This aim introduces the comparative element of the investigation.)

Aim 3: To apply these to Robin Lakoff's 1975 theory, *Language and Woman's Place*, examining whether and how the use of politeness strategies has changed. (This is what the features of Aim 1 will be tested against. The framework part of the methodology will identify the particular aspects of the theory to be used.)

The investigation is looking at *Who uses a particular type of language?*

2 An investigation into the language techniques employed on BBC and Channel 4 news programmes

Question: Are there any significant differences in the language strategies of the BBC and Channel Four News, and do these reflect differing news values?

Aim 1: To find out how the programmes use syntactical and grammatical techniques to create dramatic effect and to position their audience. (This is the main aim and focus of the investigation in which the particular types of language to be investigated are highlighted.)

Aim 2: To highlight any differences in the use of these techniques by the two programmes. (This is the comparative element.)

Aim 3: To test whether these techniques conform to the theory of news values. (Again, the use of a theory, but this time from another field, will help to refine the investigation. In the framework part of the methodology the chosen aspects of the theory will be translated into language objectives. For example, the theory states that news programmes focus on things that are current and immediate. Looking at the use of adverbials of time or tense construction would be a way of testing this news value from a linguistic perspective. We will look at this in more detail in the Methodologies topic.)

> **Study tip**
>
> Make sure your aims work together as a unit. Multiple aims can be used to look at different aspects of the same key question or to develop the depth or range of the investigation. They should not, though, be 'pulling in different directions'.

> **Study tip**
>
> To test whether an aim is an appropriate one, ask yourself whether it will help you to test your hypothesis, or answer your key question.

The investigation is looking at *What is the language being used to do?*

Coursework activity 5

Now, have a look at the following examples of aims, hypotheses and questions. In each case, decide whether, together, they suggest approaches which are Promising, Useful, Precise and Obtainable, and whether they represent a good foundation for an investigation. If not, what particular problem does each present?

1 **An investigation into child language development in boys**

Hypothesis: An older child will display a greater complexity in language use than a younger one.

Aim 1: To find out how a four-year-old child's spoken language compares with that of an eight-year-old.

Aim 2: To discover whether the language of the older child is more sophisticated.

2 **An investigation into the use of politeness strategies by women**

Hypothesis: Younger women will use fewer politeness strategies, reflecting their more dominant role in contemporary society.

Aim 1: To find out how the use of the tag question differs in the conversation of women from different age groups.

Aim 2: To examine how the use of adverbs differs in the conversations of the two groups.

3 **An investigation into the use of metaphorical language in the conference speeches of the leaders of political parties**

Question: Do the three party leaders use metaphor in similar ways and for similar purposes?

Aim 1: To find out how metaphorical language employs rhetorical and grammatical techniques to create dramatic effect in political speeches.

Aim 2: To discover whether the features of metaphor use are consistent in the speeches of politicians.

Topic revision summary

- Your submission will need a set of aims that breaks down the different parts of your investigation.
- Each aim should help in testing your hypothesis or answering your key question.
- Your aims should be Promising, Useful, Precise and Obtainable and should work together.
- Aims should not contain a discussion of methods to be used or specific features to be explored – these should be included in the methodology section.
- The aims you choose, though, will directly affect the design of your methodology.

Methodologies

Key terms

Validity: a measure of how the design of the methodology allows the conclusions of an investigation to carry weight. Internal validity refers to whether the conclusions drawn from data used in a specific investigation can be justified within the context of that investigation. External validity refers to whether these conclusions can be applied in a wider context.

Ethical issues: issues relating to the collection and presentation of data that may affect the rights of the participants. These can include confidentiality and whether permission is gained from participants to collect or publish data.

Your methodology is where you explain your method for and reasoning behind data collection. You will also outline how you intend to analyse your data through the selection and discussion of a set of linguistic frameworks. In this section of your investigation coursework you must describe what you are going to do and why. In doing this, you need to show an awareness of some important considerations that must be made in the collection of data, specifically **validity**, and **ethical issues**. Before you look at these, you need to think about different types of data and the different methods that could be used for collecting it.

Data

Types of data

Primary data is data that you will gather yourself specifically for your project; it is the language being studied. Primary data could be in the form of recorded or transcribed speech, word lists, scripts or questionnaires. For the purpose of this investigation, primary data would also be any examples of spoken language that you use in a questionnaire or interview to test attitudes towards language varieties.

Secondary data refers to data previously collected by other individuals or researchers. It could be in the form of other research projects, news articles or reports, surveys, statistics, etc. Secondary data is good for generating useful approaches to investigations. You could use the results of the research of others to plan the aims of your investigation or to create a hypothesis. In an attitudes-based investigation, the results of your interviews or questionnaires would also be classed as secondary data.

Data can also be studied as quantitative and qualitative. **Quantitative data** is based on numbers and is therefore easy to analyse statistically. Counting the number of times a child makes a particular virtuous error would result in a quantitative study. This type of data can be used to make concrete and objective points about language. Comparing the average number of words in the utterances of two children would lead to a definitive result – one using longer utterances than the other. This may then allow you to draw certain conclusions: in this case that the child with the greater average is more advanced, perhaps. However, you must be careful in doing this as these conclusions may be challenged on the grounds of validity. In the example given, it may be that the child with the shorter average utterance is actually expressing more complex ideas in more complex ways. For this reason, you must take care in considering the implications of results obtained through this method. Additionally, investigations using quantitative data only can be dry and over-statistical, and often struggle to deal with the more subtle points of language use.

Quantitative data is useful though and is seen generally as more scientific than qualitative. It would allow you also to present some of your results in the form of graphs or tables and can give an investigation a solid foundation from which to move on to a more detailed analysis of language.

Key terms

Quantitative data: data measured in numbers. This kind of data can be analysed using statistical methods, and results can be displayed using tables or charts.

Qualitative data: data concerned with describing meanings and effects, rather than with making statistical analyses.

Fig. 11 *Quantitative data is made up of numbers*

Qualitative data is concerned with meanings and effects. It is less 'scientific' as it cannot be analysed statistically, but it often leads to more subtle and in-depth analyses. Analysing the effect of the language used by a child to describe a toy would be studying data qualitatively. In this particular example, the child's language would be analysed in non-statistical terms and conclusions may be drawn on the basis of the types of adjective used or the order of words in an utterance for example. Qualitative data tends to be more subjective and people may disagree on its findings; therefore, it is important to take care when drawing conclusions from it.

Many good research projects use both types – the examples above could be used in the same project on language development. Indeed, sometimes research will combine the two in one approach. Asking people to rate their opinion of a particular type of language on a scale of 1 to 10 would allow you to present qualitative information in a quantitative way.

Methods for gathering primary data

Recording and transcribing speech

Because of the focus on spoken language, many investigations will involve the collection of the actual speech of individuals or groups. This is not always easy for a number of practical reasons:

The collection of speech through a recording device (digital voice recorder for instance) often leads to data which is indistinct and unclear. Real people don't always speak clearly and precisely; speakers overlap and interrupt each other, blurring the words themselves; and speakers are often most inconsiderate to the poor researcher in choosing to have their conversations in 'real' locations where recording is difficult and background noise can disrupt the clarity of what they are saying. These factors need to be considered in planning a methodology which involves the recording of speech. There are, though, a number of things you can do to reduce the impact of these factors.

■ The quality of your recording equipment will go a long way to determining the quality of your data. The kind of recording devices most of us own or are familiar with are not designed for the purpose of high-quality recording, so check with friends or teachers to see if they have access to something more sophisticated that you can borrow. You may know someone who owns a more professional system or you may have a department in school or college (Media, Performing Arts, Foreign Languages) which routinely uses this type of technology.

In some investigations you may look at using digital video for added context (it would allow you to comment on how non-verbal communication reinforces spoken language for example), or different microphones for different situations to enhance sound quality. Of course, the more technical the equipment the more can go wrong with the procedure, so you will need to ensure that you are competent in the use of the equipment and find out about things like file formats and compatibility issues when it comes to storing and using the data.

■ Think about where you are going to record your data. Ask yourself whether another location might be better in terms of disruptive background noise. Recording conversations in a busy bar or café will inevitably result in problems, so perhaps recording at home or in a situation that you have artificially set up would be better. However, a café location, though noisy, would be more representative of an authentic model for conversation and we would expect speakers to act more naturally in this environment. The pre-planned situation (a private room for example) would result in clearer data, but would the artificiality of the situation lead to speakers changing their normal behaviour? For example, an investigation into the use of taboo language involving recording the conversations of teenagers could be compromised by their awareness of the researcher. The presence of recording equipment could lead to a decrease or increase in the use of such language and would therefore invalidate the results. An awareness not only of the researcher but also of the focus of research can lead to behaviour being affected even more radically as participants consciously or subconsciously conform to or diverge from standards or expectations.

This phenomenon is known as observer's paradox and should be considered when carrying out research like this. Thus, in recording speech, there is always a play-off between clarity and reality, and you will need to decide which situation would be best for your particular project. The reasoning for your decision needs to be explained in your methodology.

Another factor to consider is whether you can get access to a particular location to record live speech. If you intend to record interaction in a primary school class or a business meeting for example, you will need to get permission from the relevant parties – schools and businesses can be quite strict on who they allow on to their premises. The same difficulty could be encountered in any public situation. To record in a café you would need the agreement of its owners, and town or city councils may have their own rules for what 'research' is allowed in their shopping centres, libraries, etc. You will need to research this and be prepared to write letters asking for permission for your study.

Whether you are recording speech in the 'real world' or from other sources such as radio or television, you will need to include the audio or video recordings of your data in your appendices, but you will also need to transcribe the data so it is more suitable for analysis. There are a number of systems for transcribing speech and they vary in their style and complexity. In choosing one, you need to consider what your investigation is focusing on. If you are looking mainly at the words, syntax and structures of speech, a fairly simple method would do (as shown in the transcript on page 151).

■ Link

For a good example of the possible effects of observer's paradox, look back at the results of an investigation into accents on page 51.

Fig. 12 *One way of avoiding observer's paradox, but is this ethical?*

■ Key terms

Phonemic alphabet: a system containing 44 symbols to represent a range of vowel and consonant sounds in English pronunciation.

If, however, your investigation will be discussing aspects such as intonation, pronunciation or accent you may need a more developed system. You may need to use the **phonemic alphabet** or even phonetic transcription (see Table 1 for examples of phonetic alphabet symbols for the sounds of the letter 'a'), which give more detailed information about the sounds of words, or you may need to employ more refined symbols that describe intonation, pitch or stress in more detail. Remember, though, the more complicated the system, the longer it will take. Ask your teacher about these other transcription methods and see the Further reading at the end of the unit on page 204.

Table 1

Symbol	Examples
æ	Cat, hat
ɑː	Rather, father
ə	Ago, away
eɪ	Page, sage
eə	Care, hair

Another thing to take into account is the amount of transcription you are going to undertake. One minute of speech takes between one and two hours to transcribe using the most basic of systems. So five minutes of conversation represents up to 10 hours' work before any analysis work has even begun. Because of this, you should not necessarily aim to transcribe everything that you record. This means you will have to make decisions as to what parts of your recordings to focus on, and the reasons for your choices must be discussed in the methodology.

Simple transcription method

■ Label the speaker (by name, or letter indicator) to the left of each utterance.

■ Begin a new line for each speaker's new utterance.

■ Do not use punctuation (such as full stops, commas and question marks) in the transcript, other than those in the key.

Key:

(.) Pause of less than a second
(2.0) Longer pause (number of seconds indicated)
Bold Emphatic stress
[ ] Simultaneous speech
[*Italics*] Selected non-verbal features

Study tip

Transcription is a time-consuming business and you will need to factor the time spent on it into your planning. If you are intending to examine non-verbal aspects of speech like intonation or stress, you will need a complex and even more time-consuming transcription method. That is not to say that this type of investigation is not worthwhile, but you will need to consider these factors before choosing this type of investigation.

Colin	alright (.) I see from the information that I've got [inaudible] you (.) is that you spent er (.) twelve months working for a builder in the south of France
Tony	um well (.) yeah I did actually I I spent (1.0) **two** years over there (.) I worked in a boat yard for some time (.) and [clears 5 throat] I worked for a builder as well and (.) you know (.) I did some bricklaying over there (.) I suppose that's what got me interested you know
Colin	yeah (.) erm alright (.) you did some bricklaying over there (1.0) what kind of things were you doing 10
Tony	well all sorts of things (.) we would do (.) putting flats up you know and (.) oh just laying bricks (.) that sort of thing you know (.) general building really (.) drain work and that sort of thing
Colin	flagging (.) that kind of ⎡thing ⎤ 15
Tony	⎣yeah flagging⎦

J. J. Gumperz, *'Discourse Strategies' from P. Drew and J. Heritage, (eds.)* Talk at Work, 1992

Interviews

An alternative to recording live conversation is to obtain data through interviews. These can be used to get examples of people's speech through direct questioning. One advantage of this is that you can manage the responses of the participants more closely through your interaction with them – when remotely taping a conversation, you will have no control over the topic or direction of the interaction. For interviews you could, again, use audio or visual recording equipment, in which case you should follow the advice on recording and transcribing given previously. You may be using interviews to get more quantitative data (the results might be made up of simple yes or no answers), in which case recording the actual language may not be important.

As with the recording of conversations, you may need to find out whether you require permission to carry out your interviews in a particular place; if so, you will have to get this in writing before you begin.

A vital consideration when using interviews is the selection of interviewees. The choice of who will be interviewed must comply with the aims of the investigation and be representative of the population being investigated. You must take into account how the identities of the interviewees may affect the results. On a basic level, an investigation into the attitudes of teenagers to politically correct language must use a sample made up of teenagers. But other variables need to be taken into account too – aspects like gender and ethnicity should be considered in the selection process. Good investigations often fall down because not enough thought has gone into this process. Even when investigations take into account some of these variables, they still often overlook other factors that can invalidate results. Using friends from your English Language class as interviewees may fulfil the focus on teenagers, and may address issues of gender and ethnicity, but is flawed in other ways: your sample will be made up of well-educated individuals; they will probably come from the same geographical location; their presence on an English Language A Level course will give them an insight into language issues that others don't have; and the fact that they are your friends probably means they share other similarities or interests. All of these factors make them unrepresentative of the teenage population and would prevent you from drawing conclusions that are externally valid from your research. Of course, the limited nature of your investigation means that it will be impossible to satisfy all possible variables, but you need to demonstrate

■ Link

A more detailed examination of issues of validity can be found later in this topic on pages 154–5.

that you have considered the importance of their impact and have planned and managed your interviews accordingly.

The other important aspect of the interview concerns the questions you are going to ask and you will need to think carefully about this before you begin the interview process. You should discuss your choice of questions in your methodology. Below is a summary of things to consider when framing questions.

- Draft your questions in detail before you begin interviewing. To make your investigation valid, you must be asking precisely the same question to each participant.
- Think about the precise wording of questions (denotations and connotations), as changing just one word could lead to different responses. Try to use language which is as neutral as possible.
  - Do you find the Birmingham accent *pleasing*?
  - Do you find the Birmingham accent *attractive*?

  Notice how the choice of adjective (*attractive*) in the second question introduces a whole set of different ideas; its more emotive connotations could result in different responses.
- Think about the order of the questions. A general rule would be to go from the simple to the more complex (e.g. a broad question on attitudes to an accent would come before a more detailed question on a particular aspect of it). Make sure you apply the same order to each interviewee as a previous question could alter the response to a later one.
- Be precise about what you are asking. A question like 'What do you think about language change?' is too vague. Something like 'Do you see changes in English vocabulary as a good or bad thing?' is more focused.
- Think about your use of **open** or **closed questions**. Open questions lead to more varied data but are less precise than closed questions which limit the number of possible responses to them.
- Don't ask **leading questions**. For example asking 'Do you think Estuary English is an unpleasant and lazy form of English?' is pushing the interviewee towards a particular response.

Questionnaires

Using questionnaires is another good way of obtaining data. Questionnaires are useful for getting information on attitudes to language issues. One advantage of this method is consistency. Even an interview which is repeated exactly for every participant will have subtle differences (the intonation or emphatic stress used in phrasing a particular question). With questionnaires you remove this variable. They are also good for getting quantitative data, such as the proportion of people who agree or disagree on a statement. On the other hand, the questionnaire, as a written medium, is pretty useless in getting examples of spoken language.

As with interviews, two vital components in planning the questionnaire are the selection of the sample and the framing of questions. In deciding who is going to complete your questionnaire you must take into account key variables such as respondents' age, background, gender, ethnicity, etc. If you decide on a questionnaire, read through the advice on validity on pages 154–5 and drafting questions on this page.

Questionnaires can be distributed in a number of ways. You could simply hand them out physically or send them by post or email. You will have to bear in mind that not everyone you send a questionnaire to will complete it, so in aiming to get 20 responses you would have to send more than 20 questionnaires. Technology offers alternative methods of questionnaire distribution. An online questionnaire could be employed, or your school or college may use a Virtual Learning Environment (VLE), like Moodle, which you could use. As with the recording of speech, you need to find out what resources are available to you and ensure that you understand how to use them correctly. Key to getting a response is that you clearly explain on the questionnaire what you are doing and why. If people know the reason for the effort you are asking them to make, they are more likely to help you.

Fig. 13 *Where and when an interview takes place can affect results*

Coursework activity 6

Look at the following pairs of questions taken from an investigation into language variation. The questions, which could be used in an interview or questionnaire, are asking for opinions on accent and dialect. For each pair, decide which is preferable and why – in some cases, arguments could be put forward to support or challenge either alternative.

1 a Which accent of Great Britain do you prefer?

   b Which of the following accents do you prefer?
      Birmingham, Newcastle, Cardiff, Edinburgh, Belfast

2 a Where would you place the Edinburgh accent on the following five-point scale?

      1 – I find this accent very pleasant.

      2 – I find this accent pleasant.

      3 – I am indifferent to this accent.

      4 – I find this accent unpleasant.

      5 – I find this accent very unpleasant.

   b The Edinburgh accent has been described as one of the most attractive accents in Great Britain. How far do you agree?

3 a What makes you like or dislike a particular accent?

   b Do any of the following influence whether you like a particular accent?

      1 – The place associated with the accent

      2 – A person or people you associate with the accent

      3 – A quality you associate with the accent (e.g. education, honesty)

      4 – Other (insert your reason)

Study tip

You should be prepared to draft and redraft your questionnaire a number of times before distributing it.

Scripts and written forms

In investigating language that is intended to be spoken, you may find yourself collecting written data. In this case you won't be faced with some of the complications involved with other collection methods, but you will still have to show that you have made logical decisions about the process. For example, in investigating the use of metaphor in the speeches of politicians (an example we have looked at in Coursework activities 3, 4 and 5) you would need to decide exactly where your data is going to come from. Simply using the first examples of political language that come to hand would not constitute a good methodology and would therefore get few marks in this area. A good methodology would consider some key questions.

- How many politicians would you include and how would you decide which ones to look at? (Selecting the leaders of the three main parties would be an example of a manageable and representative choice.)

- Which particular speeches or sections of speeches would you choose? (Using the party leaders' conference speeches from the same year would give consistency.)

The speeches would all be given to the politicians' own parties; therefore the audiences would be comparable. Focusing maybe on the opening and closing 500 words of each speech would give precision and could be justified, as we would expect these sections to contain the key ideas and to employ the most dramatic and emotive language. All of the decisions that you make in selecting your data must be discussed and justified in your methodology.

You need, also, to make sure that you can get hold of the written sources you are going to use. Film, television and radio scripts, for example, are not easy to acquire and getting hold of them may be expensive and time-consuming. You can't start your analysis until you have the data so research its availability before deciding to use it.

Collecting secondary data

Secondary data, like language theory, can be very useful in giving some background to an investigation or helping to build hypotheses about language. For example, an investigation into the influence of gender on children's language development could begin with a brief discussion of national trends in SATS results. These results could then act as the foundation of the hypothesis which the investigation would go on to test. Using secondary data in this way can give your submission academic rigour and a sense of purpose. Alternatively, secondary data can be used to lend weight to the analysis.

Validity

There are a number of key questions about data that the person who marks your project will consider when assessing its merit. The answers to these questions will dictate whether your investigation, and the questions it attempts to answer, is seen as having validity.

■ **Is the data representative of the area of language you are looking at?**
You must be able to show that the data you collect is representative of a type of language in its broader sense. For example, if an investigator was analysing the use of dramatic language in news programmes but decided to record his or her data on an unusual news day (e.g. the day of a catastrophic world event), the validity of the data as reflecting usual news language could be questioned. That is not to say that the data would not be interesting or worth analysing, but it might not be appropriate for that particular project. In this case, the data may be valid internally (within the confines of the investigation) but invalid externally (in its application to a wider context).

■ **Does the data collection method take into account certain variables which may affect it?**
Variables are things that can affect data in numerous ways and good researchers always consider their implications on their projects.

- The **time** when data is collected can affect results. Interviewees may be more likely to respond in certain ways at particular times of the day, days of the week, or weeks of the year. This is especially true of younger children, and would need to be considered in planning an investigation into language development.

- **Where** data is collected can affect results. Choosing a place to record or interview is an important aspect of your methodology and must be considered. In aiming to survey a cross-section of the population for an investigation, the survey would need to be conducted in a place that is visited by a range of people that reflects this. Choosing a location such as outside a gym or a health food

Fig. 14 *A representative group of interviewees?*

shop could mean that you are selecting people of a particular type (people interested in fitness and healthy eating) and therefore the data may be skewed in a particular direction.

 – The **identity of participants** can affect data. Gender, ethnicity and age are some of the factors that may lead individuals to respond or behave in different ways. In investigating speech patterns or attitudes of the population as a whole, your sample should reflect its differences in terms of these types of variable. Alternatively, as this can be difficult to manage, you could specify that you are looking at a specific group or **target population**, females under 20 years of age, for example, which will allow you to ignore some variables. In doing this, though, your findings can no longer be applied to the wider population as your sample is no longer representative of it.

■ **Has the data been used in a way that is consistent with standard research methods?**
The answer to this question will hinge on the ways in which you use your data. Imagine that you are investigating problem-solving language, for example, and have recorded 10 conversations between the same people to give you a good representation of their language use. You have a range of data that may be able highlight some standard features. However, if two of the pieces of data don't seem to suggest the same things as the others, you can't simply throw them away and focus on the other eight. As part of the investigation their implications must be taken into account, even if you feel they detract from your main findings. To ignore them would be to undermine your whole methodology.

Furthermore, finding unusual results in data often leads to opportunities for interesting discussion. Life and language are not simple, and when research seems to indicate that they are it is often viewed with suspicion.

Discussing how you have gone about ensuring that your investigation is internally valid and the extent to which its findings can be applied more widely (its level of external validity) is a key part of your methodology.

Ethical issues

One more thing to think about and discuss in your methodology is how any ethical issues involved with your project have been considered and handled. You should include a discussion of ethical issues in your methodology, explaining how they affected the collection and presentation of your data. These issues can be broken down into four key categories.

Informed consent

In presenting the results of your interviews and recordings you must have the consent of the participants. You should provide each participant with a written summary of your research, informing them of what you are doing and telling them exactly which bits of the data you intend to use. Each participant should then agree to take part by signing and dating this form. If your research involves children under the age of 16, consent must be given by parents or carers. You should keep copies of the signed informed consent forms until after your research is completed and should include a blank copy in your appendices as an example. One problem here is that if participants know what a researcher is looking for, this can influence their behaviour. This phenomenon, similar to observer's paradox as discussed on page 149, is commonly known as **demand characteristics** and is a common problem in research. One way around

■ **Key terms**

Target population: the population group that the researcher wishes to draw conclusions about. The target population will be dictated by the people in the data sample.

Demand characteristics: a problem in research, where participants in a study behave, act or answer questions in the way that they think the researcher wants them to.

Study tip

Being very clear about the target population of the study in the introduction section of your coursework will increase the validity of your investigation.

Study tip

A useful way to assess the strength of your methodology is to put yourself in the position of someone wishing to attack it. Are there any issues with the validity of the data or the collection methods that could be used to undermine any of its future findings? What criticisms could be made, and how would you respond to them?

this is to inform participants of the area you are looking at, but not of the exact aims or hypotheses of the research (for example, participants are told that the study is focusing on dialects but not that it is exploring attitudes to how dialects are changing). In this way you can avoid demand characteristics but also fulfil your ethical obligations.

Right to withdraw

All participants should be informed that they have the right to withdraw from the research at any point, either during or after the study. It is unlikely with the type of research you will be doing that this will happen, but this right is a key principle of research ethics and should be followed.

Confidentiality

All results of your research involving participants should remain confidential, and participants should be informed of this at the start of the study. It may be that in the recording of your data something emerges that should be treated with sensitivity, so names and details of those taking part should be omitted from the data. When using transcription of speech you shouldn't use the names of participants or any other data that could help in identifying them. This is especially true with regards to children. Names of speakers can be abbreviated ('V' for 'Victoria') or replaced with neutral labels (for example, Speaker A). You should also examine instances of names, addresses, specific locations or similar information in the data and decide whether they are likely to make identification of participants likely. If so, don't include them in full. Below is an example of how this might be applied.

Original transcription

David   went out in oxford last night (.) chucking it down with rain
and Jason turns up outside the dog and gun …

Modified version

D   went out in oxford last night (.) chucking it down with rain and J
turns up outside the (name of pub) …

The name of the speaker has been abbreviated along with other names mentioned in the transcript. The pub name has been omitted but Oxford has been retained as it is not specific enough to cause concern.

Debriefing

At the end of the data collection, those taking part should be debriefed by the researcher. This will involve you explaining to the participants exactly what your study was about and what you were hoping to find, as well as details about how you wish to use the data. When your investigation is finished, participants should be given the chance to read through the report, including the actual data you will publish. This final opportunity for participants to confirm their willingness for it to be used shows courtesy and an awareness of the nature of research ethics.

■ Linguistic frameworks

What are linguistic frameworks and why are they used?

A linguistic framework is the part of the methodology that will identify the precise features of language that you intend to analyse. The framework section, although small, is vital in creating logical connections between your aims, your data and your analysis, and you need to think carefully about what to include in it. Don't rush this stage of the investigation in order to move on to the analysis stage. This inevitably leads to problems further down the line.

Broadly speaking, your frameworks should specify the particular language features you intend to examine. As well as listing the features, though, you will also need to explain the reasons for the selection of these features and how they connect to your hypotheses, questions and aims. The language features selected for the framework need to make sense in the context of what you are investigating.

A common pitfall at the framework stage is to simply list features for analysis in a very broad way (nouns, verbs, adjectives) with little or no explanation of why they have been chosen. Frameworks must tie in with aims in the same way that aims tie in with hypotheses and questions. A haphazard approach to frameworks frequently leads to irrelevant discussion in the analysis section where students examine the use of nouns, for example, with no clear idea of why they are being discussed and how their use answers questions posed by the investigation. Different investigations demand different frameworks and you will need to think carefully about your selections.

Range in frameworks

Your analysis must examine enough features to give it a chance of meeting its aims. If in studying language use and gender you focus simply on the use of nouns, you will be able to say little about men's and women's conversational strategies. The framework would need more range before it could give any kind of commentary on this topic.

On the other hand, an investigation that attempts to use too wide a range will also encounter problems. An investigation that contains 20 (or even 10) framework points will have so little time to focus on each one that its analysis will be thin and superficial. It is difficult to generalise about how many features a framework must contain, but when considering the issue think about whether each feature listed can be discussed in enough detail to warrant its inclusion and to conform to the word count.

Depth in frameworks

Make sure that your investigation is going to look at least at some 'higher order' features. This could include clauses and phrases, tense and aspect, active and passive voice and more precise definitions of word classes such as abstract nouns, comparative adjectives and adverb types. However, this is by no means a complete list and an investigation looking closely at pragmatics or speech acts could be examining features of a similar complexity.

An investigation looking simplistically at nothing more than alliteration and semantic fields, though, would need more range and/or depth to give the investigation some weight.

Bear this in mind when planning your framework but don't go overboard by trying to stuff lots of complex language features into it for the sake of it. Ask yourself whether the things you are focusing on allow you to examine language in enough depth to make insightful comments about its use. If the answer to this is yes, you are probably on the right track.

Study tip

Check whether your framework contains enough depth by looking at the mark scheme for Unit 3 on the AQA website.

Approaches to selecting frameworks

Approach 1: focus on aims

You should begin planning your framework by looking back at your aims and asking yourself 'what could I look at that would help in trying to answer the language questions I have raised?' Look at the example project below that we have already discussed.

An investigation into the use of metaphorical language in political speeches

Aim 1: To find out how metaphorical language is used to create effect. (This is the main aim and focus.)

Aim 2: To discover whether the features of metaphor use are consistent in the speeches of politicians. (This is an extension of Aim 1 and gives the investigation a clearer objective.)

Question: Do the three party leaders use metaphor in similar ways and for similar purposes?

The aims have already stated the focus of the investigation: the use of metaphor. But the frameworks need to be more specific and must break down exactly what it is about the metaphor that we want to analyse. One way to do this is to think abstractly about the different ways in which metaphors can be used, but this is not easy. A better approach would be to do some research on the metaphor and the different ways it can be analysed. There are thousands of books and websites that could supply us with useful ways of approaching our data and could act as the foundation for the framework. Of course, in using the web to research technical language ideas, we need to make sure, for the purpose of validity, that we are using legitimate academic websites. Below is one way that the metaphor might be categorised on one such site.

Metaphor

The metaphor consists of two parts: the tenor and vehicle. The tenor is the subject to which qualities are given. The vehicle is the subject from which the qualities are borrowed. The vehicle can take the form of various parts of speech.

- **Adjectival metaphor**: e.g. Her love was *dead*. The adjective works as the vehicle giving the subject a metaphorical quality.
- **Verbal metaphor**: e.g. Rage *burned* inside him. The metaphorical use of the verb emphasises or dramatises the action.
- **Adverbial metaphor**: e.g. He walked away *sheepishly*. The adverb works as the vehicle presenting the way something is done metaphorically.
- **Noun metaphor**: e.g. Crime is *a virulent disease*. The use of a noun (a noun phrase in this example) gives the subject a metaphorical alternative identity.

We can see that this system of categorisation contains key linguistic terms already and that it has the potential for both range and depth – in looking at the verbal metaphor we can introduce ideas of tense and aspect, and the example given with the noun metaphor indicates the possibility of examining phrase and clause structures. Some minor tinkering could result in a promising framework that we could then apply to our data. Of course we would need to explain how the framework points are going to help us to achieve our aims and to illustrate useful points about the data.

Look at Framework 1 to see how the first couple of features in this system of categorisation could be developed and translated into a framework that can be applied to our political language data.

Framework 1

▓ **Adjectival metaphor**: These metaphors help to describe people's ideas and issues.

– I will look at how they are used to create positive and negative ideas about the political parties through **connotational** and **denotational** meaning and whether any significant **semantic fields** are consistently used.

Fig. 15 *An extended metaphor*

▓ **Verbal metaphor**: These metaphors use verbs to describe action and drama.

– I will analyse how the politicians use them to create ideas of change, growth and deterioration.

– I will examine how the use of **tense** and **aspect** in these metaphors presents ideas of time and duration, key considerations in the world of politics.

– I will analyse how the use of **active** and **passive voice** in these metaphors creates ideas of control and victimhood.

Comment

Each framework point is explained along with the reasons for its inclusion and how it links with the aims of the investigation. The point is then refined and the key features are identified. The words in bold are highlighted to show the range and depth of linguistic terms which will be discussed. Notice, also, how the verbal metaphor has spawned a number of features for analysis. By adding a few more (finite and non-finite verb forms, and verb position in the clause for example), the project could be narrowed down further to look just at the use of the verbal metaphor. Throughout your investigation, be prepared to adjust your thinking and approach.

Approach 2: focus on data

Another way of beginning to think about frameworks is to have a look at an example of your data or, if you are yet to collect it, data that you think would be similar. Often a broad analysis of data will suggest ways of discussing it that can be used to formulate your frameworks. If you think about it, much research is done in this way anyway. Preliminary analysis of your data may lead to the formulation of interesting frameworks and may even persuade you to go back and reformulate your aims. Good investigations evolve with, and react to, the implications of their data.

The edited extract given is from Gordon Brown's 2006 Labour Party Conference speech. In this speech, Brown employs many standard features of rhetoric and metaphorical language that have been used by politicians for centuries. Try to identify some of the semantic fields that he uses in his metaphorical language and whether these could be used to formulate some framework points focusing on fields of language.

Fig. 16 *Gordon Brown speaking at the 2006 Labour Party Conference*

This approach to selecting frameworks uses a more 'inductive' method of analysing data. Inductive methods like this are being used increasingly in fields such as psychology and business management. The key to the inductive method is that it looks for themes or ideas in the data and uses these to help identify an appropriate framework to use, instead of setting a framework beforehand and hoping that it fits with the data being studied. The inductive method allows more flexibility and means that you can change or adapt your framework features as you read and reread your data. By completing Data response exercise 1, you should arrive at a possible framework that emerges out of the extract. You can then use this framework to explore the data in more detail.

> New Labour (is) strengthening and entrenching our position in the mainstream as the party of reform. I tell the country: This is not reform for reform's sake but reform to deliver the best service possible, and Britain cannot lead the world by standing still. I know where I come from, what I believe and what I can contribute. And 5
> I am confident that my experience and my values give me the strength to take the tough decisions. I would relish the opportunity to take on David Cameron and the Conservative Party. And in that endeavour I would be determined to draw on all the talents of our party and country. 10
>
> And why? Because I know that in Britain today there are great causes left, noble purposes worth fighting for, a progressive future still to be built, and this is the task that falls to our Party and our Government. A few months ago a primary schoolteacher told me that despite the improvements in education, in all her 34 years 15
> of teaching just a small handful of her pupils – just one every few years – had ever gone on to university. Don't try and tell me so few of these pupils ever had the ability. Don't tell me we couldn't have done better for them. And it falls to us now to address this poverty of opportunity and aspiration. So there is a vision of the 20
> good society. A Britain where we can do better than we are. Where we do feel and share the burdens of others. Where we do believe in something bigger than ourselves. Where we can be inspired by the driving power of social conscience. And where by working together we grow more prosperous and secure. 25
>
> This is the Britain I believe in. A Britain where by the strong helping the weak, our whole society becomes stronger and where by all contributing, each and every one of us is enriched. Let this message go out from our party to the people of Britain. Your values are our values. And working together the good society can and will be built. 30

From *Gordon Brown's Labour Party Conference speech 2006*, The Guardian, *25 September 2006*

Approach 3: focus on a theory

As we have previously seen, an alternative way of focusing an investigation is to 'hang' it from a theory with the broad aim of testing that theory's validity in a particular situation. You will have met a range of different theories throughout the course that could be used in this way, for instance theories about language and communication or language development. Alternatively, you could take a theory from another area of study and 'translate' it into a linguistic model that could be analysed. Have a look at a previous example of an investigation topic to see how this might be done.

An investigation into the language techniques employed on Channel 4 news programmes

Aim 1: To find out how the programmes use language techniques to create effect and to position their audience (main aim and focus of the investigation in which the particular aspects of language to be investigated are highlighted).

Aim 2: To test whether these techniques conform to the theory of news values.

Question: How does the language used by Channel 4 conform to set news values?

The student has here identified a non-linguistic theory and is intending to use it in a linguistic analysis of data. Don't worry about the detail of this particular theory as it is only used here as an example. Broadly speaking the theory identifies some particular aspects of how news programmes tend to present their stories, suggesting that they conform to certain key ideas such as frequency, negativity, unexpectedness and personalisation. The project has picked two of these, personalisation and negativity, and will use these to build a linguistic framework that can be used to analyse the data.

Framework 2

- **News value**: Personalisation and negativity
- **Representation of the victim/accused**:
  - metaphors – dramatisation of events and conditions
  - verbs – action and inaction
  - adjectives – descriptions of individuals
  - active/passive voice – control/lack of control
  - adverbs/adverbials and tense – representation of change/contrast.

I will explore how these features are used to personalise the story and to draw audience sympathy. I will analyse how ideas of negativity and decline are represented through these features.

Comment

Here, some key ideas from a non-linguistic theory have been used to build a set of framework features. The non-linguistic ideas have been 'translated' into language features that can be analysed to achieve the project's aims.

Topic revision summary

- Your methodology should explain your method for carrying out your research and the reasoning behind it.
- It should also list the framework you intend to use in your analysis and discuss how this will help you to achieve your aims.
- Data can come in different forms and can be collected in different ways – you will need to consider which forms and methods of collection are appropriate for your investigation.
- You will need to ensure that your data is valid, that it is a true representation of the area of language you are studying.
- You will need to take into account and discuss any ethical issues that may arise in your collection and use of data.
- The features you choose for your framework need to be related to your aims. Don't analyse features that are irrelevant or that don't help in answering your questions or testing your hypothesis.

The analysis

If your work on topic choice, aims, methodology and frameworks has been carefully thought out and considered, the analysis section should pose no real terrors; analysis, after all, is the main skill you have been working on throughout your course.

If, though, you get to this stage of the topic and are confused as to how to progress further, it is probable that your earlier sections are not focused enough. In this case it would be a good idea to go back and re-look at them.

Assuming, though, that everything's fine, you can now look at some key points that should be considered when embarking on your analysis.

■ Structure

Your analysis is not an essay and it is a good idea to break it up with subheadings to help guide the reader through it. One way of doing this is to take each framework point and to use it as the focus of each subsection. This should give you an idea of how much time to spend looking at each – remember the word limit for the whole project is 2,500 words, so if you are planning on writing 500 words on each of your 10 framework points your analysis alone will be twice the prescribed length. You may decide at the analysis stage to go back and trim down your framework.

If your analysis is comparative, if it is comparing two things, it is best to avoid looking at one and then looking at the other. This makes it difficult to make comparisons and you will end up with two analyses rather than one. A good approach is to take a feature of your framework and apply it to both sets of data – for instance, if you are looking at differences in male and female conversational strategies, take a particular linguistic feature and compare how it is used by both parties.

If you have gathered or are using quantitative data, use graphs or tables to present it. This will give it a visual presence and more impact.

Focus and cohesion

As already discussed, your investigation must have focus and cohesion. Stick to your frameworks, but ensure that your analysis is making points that link back to your aims and questions. After each point, or group of points, comment on how your analysis has helped to address an aim.

💡 The analytical sentence

One vital thing to remember in making points about your data is that you focus not only on the technical aspects of the language but also its impact or effect. This is true of all the analysis you will undertake on the course. If we just identify a feature as an abstract noun, for example, without any discussion of its role or effect in a text we are only doing half the job. Using the analytical sentence is a good way to do this. Look at the example on page 163 from the Gordon Brown speech analysis.

Key:
Introduction of point and quote from text
Technical identification of features
Discussion of effect
Conclusion of point

Brown describes social conscience as a 'driving power'; the noun phrase, with its emotive adjective 'driving', personifies this abstract idea and presents it as something that possesses strength and energy demonstrating how Brown wishes to emphasise his belief in the importance of a caring society.

This example shows how we can mix technical points about language with explanations of context and effect. In using sentences (or groups of sentences) in this way you will ensure that you are engaging with your data in a linguistic but meaningful way.

▮ Data response exercise 2

Have a look at an extract from an analysis of a project similar to one we have already looked at. Here the focus is on a news programme from Channel 4 only. Think about whether the student is making good points about the data, whether these are linked to the aims and whether the analytical sentence is used.

An investigation into the language techniques employed on Channel 4 news programmes

Aim 1: To find out how the programmes use language techniques to create effect and to position their audience.

Aim 2: To test whether these techniques conform to the theory of news values.

Framework

▮ **News value**: Personalisation and negativity

▮ **Representation of the victim/accused**:
- metaphors – dramatisation of events and conditions
- verbs – action and inaction
- adjectives – descriptions of individuals
- active/passive voice – control/lack of control
- adverbs/adverbials and tense – representation of change/contrast.

Key:
(.)   Brief pause
(1.0)   Pause in seconds
Bold   Stressed syllables
N1   Newsreader 1 (Jon Snow)
LM   Lucy Manning

Channel 4 news report on the poisoning of a Russian spy, 20 November 2006

N1   Good evening (1.0) this is it the first image of him since someone possibly introduced the poison thalium (1.0) after he'd met with two other Russians three weeks ago   5 (.) but was it a risk worth (.) taking for the Russian Secret Service (.) to try to kill Alexander Litvinenko (.) tonight we hear directly from the Kremlin

Fig. 17 *Jon Snow's report must convey a neutral and unbiased stance*

163

N1 Gaunt (.) weak (.) fighting for his life (.) the former Russian security agent Alexander Litvinenko (1.0) has been moved into intensive care under police guard after allegedly being given the deadly toxin (.) thalium (1.0) photographs showing his dramatic decline in health were released this evening (.) as Scotland Yard said (.) its counter terrorism unit (.) was now leading an intensive investigation (1.0) a member of the European parliament has also told Channel 4 news (.) Mr Litvinenko (.)was warned that Russian agents were trying to kill him (.) just before he fell ill (1.0) the Kremlin dismisses any suggestion that they were involved (.) as complete nonsense (2.0) well now (.) there may be a problem with this report but I'm gonna try and take it anyway (.) Lucy Manning reporting (3.0)

10

15

20

LM These pictures released in the last few hours (1.0) this is Alexander Litvinenko in hospital (1.0) given only a 50/50 chance of survival (1.0) he's lost his hair his throat is inflamed (.) and he hasn't eaten properly for days (1.0) friends say he's been left in this way after being poisoned by the Russian security services (2.0) this was Mr Litvinenko before the alleged poisoning (.) the former Russian security agent he's now under police guard (.) Scotland Yard's counter terrorism unit is now leading the investigation

25

30

LM His illness which has all the hallmarks of the murky dealings of The Cold War (.) centres on this sushi restaurant (1.0) he fell sick after visiting here with Italian academic Mario Scaramella (1.0) there's no suggestion that here made him ill (.) and he had another meeting that day in a hotel with two Russians (1.0) Mr Litvinenko's meeting with Mr Scaramella (.) was said to be about information concerning the murder of journalist (.) Anna Polikovskia whose reports on Chechnya (.) outraged the Kremlin (1.0) but MEP Gerrard Batten who yesterday spoke to Mr Scaramella (.) who has now gone into hiding (1.0) believes there was a more sinister reason (.) for the meeting

35

40

45

Analysis of extract

By using the adjectives 'gaunt' and 'weak' in conjunction with the participle phrase 'fighting for his life', Alexander Litvinenko is portrayed as a helpless human being struggling to survive. He is later described as a 'former Russian security agent', someone with typically high status and a good deal of power who is now not even able to control whether he lives or dies; this emphasises the dangerous state he is in. The use of the passive voice in constructions such as 'has been moved into intensive care' emphasises the helplessness of Litvinenko and highlights his role as a victim. All of these features conform to the news values of personalisation and negativity.

Jon Snow's report does not give away any certainty as to whether Litvinenko was deliberately poisoned. His sentences are carefully constructed and the use of qualifying adverbials such as 'possibly' and 'allegedly' is frequent so as to communicate a neutral and unbiased stance.

Many of the lines spoken by reporter Lucy Manning are context bound and use deictic features such as demonstrative pronouns ('this') when referring to photographs of Mr Litvinenko. This gives the story a sense of currency and urgency. Lucy Manning uses the metaphor 'His illness which has all the hallmarks of the murky dealings of The Cold War'.

The adjective 'murky' is often used to describe the purity of water, but used in this context suggests underhand dealings and intrigue, adding drama to the story. The reference to 'The Cold War', an emotive noun phrase packed with powerful connotations, places the story in a historical context evoking ideas of espionage, deceit and ideological warfare.

The adjective 'sinister' describes the underlying reason for a meeting between Litvinenko and Mario Scaramella, implying that it had a darker and perhaps more malevolent side. Alexander Litvinenko's health is described by Jon Snow as being in 'a dramatic decline'. This noun phrase gives the impression of a downward struggle, the use of the powerful adjective 'dramatic' helping to describe the startling way Litvinenko's health has rapidly deteriorated.

Topic revision summary

- Structure your analysis section clearly using subheadings to indicate the focus of each subsection.
- Make sure the analysis links back to your hypotheses, questions and aims.
- Use the analytical sentence to ensure you are discussing both technical features and their effect.

Conclusion and evaluation

In this topic you will:

- learn what is meant by the terms 'conclusion' and 'evaluation'

- understand what you should include in these sections

- look at effective strategies for writing conclusions and evaluations.

Study tip

When you write your conclusion, have your hypotheses and aims close at hand and cross-check to ensure you maintain this focus.

Coursework activity 7

In the light of these points, have a look at this example conclusion (right) from a project and, without worrying too much about its detail, think about whether it is an effective summary of an investigation's findings. Check your ideas against the feedback on page 175.

An investigation into the relevance of Lakoff's 1975 theory on male and female conversational strategies in a study of teenagers in 2008

Hypothesis: Females' increased social power will be reflected in their conversational strategies, challenging Lakoff's 1975 findings.

Conclusion

Your conclusion, as the name suggests, is the place where you discuss your overall findings. The analysis looks at how individual features help to address your aims, but the conclusion will summarise these findings and state what you have (or have not) found. Here are key points to remember with regard to the conclusion.

- Make sure that your conclusion addresses your aims. You may have found many interesting features in your data but if they don't relate to your initial aims, don't discuss them in the conclusion.
- Don't repeat bits of your analysis. The conclusion should be an overview of your investigation in which you discuss your findings more generally.
- Don't try to claim that you have found things that will change life as we know it. Your investigation is limited so you will need to take this into account when discussing your findings. If you have found some interesting things about language development in four children you cannot propose that this will apply to all children. Try to be considered and cautious in your claims – using phrases like 'the data suggests ...' rather than 'this proves ...' is a good way of showing caution.
- Don't be afraid of stating that your hypothesis has been disproved or that you have found unexpected results. Be honest about your findings and discuss both what you have found and perhaps what you have not found. Some of the best investigations come up with surprising results.

> I was expecting to find that females would be more outspoken than they were compared to Lakoff's theory in this investigation. Although this is partly true, I did find some factors were still relevant today. The main similarities I found between males and females were in grammatical mood and tag questions. Females used nearly equally as many declarative, imperative, interrogative and exclamatory sentences. If using imperatives determines power, then this shows that females and males are equally powerful in conversations. This proves my hypothesis that females will be more outspoken than they were in the 70s is correct. Males and females also hardly used tag questions which were a determining feature according to Lakoff; she suggested that females use them to show uncertainty and need for reassurance in conversations, but as there were none used it relates back to my hypothesis that females are more outspoken because they do not need reassurance from males. Another interesting point I found was that males tend to use the first-person singular pronoun more than females, which goes against the theory that females talk about themselves more.

> Whilst there are factors that suggest my hypothesis is right some also go against it. Females did use language overtly, such as when they use expletives they tend to be weaker than those used by males. I did find, though, that females in the study used weaker expletives to express themselves but also used stronger ones in some situations, whereas the males never used terms such as 'oh dear' and only used stronger ones, which links to the idea of covert prestige suggested by Lakoff.

> In conclusion, I feel that my hypothesis was correct in the fact that the females in my limited study seemed to behave in ways that

contradict Lakoff's findings, but I also found that they were not as dominant as I thought and parts of Lakoff's theory do seem to still have relevance today.

Evaluation

The evaluation considers the investigation's aims and the validity of its conclusions in the light of its methodology. Your evaluation should consist of a brief discussion of some or all of the following.

- An analysis of the success and validity of the methodology that you followed: you could discuss the reasons for certain decisions that you made in preparing your methodology, how you changed or modified it and why, or your consideration of ethical issues and issues of validity.
- A realistic discussion of the extent to which your findings allow you to make wider generalisations about language issues: don't claim too much here. Think about how your small study is valid in making wider statements about language use on a bigger scale.
- Possible avenues for future research: it may be that your investigation has thrown up certain questions that would be worthwhile pursuing further or in different ways. Alternatively, you might suggest ways that your investigation could be improved or extended.

Look back at the key points raised in the Methodologies topic on page 147. You could use them as a starting point for your evaluation.

> Overall, I feel my investigation was successful in testing the relevance of Lakoff's 1975 theory in a modern context. I feel the choices made in my methodology gave the investigation internal validity, allowing me to establish clear conclusions from my data. In recording the conversation of the teenagers, I decided to set up a situation rather than attempt to record from a 'real life' situation. This allowed me to select a suitable location and to position my recording equipment to ensure clarity in the data. It allowed me also to address ethical issues as the participants had given their permission for their conversation to be recorded and used in a research study. I was aware in doing this that the authenticity of the conversation might be reduced and that observer's paradox might come into play, but attempted to counteract this in a number of ways. The participants were told that the focus of the investigation was 'my favourite film' and so were not aware that I was focusing on issues of gender. This did not affect the ethics of the research, but I felt it would reduce any conscious or subconscious deviation from their normal behaviour. I started the recording process after 15 minutes of the conversation had elapsed, although the study group were not aware of this, reasoning that participants would be more relaxed at this point and therefore more likely to act naturally. As a last consideration, I was not present in the room during recording, reducing further the danger of observer's paradox.
>
> In terms of the participants themselves, the six studied were split equally by gender and were all of the same age. The limited number of participants prevented me from selecting a study group truly representative of the teenage population as a whole as this number did not allow me to reflect fully educational, ethnic, social and geographical variables. This limits the extent to which my findings can be applied to society in general.
>
> However, I felt my conclusions, suggesting a convergence of the conversational strategies of the genders, were at least suggestive of a general trend in behaviour. This conclusion could be used as the basis of a further and more wide-ranging study incorporating a much larger study group and addressing the key variables already discussed.

Study tip

Keep the interconnected nature of the investigation components in mind during the writing. Do not approach the evaluation as a separate and unrelated section.

Don't go overboard on your evaluation; it should be brief and should contain relevant discussion of the project's success.

Coursework activity 8

Consider the example evaluation (right), which is from the same investigation used in Coursework activity 7. Again, without worrying too much about the particular topic discussed, think about how usefully it evaluates the investigation's aims and the validity of its conclusions in the light of its methodology. Check your ideas against the feedback on page 175.

Topic revision summary

- Your conclusion is the section of your coursework where you discuss your overall findings.
- In the conclusion you should summarise how your investigation has met its aims.
- The evaluation section should discuss the success of your investigation, considering to what extent your findings can be applied to wider language issues.
- Your evaluation should also contain a discussion of the strengths and weaknesses of your methodology and suggestions for further research.

Bibliography, appendices and data

In this topic you will:

- learn about academic standards for presenting bibliographies
- learn where additional data can be located and the function of appendices.

Study tip

All books list the details required for the bibliography on a page between the front cover and the start of the main text. If you no longer have access to a book you have used and need its details, try a search at the British Library Catalogue website at http://catalogue.bl.uk. This catalogue contains details of over 13 million books and will almost certainly contain the details you need.

Looking ahead

The ability to produce correct references and bibliographies is a key skill required by all university courses. In fact, it is not uncommon for students on higher education courses to fail modules, or even their whole course, because of poor referencing in assignments. The method discussed here is recommended by many universities worldwide, so mastering this technique will stand you in good stead for future study.

 Bibliography

As an academic study of language your investigation needs to conform to certain rules in its final presentation. The most important of these is the bibliography.

The bibliography should be a record of all of the secondary sources you have used in your investigation. These may include books, websites, newspaper articles or the research of others. It is important that your bibliography is clear and comprehensive, and there are a number of different conventions as to how it should be set out. The most important thing is that you use a method **consistently**. Below is a suggestion for a bibliography layout based on the commonly-used Harvard referencing system.

- For books, you need to include details of author, date of publication, title, place of publication and the name of the publisher.
- The book's or article's title should be in italics.
- Always list your sources alphabetically by author; if you are listing a website, try to find out the author's name (it may be listed somewhere else on the site). If you can't find it, list it as 'anon'.
- For websites you need to include the date that you accessed the page; websites are updated and modified, and it may be that what you looked at three months ago has since been removed or altered.

The following is an example of part of a bibliography. It contains books, newspaper articles and a website. The first listing is colour coded to illustrate its different parts. Use this as a guide to setting out your own bibliography, or ask your teachers or school/college librarian about referencing.

Key
Author(s)
Year of publication
Title of book
Place of publication, followed by publisher

Clayton, D. and Kemp, B. (2008) *AQA A AS English Language: Student Book*, Cheltenham: Nelson Thornes Ltd

Crystal, D. (1976) *Child Language, Learning and Linguistics*, London: Edward Arnold

Crystal, D. (2001) 'Languages on the Web'. *Guardian Weekly*

Trippel, T. (1997) *Labov's Approach to Language Change* [online]. [Accessed 2 January 2008]. Now available from http://www.spectrum.uni-bielefeld.de/~ttrippel/labov/termpape.html

Fig. 18 *Any books you have referred to should be included in the bibliography*

Appendices and data

As well as the bibliography, your final submission should contain appendices. Your appendices will contain, most importantly, your data. All data that you collect should be included in its original form – so if you recorded conversations and then transcribed them you will need to include both the transcription and the original recordings of the data.

Additionally, you should include other relevant material in your appendices. This may consist of questionnaires that you have designed, letters of permission and any other documents such as newspaper articles or statistics that you feel will assist the examiner in assessing your project.

Each appendix should be numbered for easy reference, with a descriptive title where appropriate (e.g. Appendix 1: Letter to owner of Cafe Zee or Appendix A: Article on teenage swearing from local newspaper).

Topic revision summary

- Your bibliography should contain a list of all the sources you have used in your investigation.
- It should be laid out consistently and list author, date of publication, title and publisher.
- For online sources, you should also include the date that you accessed them.
- Appendices will include your data and any relevant secondary sources used.

Coursework preparation

In this topic you will:

■ look at what the exam board requires for this unit

■ plan your own investigation

■ evaluate some sample work

■ consider the presentation of your final submission.

Having worked through the previous topics, you should now be all set to begin your coursework planning. Before you do this, though, remind yourself of AQA's requirements for this part of the coursework.

AQA's requirements

■ Your investigation must be an original piece of work – your own ideas and data.

■ Your investigation must be based on primary language data.

■ Your investigation should be 1,750–2,500 words (excluding data).

■ Your investigation should contain the following sections.

– Introduction, hypotheses and questions

– Aims

– Methodology

– Analysis

– Conclusion

– Evaluation

– Bibliography

– Data and appendices

How the work is assessed

The relevant AOs here are as follows.

■ AO1: Select and apply a range of linguistic methods, to communicate relevant knowledge using appropriate terminology and coherent, accurate written expression.

■ AO2: Demonstrate critical understanding of a range of concepts and issues related to the construction and analysis of meanings in spoken and written language, using knowledge of linguistic approaches.

■ AO3: Analyse and evaluate the influence of contextual factors on the production and reception of spoken and written language, showing knowledge of the key constituents of language.

The project is marked out of 30 with each of the AOs being equally weighted (10 marks each). This means, as already discussed, that you must discuss language in a technical and linguistic manner, but also show an awareness of what the language is doing. The quality of your writing and the way you structure your project will also be considered in your final mark, so don't ignore this aspect of the task. The full mark scheme is available in the English Language A specification on AQA's website at www.aqa.org.uk.

What to do next

The most important aspect of the investigation is the original idea or topic that you choose so you need to spend time thinking about this. Ask yourself which areas of the course you have enjoyed the most and consider whether any of these areas would be appropriate for an investigation topic. Think about other areas of interest that you have and whether these can be translated into a linguistic study. Spend some time researching possible avenues of investigation and assess them on the following criteria.

- Is this area a legitimate focus for language study?
- Is there a non-obvious question I could ask about this area of language?
- Will I be able to get hold of the necessary data?

Always consult your teachers throughout your planning process; they will be able to tell you if an investigation has potential and will be able to suggest adjustments and modifications.

💡 Beginning your own work

Once you have decided on the topic area you wish to investigate you can begin planning in earnest. A good way to start this is to draw up a timetable of when you are going to do what.

Find out from your teacher the final submission date for the assignment and work out how much time you have for its completion. Getting hold of the data early on is vital, so make sure this fits into the available timeframe.

Finally, look back through this section of the book as your coursework progresses; students can often get a bit lost when undertaking complex investigations so using this book as a guide will help to keep you on the right track.

Presentation of your work

Below is a list of dos and don'ts in terms of how your investigation should be presented. A neat and organised project will immediately send out a positive message.

1 You must word-process the project – handwritten material is not appropriate at this level of academic study.
2 Use plain white A4 paper.
3 Examiners often like coursework to use double line spacing as it is easier to mark. Check with your teacher as to whether you should do this.
4 Spellcheck the project on your word processor and proofread the whole project for spelling or grammatical errors – a spellchecker won't pick up everything.
5 Set coursework out clearly, and use a consistent style in terms of things like headings, font sizes and types.
6 Make sure the pages are numbered – all word-processing software has an automatic way of doing this.
7 Include a title page with a broad description of your project focus.
8 Include a contents page listing each section and its page number.
9 Include a word count (excluding data and appendices) at the end of the project.
10 And, finally, make sure you put your name on your work.

■ Further reading

General

Bryson, B. *Mother Tongue*, Penguin, 1991

Crystal, D. *Making Sense of Grammar*, Pearson Longman, 2004

Crystal, D. *Rediscover Grammar*, Pearson Longman, 2004

Crystal, D. *The Stories of English*, Penguin, 2005

Russell, S. *Grammar, Structure and Style*, Oxford University Press, 2001

Thorne, S. *Mastering Advanced English Language*, Macmillan, 1997

Language investigation

Andersson, L. and Trudgill, P. *Bad Language*, Penguin, 1992

Cockcroft, S. *Living Language: Investigating Talk*, Hodder & Stoughton, 1999

Goddard, A. *Researching Language: working with English language data at AS/A level and beyond*, Heinemann Educational, 2000

'Hot on the Trail', Teachit, available from worldwide web: http://www.teachit.co.uk/

Langford, D. *Analysing Talk: Investigating Interaction in English*, Macmillan, 1994

Sebba, M. *Focussing on Language: a student's guide to research planning, data collection, analysis and writing up*, Definite Article Publications, 2000

Wray, A. and Bloomer, A. *Projects in Linguistics*, Arnold, 1998

■ Topic revision summary

- Spend time considering possible topics for your investigation before making a final decision.
- Take into account factors like ease of data collection in your decision making.
- Make sure that your work is presented clearly and conforms to academic standards of presentation.

ASKHAM BRYAN COLLEGE
YORK

Feedback

This part of the book provides all the feedback for the Coursework activities and Data response exercises in Unit 4, Section A.

■ Choosing an area to investigate

Coursework activity 1

1 Yes. This is a spoken language topic but you would need to collect your own data.

2 Yes. Here you would be analysing attitudes to a particular style of spoken language. Using a questionnaire or survey would result in primary data.

3 This would be fine, as long as you were looking at how the subtitles compared with the spoken dialogue. The subtitles on their own are not spoken or intended to be spoken so an investigation focusing only on subtitles would not be appropriate. In selecting pieces of the subtitles/dialogue you will be collecting primary data.

4 Yes. This is certainly spoken language. In devising a method for deciding which interviews, and which bits of the interviews, to look at, you will be collecting primary data.

5 No. Although this involves representation of speech it is not intended to be spoken. If you were to investigate whether the novels' representation of speech stands up to the conventions of actual speech, this would fall within the requirements.

6 Yes. This is spoken language, as long as you focus on what the witnesses actually said rather than how the newspaper reported them. Again, your decisions about what to look at will lead to primary data collection.

7 No. This is not spoken language, even if you feel it has spoken elements to it.

8 No, politically incorrect language is not necessarily spoken language. If you looked at attitudes to the politically incorrect language of a particular comedian's performance, for instance, this would be OK.

9 Yes, the judge's speech may be pre-planned but it is still language intended to be spoken.

10 No. Seamus Heaney may read his work at poetry readings, but it couldn't be said it was intended to be spoken.

■ Narrowing it down

Coursework activity 2

The following are only suggestions, and there are plenty more possibilities.

1 **Language of sport**
- Sports commentaries
- Interviews with sports people
- Press conferences
- Sports news channels
- Sports quizzes on TV/radio
- Football crowds' chants at matches

2 **Language of comedy**
- Scripts from comedy films/programmes
- Stand-up routines
- Comic improvisation
- The telling of jokes

3 **Language of film**
- Spoken film reviews
- Scripts for films
- Interviews with film stars
- Award ceremonies
- Trailers for films
- Subtitles and scripts

Coursework activity 3

1 This has potential. Using language and gender, a topic you have studied in Unit 3, will allow you to use the conclusions of a theory or other piece of research as something to test or challenge. Predicting what you might find is not straightforward so the topic isn't obvious. Collection of data shouldn't be a problem.

2 Again, as a topic previously studied, research and theory are available to inform this task. The 'answer' isn't obvious, so the question is significant and if you could find suitable opportunities for data collection this could be successful. This is the kind of topic where knowing someone who could help with the data (i.e. a family friend who is a primary school teacher) might influence your choice.

3 This topic could be interesting, again depending on opportunities for data collection, though you would have to be careful that your questions didn't lead to obvious answers. Having studied dialect in Unit 3, you would probably expect its use to decrease in younger generations, but there might be some more subtle questions you could ask, e.g. What particular dialect features are retained?

4 Having watched the two versions of this film, you might have had the impression that something was different in the presentation of the main character. This is where looking at data first can help to spark ideas for investigations. The data would be available through scripts or your own transcripts of the films and, again, the 'answer' is not obvious.

5 Here, a very precise focus will help to sharpen the investigation. The data is fairly easy to get hold of and the answer is not obvious.

6 Here the focus is a good one, but getting hold of the data could be difficult in practical terms. There are also issues of getting permission from the people and the supermarket involved in the study, which could prove problematic. This would be a good example of a project where you might keep the focus of the investigation but change the data.

7 This looks good and, again, is very clearly focused on a particular idea. Data collection shouldn't be a problem and the 'answer' is not obvious.

8 You could get help from your own teachers on this one, so data collection shouldn't be difficult, although you would need the equipment to collect it, a good recording device and microphone for instance. The results could be quite interesting, though there may be the danger of observer's paradox, an issue we will discuss in more detail on page 149.

9 This attitudes topic has potential and by focusing on attitudes and age it has clarity. You would need to be careful that you choose an aim which is not too obvious – you might expect that older people would be more negative towards new accents – and also that the analysis has enough depth – just recording whether people like or dislike the accent would lead to simple and unrewarding results.

10 This could be good as long as you make sure you have a clear idea of your question. You would need to decide whether you are looking at common features of news language, for instance, or at what the language is being used to do.

Introduction, hypotheses and questions

Coursework activity 4

1 The title of this investigation is very specific, its focus on turn-taking clearly indicating that it will be looking at language on the interactional level. By looking at the content of the utterances, perhaps to examine why different turn-taking strategies are used in different parts of a conversation, the investigation may deal, also, with language on the speech or lexical-semantic levels.

2 Here, the language level will depend on what aspect of language development is to be investigated. For pronunciation features, the phonological level; for the complexity of words, the lexical-semantic or grammatical level; for sentence construction, the syntactical level. One possible approach would be to look at a number of these, the range giving an overview of language development. An alternative would be to concentrate on one particular aspect, giving detail and depth.

3 The selection of levels here will depend on what aspects of the metaphor are to be explored. Analysis of the persuasive effect of the metaphor will almost certainly be used, and this falls within the rhetorical level. Analysis of the design of the metaphor would involve using the lexical-semantic or grammatical-morphological levels.

Aims

Coursework activity 5

1 This example has many weaknesses. Most importantly, the hypothesis is not a good one and this will inevitably cause problems: it is fairly obvious that an eight-year-old will be more developed than a four-year-old in terms of language use so the investigation is not pursuing a useful line of enquiry and is fundamentally flawed.
At least the first aim does attempt to show how the hypothesis will be tested, but the second aim is imprecise and doesn't clarify what exactly is meant by 'sophisticated' language – is this grammatical, lexical or pragmatic sophistication, or all three? Although much of this kind of detail should be explained in the frameworks section (from page 156), the aim could do with a bit more detail.

2 This is similar to the first worked example discussed earlier, but it shows how a promising topic can be weakened by its aims and hypothesis. Its focus on the changing use of politeness strategies in a particular group could be a useful area to investigate. One problem, though, is that the aims are too precise. A list of the actual features to be examined is part of the method and should go into the frameworks section not the aims.
Another problem here is that, in focusing simply on the tag question and the use of adverbs, the investigation could lack range and depth. These are fairly simplistic features and more complexity is needed to make these aims promising.
Finally, it is not clear how aim 2, the use of adverbs, will help in assessing levels of politeness. This is a common error made by students, at both the aims and frameworks stages, where a feature is investigated that has little or no relevance to the task's hypothesis or question.
This is a good example of where secondary data or a language theory could be used to inform the aims. A broader set of aims testing the language of the groups against the politeness theories of Brown and Levinson, for example, would be a better foundation.

3 This example is much better. Focusing on the party leaders and their conference speeches gives it precision, and the focus on metaphor, and the aspects of it which will be examined, is also precise and could lead to the discussion of a promising range and depth of features. This precision is different from example 2, though, because metaphor is not a feature here, but the focus of the investigation. The frameworks will go on to explain precisely what rhetorical and grammatical features of the metaphor will be explored. The two aims summarise the key proposals and link together well. The proposal uses a question rather than a hypothesis, which is appropriate in this case as the investigation aims to explore a language issue rather than support or challenge a particular piece of research or theory.

■ Methodologies

■ Coursework activity 6

1 a) is an open question and could lead to a range of answers which might prove useful in some preliminary research. On the other hand, the range of answers given may be unhelpful (20 respondents asked giving 20 different responses for example) and may not supply any useful information about general preferences. Another problem is the definition of Great Britain; Great Britain does not include Northern Ireland but the United Kingdom does – will your interviewees be aware of this fact? This is an example of how you must consider any ways in which the wording of your questions could cause confusion or ambiguity. Anything that you think may be unclear should be explained fully in the question. As a closed question, 1 b) resolves both of the issues above. Its narrower focus limits the range of answers but this limitation should produce results that can be analysed usefully.

2 b) is a leading question and could sway respondents to agree with the view stated. Additionally 'How far do you agree' is vague and unhelpful. 2 a) is much better as it takes a neutral stance and gives a range of options from which the respondents choose. The results from 2 a) could also be used quantitatively to give a statistical backbone to an attitudes-based piece of research.

3 a) is another open question and lacks focus – in asking about factors that influence liking and not liking it is asking too much. On a questionnaire it would produce rambling imprecise answers or, more probably, would be unanswered as it requires much effort on the part of the respondent. 3 b) is much better as, again, it has focus, simplicity and also considers the possibility of responses outside the confines of its answer options.

■ Data response exercise 1

In the opening line, Brown uses two verbs, 'strengthening' and 'entrenching'. These are from the semantic field of warfare so we might include this field of language as a framework point. In using these verbs he is also personifying the Labour Party so this could be something to include. In line 4 he uses the metaphor of Britain 'standing still', and in line 24 he describes social conscience as a 'driving power' and talks about his wish for society to 'grow'. The language here relates to ideas of action and inaction and could lead to the formulation of a framework point focusing on the language of activity and energy. In line 20 he describes the 'poverty' of opportunity. This abstract noun is very emotive and is an example of the use of financial language to highlight ideas of physical and spiritual wealth and wellbeing. Again, this could be included in the framework. In line 26 his labelling of the country as 'A Britain' is interesting and is working metaphorically. He seems to be using the indefinite article 'a' to highlight a particular perspective on the nation as opposed to other possible ones. Its use also seems to be linked to the idea of possibility and the future which might lead to the inclusion of the language of time in your framework.

Just this cursory glance at the data could lead to ideas for framework points. A couple of framework points built from the above commentary could look like this.

Framework

The language of warfare

I will look at how implements of war, through **nouns**, and actions of warfare, through **verbs**, are used in creating ideas of political conflict.

The language of activity

I will look at how the use of **verbs** in the metaphors sets up ideas of action or inaction, and how these help to present ideas about the state of the nation and its politicians.

The use of personification

I will examine how the use of personification creates emotive images of the nation and its politics and how **abstract nouns** are used in giving human attributes to ideas and issues to create dramatic effect.

Comment

By using an alternative approach we have come up with part of a framework that differs from Framework 1 (see page 159). But, again, it is worded so that the reasoning behind our choices is explained and connected to our aims. The words in bold highlight the range and depth of language features to be analysed. Framework 1 started with linguistic terms and used them to focus on semantic issues, whereas this framework starts with semantic issues and then describes how they will be analysed linguistically.

■ The analysis

■ Data response exercise 2

Comment

AO1 Select and apply a range of linguistic methods, to communicate relevant knowledge using appropriate terminology and coherent, accurate written expression

This is an effective piece of analysis. The range of features discussed is good and features are looked at in some depth (phrases and voice for example) and are accurately identified. This will help meet the assessment objective, one part of which is concerned with testing range and depth of knowledge of linguistic features. Each feature is used to address the investigation's aims, so the analysis has precision, avoiding the identification of irrelevant or unimportant words or phrases. The analysis doesn't stray out of context and the frameworks chosen are relevant. The writing is fluent and there are few technical errors.

AO2 Demonstrate critical understanding of a range of concepts and issues related to the construction and analysis of meanings in spoken and written language, using knowledge of linguistic approaches

In focusing on news values and using these as an underpinning theory to analyse the data, the analysis will score well on AO2 which is concerned with knowledge of linguistic theory and research. Notice, also, how periodically the analysis links back to a discussion of how it has addressed some of its aims giving it focus and cohesion. It provides a good overview of issues raised by the data.

AO3 Analyse and evaluate the influence of contextual factors on the production and reception of spoken and written language, showing knowledge of the key constituents of language

Each technical point is followed by a focused discussion of its effects, and this is often done through the use of the analytical sentence where key features and their impact on audiences or readers are clearly linked. This will help meet the assessment objective, which looks for an awareness of how language creates effects in its particular context.

Conclusion and evaluation

Coursework activity 7

Comment

AO1 Select and apply a range of linguistic methods, to communicate relevant knowledge using appropriate terminology and coherent, accurate written expression

The conclusion is well written with rare errors. In summarising the types of feature identified in the analysis, the conclusion demonstrates range and depth in the investigation's framework, a key aspect of the assessment objective.

AO2 Demonstrate critical understanding of a range of concepts and issues related to the construction and analysis of meanings in spoken and written language, using knowledge of linguistic approaches

The conclusion refers back consistently to its aims and discusses how its findings address them. It groups points together well and looks at the ways in which the analysis both supports and challenges its hypothesis. It takes language features, links them to Lakoff's gender theory and then discusses their relevance. All of these are pointers to a good response that demonstrates knowledge of theory and research and the ability to challenge views and standpoints.

AO3 Analyse and evaluate the influence of contextual factors on the production and reception of spoken and written language, showing knowledge of the key constituents of language

The key part of the AO3 mark is the ability to evaluate an investigation (the strengths and weaknesses of its findings) and to see how it fits into a wider context. Occasionally this conclusion is perhaps a bit overconfident in claiming successes and does tend to use words like 'prove' a bit too loosely, where perhaps words like 'suggest' or 'imply' would be better. But it ends well, summing up how the investigation has achieved its aims and tempering its claims by indicating that the findings are within a 'limited study'. In doing this it shows an awareness of how this investigation relates to language and behaviour in a wider context.

Coursework activity 8

Comment

AO1 Select and apply a range of linguistic methods, to communicate relevant knowledge using appropriate terminology and coherent, accurate written expression

Because the evaluation section of the coursework is focused on an assessment of the success of the investigation, it will not contain the 'raw' analysis of other sections, so that part of the AO1 assessment is not really applicable here.

However, another part of AO1 (an assessment of the investigation's methodology) certainly is. This example considers the choices made in the methodology, explaining why certain decisions were taken. The evaluation discusses ethical issues showing an awareness of their importance in this type of investigation.

The discussion of observer's paradox, its implications and ways to reduce its impact, shows a firm grasp of methodological approaches. The validity of the data is considered and variables are discussed. Even though certain factors were not fully addressed in the methodology, they are recognised and commented on in the evaluation. All of these decisions are then justified and weighed up against possible alternative approaches.

The final part of AO1 – using accurate and correct expression – is tested in all sections of the coursework. In this particular example there are few errors and the evaluation is structured into clear and well connected paragraphs. This level of organisation and accuracy applied consistently throughout the investigation has resulted in a good response.

AO2 Demonstrate critical understanding of a range of concepts and issues related to the construction and analysis of meanings in spoken and written language, using knowledge of linguistic approaches

This example summarises its findings and evaluates them in the light of the theory used to underpin the investigation. It is concise and focuses only on the key considerations mentioned in the advice. Weak evaluations are often 'tacked onto' investigations as an afterthought, making broad generalisations about findings, repeating bits of the conclusion or analysis, or discussing irrelevant issues. In tentatively suggesting findings that go against Lakoff's gender theory, the evaluation identifies and challenges theoretical standpoints, another pointer to a good response.

AO3 Analyse and evaluate the influence of contextual factors on the production and reception of spoken and written language, showing knowledge of the key constituents of language

The focus is this assessment objective is on the students' ability to identify findings and to discuss them in a wider context. The evaluation contains a careful statement about the success of the investigation, including discussion of the strength and implications of the conclusions. The limitations of the research (its appropriateness) are highlighted showing a consideration of contextual factors – weak evaluations often claim too much in terms of success, showing a lack of awareness of wider issues. Suggestions for further research are made in recognition of the limited scope of the investigation, and the conclusion is evaluated in terms of its external validity. As a whole, the piece is thoughtful and confident in tone but shows a firm understanding of the extent to which the investigation's findings are limited by its scale.

B Language intervention

Introduction

In this section you will:

- develop an understanding of the requirements of this part of the coursework

- examine a range of debates about language from Unit 3, which could be used as a focus for an intervention

- examine a range of forms that could be used for the intervention

- assess the success of examples of intervention texts

- look at how to present your final submission.

Link

For a full explanation of these forms, see page 180.

Key terms

Form: the outward appearance or structure of a text, e.g. novel, play, newspaper article.

Further reading

Read Chapter 1 of David Crystal's *Internet Linguistics* (Routledge, 2011) for more ideas on how the internet is shaping language in the 21st century.

In this section you will look at how to approach the second part of the A2 coursework, the language intervention. The language intervention is your chance to produce a creative text which contributes to a debate about language; your piece will 'intervene' in this debate, adding ideas, suggesting views or arguing standpoints.

Your planning for this part of the coursework will involve the examination of the range of different topics that your piece could focus on, as well as the variety of **forms** in which it could be written.

This part of the unit links in with the work you have already done on language change and variation in Unit 3, Section A and also with the text types you looked at in Unit 2, Section B Producing representations.

Basic requirements for the intervention task

To begin with, look at the following basic requirements for this part of your coursework.

- **You should write about a language debate in a particular form for a non-specialist audience.**
  This means that the people reading your work should not be expected to have a high level of knowledge about language issues, so you will need to think carefully about how to present these debates in a way they can understand.

- **The purpose of your piece should be to inform, argue, instruct or persuade.**
  Examples of the type of piece you could produce would be articles, editorials, letters to the editor, scripts, etc.; though, as long as it is fulfilling one of the stated purposes, most forms would be appropriate. Most texts attempt to achieve more than one of these purposes – informing and persuading for example. Because of this, rather than looking at what is involved with each, we will focus on some real examples of texts and consider how they achieve these purposes.

- **The topic for the intervention should come from the subject matter that you studied for Unit 3.**
  Ways of doing this are looked at on pages 177–8.

- **You need to produce one or two texts totalling 1,250 words.**
  One decision you will have to make fairly early on is whether to produce one or two texts for your submission of coursework. Letters and short leaflets, for instance, would normally not reach the 1,250-word limit, so you would probably need two of these to fulfil the requirement. A feature article, however, would often reach this length so, if this is your choice, one text would be better. This is looked at in more detail on page 188.

- **The coursework will be assessed using only one assessment objective – AO4.**
  This AO requires you 'to demonstrate expertise and creativity in the use of English in a range of different contexts, informed by linguistic study'. We will look at what this exactly means on pages 201–4.

Choosing a topic

In this topic you will:

- examine the range of language topics that could be used for your assignment

- identify issues and debates within these areas that could be used as a focus.

Study tip

When choosing a language debate, try to find something that people have different opinions about, or something that can be argued about from different perspectives. Debates that are truly debated (rather than issues where most people agree) will give you more scope for creativity and authenticity in your intervention piece.

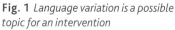

Fig. 1 *Language variation is a possible topic for an intervention*

Choosing a topic that interests you

As already mentioned, the topic for your language intervention should come from the subject matter studied in Unit 3. You have either just studied this unit or are in the middle of doing so; therefore, the types of issue and debate concerned should be fairly fresh in your mind. But, as a reminder, below is a very simplified summary of the types of thing we are talking about when looking at change and variation.

Table 1

Language change	Language variation
How language changes Process of change and the history of change **Why language changes** Society, technology, the media, etc. **Attitudes towards language change** Descriptivist and prescriptivist approaches	**How language varies** Why it varies, attitudes to and theories of variation, debates on variation looking at a wide range of variables: Regional variation – accents and dialects Language and gender Language and social variation – class/ occupational groups/age English as a world language

As with your investigation coursework, when considering a topic for your intervention think about those areas of the course that you have enjoyed or found particularly interesting. Go back through Unit 3, Section A in this book, and through your notes, and get a more detailed reminder of the debates and issues that you have covered. Make a list of those you enjoyed.

Making the topics manageable

A good idea is to think about the broad list of topics available (see Table 1) and see how you can break them down into more detailed and focused issues – for instance, rather than tackle the rather large topic of English as a world language, you might focus on one aspect of this, such as English and the rise of the internet, creoles of British English, or attitudes towards American English.

Coursework activity 1

Try this narrowing-down exercise with two of the other listed topics, why language changes and language and social variation. For each, make a list of five mini-topics (specific debates within the wider topic) that could form the focus for an intervention piece. Don't worry about the type of text at this point or its purpose, just the topic on which it could focus.

Deciding on a purpose

Once you have decided on the broad topic area for your intervention, you need to move on and make some more detailed decisions. You are required to make an 'informed contribution to social debates about language' and you must do this through a text (or texts) that inform, argue, instruct or persuade. So, you now need to decide what type of text you want to write. Letters to the editor usually attempt to argue or persuade, whereas an educational textbook is more likely to inform. Think about the type of writing you are good at or prefer to use when considering your purpose.

> ### Topic revision summary
> ■ You should choose a language debate from those you have studied in Unit 3 Language change and variation.
> ■ Think about how a broad debate can be narrowed down into a smaller and more manageable topic.

Choosing a form

Key terms

Discourse structure: the structure of a text, in terms of how its component parts fit together to give cohesion and form a whole.

Convention: a set of agreed, stipulated or generally accepted rules of layout and language use for a particular form or genre.

Genre: the category or type of text within a form, such as romance or thriller (novel); comedy or tragedy (play); review or editorial (newspaper article).

What do we mean by form?

The **form** of a text is to do with its characteristic structural elements and is the key consideration in choosing a text or texts for your intervention. Novels, for example, have particular features which distinguish them from other written texts – they have a narrative **discourse structure** and are usually written in chapters. Plays, on the other hand, replace the narrative with dialogue between characters and are written in acts, scenes or both. There are novels and plays which don't follow these **conventions** – perhaps to challenge the idea of form – but, generally speaking, chapters are form conventions of novels, and scenes are form conventions of plays.

Genre, on the other hand, is a variation within a form: in terms of form, *Dracula* is a novel, but in terms of genre it is horror. The choice of genre will obviously affect the content of the story, but it will also dictate how the novel employs things like address, use of descriptive language, objectivity, tone and sentence structure. This is not only the case with novels but is also true of all kinds of text. These factors should be considered when you choose an appropriate form for your intervention piece.

As already discussed, the range of texts that you could choose for your intervention is wide and all the possibilities can't be covered in this book. What can be done, though, is to look at some of the most popular forms of text and consider the features and styles that they employ. We can also examine some of the variations within each form. Before we do that, however, take a look in more detail at how your piece is going to be assessed.

Fulfilling the requirements of AO4

The AO that is central to the language intervention is AO4 (Demonstrate expertise and creativity in the use of English in a range of different contexts, informed by linguistic study) and this is split into three distinct parts in the mark scheme. You need to be able to demonstrate your ability to use a convincing form, an appropriate style and to include content in your piece which demonstrates your understanding of language issues and debates. Table 2 lists the things you need to do to satisfy these three requirements.

Table 2

Form	Style	Content
■ Use a demanding form effectively. ■ Be original and innovative as appropriate. ■ Produce a polished and impressive piece. ■ Give a well-shaped and structured tour of issues.	■ Demonstrate flair, precision, deftness. ■ Use technical aspects for stylistic effect. ■ Use vocabulary and syntax subtly to express arguments. ■ Combine information and argument, with stylishness, wit and playfulness. ■ Use language to entertain as well as inform and argue.	■ Demonstrate a conceptualised overview of theories and research. ■ Analyse and evaluate alternative views. ■ Identify and challenge standpoints. ■ Adopt an exploratory/original/ evaluative approach.

Form

In choosing to write in a certain form you must ensure that your piece is shaped and structured in an appropriate manner. As we have seen, texts have particular forms that we expect them to adhere to. Newspaper articles, for instance, have fairly standard structures and conventions but these will vary depending on the article type. You will need to ensure that you are aware of these conventions so that your piece feels and looks like the real thing. Some forms are less easy to generalise about. Fiction texts for instance can have a variety of structures and can be more experimental and creative in form. However, they still have an organised structure and form, and you need to think carefully about this aspect of your writing during the planning stage. We shall look at a range of forms in more detail on pages 182–200 but it is vital that, whatever genre you choose, you do some background research into it so that your piece mirrors the form standards expected for that particular type of writing.

Style

The form that you choose and the particular genre within that form will influence the style of writing. You will need to ensure that you are using an appropriate **register** for your chosen piece. Media texts, for instance, use particular types of address, and different genres of media text vary in their use of things like tone, reader positioning and descriptive language. A successful intervention piece needs to look and feel authentic; conforming to the style expectations of form and genre will help you in achieving this.

You will also be rewarded under this part of the assessment scheme for using interesting and entertaining language. Most of the genres available for your intervention will involve an aspect of entertainment in their purpose, so using language creatively and imaginatively is important. This is especially true for certain types of text: fiction and feature articles for instance commonly use figurative language and highly creative styles.

Content

The content part of the assessment looks at how well you have demonstrated your understanding of language issues and debates. To score well here you will need to show an overview of the issue that you are focusing on. The key word from the mark scheme here is evaluation,

Fig. 2 *Understanding assessment objectives is important in achieving good marks*

which means you will have to show an awareness of different ways of looking at an issue or debate, even if you are arguing for a particular position or standpoint. Remind yourself about the evaluation section of your language investigation. In it, you considered the strengths and weaknesses of your methods and conclusions. A similar approach is required here, the difference being that now you may well be assessing the theories and research of others, or evaluating ideas about language in a wider context.

Remember, though, you are writing for a non-specialist audience so you must be able to translate complex linguistic ideas into language that is comprehensible to a general non-expert readership. The key here is getting the right balance between complexity and accessibility, and where that balance lies will depend on the type of text that you choose to write – an editorial in a broadsheet newspaper will demand a higher level of complexity than a textbook for GCSE students, for instance.

■ Think about it

Before you read the next topic, which will go through the features of various forms, try to come up with a list of features that are usually associated with the following forms. Think about structure and style as well as content.

- News articles
- Educational textbooks
- Novels or short stories

■ Extension activity

Using a standard search engine, perform an internet search using the key words 'accent and dialect'. Concentrating on the top 20 hits, list the different forms of text the search throws up (e.g. educational resources, news articles, user guides). Consider:

- how the forms differ in structure and style
- how the key purposes (inform, argue, instruct or persuade) are addressed by each
- whether each text would be suitable for an intervention piece in terms of its content and level of evaluation.

■ Topic revision summary

- All texts can be described in terms of form.
- You need to match the language and structure of your intervention to its chosen form and genre to give it authenticity.
- Your piece will be assessed on its use of form, style and content so you need to be aware of the conventions of your choice of text.
- In writing for a non-specialist audience, you need to translate complex linguistic ideas into ones more generally accessible.

Printed and online articles

In this topic you will:

- look at a variety of media texts considering aspects of form and genre

- look at the features and styles typical of a range of media texts

- examine examples of media texts and consider their use of language.

The popular choice

One of the most popular choices for this type of task is a written media text, i.e. the kinds of text you would find in newspapers, magazines and online publications. As you found in the Extension activity on page 181, they come in a variety of forms and have a range of purposes. Getting to know their conventions in terms of form and style is important before you attempt to produce one. Here we shall focus on three types of media text: news articles, editorials and feature articles.

News articles

News articles can be found throughout newspapers though they tend to take up the prominent pages at the front. They are topical and focus on current events of importance or interest. A news article that would fit in with the focus of an intervention might include a report on some interesting research findings about language, a government's or other institution's announcement on a language issue (the teaching of English in schools for example), or a review of a book that raises interesting ideas about language.

Data response exercise 1

Look at the example of the news article on research into language change that follows. What distinctive form and style conventions does it seem to be following? Think about the features listed below (framework).

1. **Address:** How does the article establish a relationship between writer and reader? Does the writer directly address the reader by using second-person pronouns? Does the writer refer to him or herself through the use of first-person pronouns? How does the piece use sentence moods (interrogatives, imperatives, declaratives)? Do these moods help in creating closeness or distance between writer and reader?

2. **Descriptive/factual language:** Does the text employ figurative language (metaphor, personification) to describe people or events or does it use more straightforward literal language?

3. **Objectivity, bias and tone:** Does the piece present its content objectively, from a neutral point of view, or does it take a stance or particular perspective? Does it present ideas in a formal, serious manner or does it use elements of humour to illustrate ideas?

4. **Sentence/clause/phrase structure:** How does the piece use different types of sentence, clause or phrase? Are the sentences long and complex, or are short simple structures used? How do these structures create impact and effect?

5. **Discourse structure:** How does the piece introduce and then go on to develop its topic? Does it have clear structural elements (introduction, conclusion)? How do the paragraphs link together to give a sense of direction?

School bans slang! Pupils ordered to use the Queen's English in the classroom 'to help children get jobs'

By Leon Watson

Parents can breathe a sigh of relief – but the local MP isn't impressed.

A school has ordered youngsters to leave slang at the gates and learn to speak the Queen's English.

Sheffield's Springs Academy hopes to give its pupils a better chance of getting a job, so slang or 'text talk' has been banned while they are on the premises.

The United Learning Trust which runs the school, which has 1,100 students aged from 11 to 18 and is in a working-class area of the city, believes slang creates the wrong impression during interviews.

Kathy August, deputy chief executive of the trust, said: 'We want to make sure that our youngsters are not just leaving school with the necessary A to Cs in GCSEs but that they also have a whole range of employability skills.

'We know through the close relationships we have with business partners and commercial partners that when they are doing interviews with youngsters, not only are they looking at the qualifications, they are also looking at how they conduct themselves.

'What we want to make sure of is that they are confident in using standard English. Slang doesn't really give the right impression of the person.

'Youngsters going to interviews for their first job need to make a good impression so that employers have confidence in them.

'It's not difficult to get youngsters out of the habit of using slang.'

Mrs August continued: 'When youngsters are talking together they use text speak and that's absolutely fine, that's what you do in a social context, but when you are getting prepared for life and going for interviews you need to be confident in using standard English.

'I'm a parent and when youngsters are at home we all have to make sure that we are all working together because this is for the benefit of those young people and their future.

'Using slang is a habit but youngsters are very adaptable and once they know that is what is expected and they know the reason is to help their employability skills, they will pick it up very quickly. It is not a big problem at all.

'It's something new and people are saying why are we doing it but once we have explained, it hasn't been a problem.'

However Penistone & Stocksbridge MP Angela Smith has criticised the school's decision.

Ms Smith, a former GCSE English teacher at a South Yorkshire secondary, said: 'The school is wrong to ban slang. How will the school police this?

'Who will say what the difference is between slang and dialect? It could completely undermine the confidence of the children at the school.

'If someone tells them how to speak they could dig in their heels and do it all the more. I really think they have set themselves a task that is impossible to achieve.'

Ms Smith said: 'Who is going to adjudicate? Who is going to say slang, dialect or accent? And which one is right and which one is wrong?

'Most people know when to put on their telephone voice because that is what we are talking about. When people go on the phone or talk to anyone in authority they put on a different voice.'

Mrs August responded: 'We are not trying to stamp out dialect or accents, it is simply the use of slang words.

'For example if someone goes for an interview it is preferable to say "Good morning" rather than "Hiya" and when the person leaves an employer would much rather hear the words "Goodbye" rather than "Cheers" or "Seeya".

'"Thank you" is a better word to use than "Ta". And it's not a case of policing or enforcing this policy at Springs Academy, we are simply encouraging it among the students.'

http://www.dailymail.co.uk/news/article-2101097/Sheffields-Springs-Academy-bans-slang-Pupils-ordered-use-Queens-English.html

💡 Op-ed articles

An op-ed article (an abbreviation for 'opposite the editorial page') is an article written by a named writer about a current issue or debate. The writer is often an expert or authority on the issue at hand, which is usually presented in the paper's editorial for that day.

The op-ed article has many similar features to an editorial where the newspaper gives its views on a topic or topics, often ones that have featured in recent news stories: it lacks the objectivity of a news article and attempts to persuade rather than simply inform. This type of article can also vary in tone, from a serious discussion of a social issue to a satirical swipe at an individual or institution. The main difference between the op-ed and the editorial is that the op-ed is written by an individual who is not directly employed by the newspaper, so they tend to have more freedom in the views that they express and the ways in which they do so. This gives writers scope to discuss alternative and even radical views on topics and to employ more creative and original strategies in their writing. As these elements are responsible for two-thirds of the marks for this element of the coursework (content and style), an effective op-ed article has the potential to score high marks as an intervention piece.

Look at the example op-ed article on pages 185–7 above the increasing use of text-speak by schoolchildren. The key features of the article have been highlighted. When reproducing an article like this it is important to have a clear idea of the exact style model, target publication and ideal audience for the piece.

Text-speak: language evolution or just laziness?

Pupils are becoming increasingly "bilingual" in English and text-speak, a new study claims. But is it just a simple decline in proper language skills, asks Anne Merritt.

Text-speak: shortened bits of language like "m8" and "b4" are altering the way that children communicate. Photo: Alamy

By Anne Merritt

9:34AM BST 03 Apr 2013

💬 **69 Comments**

Schoolchildren as young as eight are showing a growing proficiency in bilingualism, according to a recent poll of UK parents and teachers. The only hitch? They're bilingual in English and "text-speak" – the phonetic or acronymic bites of language such as "L8R" or "LOL."

What's more, this text-speak is creeping beyond their smartphones and into pupils' everyday language. Mencap, a charity for learning disabilities, sponsored a poll of 500 UK parents and teachers. Two-in-three teachers reported that they regularly find text-speak in pupils' homework. Over three-quarters of parents say they have to clarify the cryptic text-speak in their children's texts and emails.

Almost all participants surveyed (89 per cent) said that this growing prevalence of text speak is creating a **veritable language barrier between themselves and children**.

Clearly, these shortened bits of language like "m8" and "b4" aren't just for concise texting with friends. They are altering the way that children communicate.

The headline sums up the topic (text-speak) and immediately presents the two sides of the debate: language evolution or language decay.

The strapline gives more detail as to the nature of the debate. The coordinating conjunction 'But', which begins the second sentence, acts as a grammatical fulcrum, weighing up both sides of the argument.

The strapline, like most of the article, is written in the present tense, emphasising that this is a current issue, and the writer's name is included to stress that the article will put forward the views of an informed individual.

The photograph sums up in pictorial form the issue at hand (schoolchildren, mobile phones and computers denoting technology, and a teacher representing education). The rather 'relaxed' attitude of the schoolgirl with her feet on the desk perhaps suggests that the writer will take a critical stance on text-speak, linking it with laziness and a decline in general standards of behaviour.

The caption under the photograph gives some examples of the kind of language use the author is discussing.

The exact time of publication and the opportunity for readers to comment through a forum indicates the online nature of the article and website. These kinds of feature give online texts a sense of immediacy and an interactive feel that more traditional printed media texts cannot achieve.

The use of the noun phrase 'The only hitch?' acting as a direct question gives readers the feeling that the writer is directly addressing them, creating writer–audience rapport.

Support for the 'decay' side of the argument is given through a third-party poll suggesting text-speak is affecting educational standards. The use of facts and statistics from other organisations and individuals presents the idea that the issue is widely debated.

The article uses a hyperlink here, which sends readers to another article that translates text-speak for adults. Again, the use of this type of feature highlights the technological nature of the text.

The use of three questions repeats the key issues involved and reminds readers of the two conflicting views on the topic.

But is this linguistic evolution, or just laziness? Do children use text-speak because they no longer understand the boundaries of formal and informal English? Or, are children consciously changing those boundaries through a one-size-fits-all communicative tone?

Related articles are listed and hyperlinks allow the reader to move around the site and learn more about the topic.

Related Articles

Text speak does not affect children's use of grammar: study

05 Sep 2012

Baffled by text speak? New app will help puzzled parents

25 Aug 2012

Why bother learning a language?

28 Feb 2013

English teenagers 'worst in Europe' at languages

15 Feb 2013

Five completely free ways to learn a language

20 Feb 2013

The 10 easiest foreign languages

05 Dec 2012

At this point the article, for the first time, uses the first person, the repetition of 'me' announcing the introduction of the author's views into the article.

Call me a traditionalist, but it doesn't look like a revolution to me. Instead, it looks like a simple decline in proper language skills, born out of a digitally literate culture that has grown too comfortable in an age of abbreviations and spellchecks.

A third-party view from a respected institution is used to counter the earlier Mencap poll that suggested text-speak is having a negative effect on formal writing skills.

Yes, recent **studies from Coventry University** and the University of Hawaii have reported that children can still distinguish between formal and informal speech. They also note that frequent use of text-speak doesn't necessarily correlate with poor essay writing skills.

So students are still capable of developing arguments, writing thesis statements, and structuring their thoughts. They're just doing it with "u" instead of "you".

It's a problem of productive language skills. Though children learn proper English in school, they're not applying it outside the classroom, and the lessons aren't sticking.

Experts say that children write more these days than they did 20 years ago, because of texting and social media. Most of that writing, however, is in text-speak, and that form of language becomes a bad habit. Students are now so used to writing in text-speak that they can't easily remember (or apply) proper language rules.

Communication is becoming more global in scope and more electronic in form. By the time these children finish school and enter the workforce, this decline in the spoken word will become greater. Written communication, in a formal report, an email, or even a text, isn't just happening on the colloquial level anymore, and children need to be educated on how to use technology in formal, professional contexts.

Teachers and parents need to encourage children to discern the right time and place for casual language. Children also need to hone their proper English skills so that they can call upon correct spelling and grammar when it's needed. Text-speak in pupils' essays may be amusing, albeit cringeworthy, nowadays. It's not as amusing to imagine our children 10 years from now, as adults, texting "can u plz c me?!?" to their bosses.

> The use of the verb 'need' sees the writer instructing parents and teachers on what they should do. This persuasive element is central to editorial and op-ed articles.

Top 10 bizarre text-speak spellings

> The 'Top 10' feature gives some more concrete examples of text-speak and adds some variation to the presentational style of the piece, making it look lively and interesting.

After – Rfd

Tonight – 2nite

Great – Gr8

Before – B4

Tomorrow – 2moro

Cool – kwl

Mate – M8

Pizza – Peetsa

True – Churoo

That – Dat

(source: Mencap/Del Monte Fruit Burst poll)

Anne Merritt is an ESL lecturer currently based in South Korea.

> The author's credentials are listed, her job as an English teacher giving her views authority.

More by this author:

> This section, like the 'Related Articles' section, uses hyperlinks to point the reader to other articles written by Anne Merritt.

Will a new phonetic alphabet catch on?

What motivates us to learn foreign languages?

Learn a foreign language for free: top five resources

Foreign languages: how to memorise vocabulary

Learning a foreign language: five most common mistakes

Foreign languages: the 10 easiest to learn

How to avoid embarrassing foreign language faux pas

http://www.telegraph.co.uk/education/educationopinion/9966117/Text-speak-language-evolution-or-just-laziness.html

Feature articles

The feature article is not so much a genre of article as a label for a whole range of different types of writing. Feature articles can be found in all newspapers and magazines – in newspapers often after the important news stories.

Perhaps the main difference between the feature article and the news article is that feature articles can focus on a wide range of issues rather than simply the reporting of day-to-day events. For this reason they do not need to focus on situations that are current, although they are often used to give background to or additional information on a news story.

A feature article may take an individual, issue or debate and look at it from a number of perspectives. This type of writing can be persuasive, instructive, argumentative or informative and may use a variety of styles and approaches.

Extension activity

Collect three different newspapers from the last week. Go through them identifying the different kinds of feature article by purpose and genre. Take three of these article types and list the features that appear typical of them using the five-point media text framework that you used in Data response exercise 1 and Coursework activity 1.

Below is a list of some common structures of feature articles, along with some suggestions as to how they might be used to address a language issue.

- **An interview:** a leading linguist discusses attitudes towards language change.
- **A personal/opinion piece/column (the article may be a one-off, or an article written by a regular columnist):** an individual gives his or her own view on the differences between the language of men and women.
- **A human interest story:** an article on how a teenager with cerebral palsy perceives issues of language, labelling and disability.
- **An advice piece:** a humorous article on the 'correct' use of the Glasgow dialect.
- **A supporting article:** an explanation and elaboration on a news story about text messaging and its effect on child literacy.

Because of the diversity of this type of article it is difficult to generalise about its typical features, but, as a type of writing aimed primarily at entertaining its audience, it will often use language in a creative and experimental way. Feature articles may use dense metaphorical language, elements of fiction, such as plot lines, characters or dialogue, and may take a less stringent approach to language 'rules' utilising unusual or non-standard forms.

Data response exercise 2

The following is an example of an online feature article, together with some comments from a message board, focusing on the use of the Queen's English.

Thinking again about address, description, objectivity, sentence, discourse structure and mode, consider how the features of the article, and the comments that follow it, affect the style of the piece. What similarities and differences does the piece have with/from the other media articles?

English ain't what it was, but we should celebrate its cultural diversity

The demise of the Queen's English Society signals the end of a nostalgic fantasy

Margaret Reynolds
The Guardian, Tuesday 5 June 2012 19.00 BST

💬 **Jump to comments (229)**

'I do like your shallots!' Linguistic mistakes, and variety in speech and dialect, are among life's great pleasures. Photograph: Fox Photos/Getty Images

Who speaks the Queen's English? Certainly not the Queen. She has used many different kinds of English over the years and her way of speaking is now pretty much unique, the crossbred product of an old-fashioned upbringing and modern adaptation.

And what is the Queen's English anyway? Does it lie in pronunciation, in grammar, in correct use of terms, or in punctuation? Is it the same as Oxford English? Or received pronunciation, or BBC English? And who will help us to tell the difference?

Until this week, the Queen's English Society ("Good English Matters") did that job. But when only 22 members pitched up for a meeting, the chairman, Rhea Williams, declared the society closed. Finished, kaput, an ex-society. "People today", she said, "just don't care". Starbucks won't call her back when she tries to point out their incorrect use of less and fewer. Advertisers shrug their shoulders over misplaced apostrophes. So, felt pen in hand, she carries on her lonely crusade, adjusting notices all over the land.

Standards in English have always been going to the dogs. Once, it was too many American expressions ("I'm taking the elevator to put out the trash, dude"). Then, it was the mimicking of the Australian style of lifting the voice at the end of a sentence? As if a statement were a question? Now, it's text abbreviations, street slang, glottal stops and "it's gonna rain tomorrow" that are the problems.

Like many teachers, I sigh over essays that don't distinguish between effect and affect. I shout at the radio over improper use of "the public interest". Along with the Radio 4 announcer Harriet Cass, I don't really feel that it is polite to say toilet in a public broadcast.

But variety in speech and dialect is one of the delights of English. For more than a century now, we have been able to hear the voices of the dead, and they speak a language already strange. So Robert Browning (recorded in 1888) says, "'Pon my word, I've forgotten me own verses". And the Anglo-Irish writer Elizabeth Bowen, in a broadcast from the 1950s, recommends the need for "plorrt and kerekter".

Where I live in Gloucestershire the pronoun "it" is often replaced with "he" – "I'm offended with him", says my neighbour when his lettuce bolts. In Lancashire, people speak with a portentous emphasis – "You're a fool to yourself, Connie". In Bristol, classical music fans love the operal.

The linguistic mistakes immortalised by Shakespeare's Dogberry and Sheridan's Mrs Malaprop are among life's happy pleasures. There was the essay on Dracula in which he ends "with a steak through his heart". Or the acquaintance who commented on my divided skirt – "I do like your shallots". I didn't say anything. I expect Rhea Williams is rather more brave. Or should that be braver?

Yes, words are important, and correct usage does make for better understanding. Along with all English teachers, I correct trivial errors and general carelessness. But I care more that my students think for themselves, that they develop a critical understanding, so they can set up their own argument.

The other thing that I value is a respect for the interests and feelings of others. Mispronounced or misspelt words worry me a bit. But stumbling over names, or failing to remember them, bothers me more. Equally, I don't mind American phrases – provided we know that that is what they are. And let's add in words from other cultures too – key European monetary terms might be useful at the moment, along with the proper names for different dress codes and social expectations.

But cultural policing (even of this kind) is always dangerous, because it says that I am right and you are wrong. The magazine published by the Queen's English Society is called Quest. And that's about right. It strives to recover a nostalgic fantasy world that never did exist and never can.

Why do we have two ears and one mouth? In order that we should listen twice as much – to the Queen's English and all the other languages of the world. As she is spoke.

- This article was amended on 11 June 2012 to correct the spelling of misspelt.

BenCaute
05 June 2012 7:13pm

106

> Once, it was too many American expressions

you mean like:

> Along with the Radio 4 announcer Harriet Cass, I don't really feel that it
> is polite to say toilet in a public broadcast.

Toilet is a perfectly good English word, which Shakespeare deployed in public
broadcast.

Oh, and

> miss-spelt

Surely either mis-spelt, or better misspelt.

Miss Spelt was the Roman Bread Association's face of AD 57.

;)

AhabTRuler
05 June 2012 7:15pm

5

I feel that the beauty of the printed word in English is that it has on the one hand
lent some stability to the language while at the same time created avenues for it to
become one of the most free, open, and changing languages in the world.

I believe that this really does have less to do with cultural or economic hegemony--
although clearly that does play some part--than it is the Anglophone world's
fondness for testing boundaries and its general disdain for tradition.

moonlightninja
05 June 2012 7:24pm

68

> Why do we have two ears and one mouth? In order that we should listen
> twice as much – to the Queen's English and all the other languages of
> the world. As she is spoke.

I like this ending.

Otherwise this article seems rather strange especially for someone who clearly has
a good command of English as Miss Reynolds.

The work of the Queen's English Society was not about a mythical past which
never existed. Beautifully written English certainly did exist - one only has to read
the literature - and continues to exist. There is nothing wrong with celebrating it,
preserving it and, one hopes, endowing coming generations with the ability to
understand it and create their own.

Breaking the rules is fine as long as someone knows the rules and why they wish
to break them. There is a world of difference between Picasso's work and if I drew
some weird shapes.

Langauges are very important. Having some agreed rules, albeit flexible ones, aids
comprehension. They also frame our very ideas and throughout history one sees a
connection between language and ideas. And finally languages can be beautiful
things. When people see so-called "text speak" used in formal letters or perhaps
just in this newspaper the strange desire to use the incorrect term "female actor" for
an actress it is perfectly acceptable to react and point out their inelegance and
suggest people try to write better English.

http://www.guardian.co.uk/commentisfree/2012/jun/05/queen-english-language

Study tip

Consider including message board
comments or other interactive
features in your article to
demonstrate your ability to use
different types of sub-form and
register for differing effect.

Study tip

When considering producing a feature article for your coursework, the best approach is to start with some background research. Try to narrow down your focus and be precise about the type of writing you are undertaking. Finding a specific example on which to base your article (a particular columnist, for instance) will help you when thinking about aspects of form and style.

Think about it

News and feature articles often use clever headlines that employ humour, alliteration, ambiguity or wordplay to attract the reader. Thinking up a headline that does this will help to give your article authenticity. Come up with some short headlines for the following articles.

- A news article criticising teenagers' poor use of written English (e.g. 'Writing Wrongs').
- A news article about how the apostrophe is disappearing from written English (e.g. 'We cant see the point').
- A feature article describing how dialects of north-east England are vanishing (e.g. 'Dying Dialects of Durham').

Topic revision summary

- The media text form uses particular language and structural conventions.
- Media texts come in a variety of genres that will affect their use of address, descriptive language, objectivity, sentence and discourse structure.
- Many modern media texts can be found online and can include a range of interactive features that should be included if you choose this type of form.
- Choosing a particular publication on which to base your intervention will help you to match your piece to a particular style and structure.

Educational resources

In this topic you will:

- look at what constitutes an educational text

- look at the conventions of educational texts considering aspects of form and genre

- look at the features and styles typical of educational texts, and the ways in which they may differ

- examine examples of educational texts and consider their use of language.

Introduction

As an A Level student, you will have spent much time using these types of resources – in reading this you are studying an educational text – so this is a genre you should be familiar with. For this reason, writing an educational piece could be a good option for this part of your coursework.

The key purpose of this type of writing is informative, although educational resources can also persuade, instruct and argue and must always look to entertain and interest the reader. This type of writing will lack the forceful persuasive techniques of feature articles but may well explain issues and ideas in more detail.

Unlike media texts, which assume an equal status with their reader, educational texts, by definition, hold an elevated position to the reader in terms of knowledge. This puts certain responsibilities on the writer in terms of the need for an objective and unbiased commentary on issues and debates. Educational writing should not push the reader towards subjective standpoints, although it may instruct on things that can be categorically labelled as right or wrong.

For the purpose of the intervention piece this is complicated, though, by the nature of many of the topics where the key focus is the differing attitudes and opinions on issues of language use. More straightforward styles of writing, such as the revision guide form of Text D, often present these differing views in a clear-cut and objective way, but other styles may adopt a particular perspective on an issue: David Crystal's writing, for instance, tends to adopt a descriptivist stance on debates about language change and variation. The important thing to remember in this kind of writing is that any bias or subjectivity is measured and is supported by a consideration of a range of different viewpoints.

The elevated position of the writer should not spill into the style of writing in the form of a patronising style of address. Fitting the appropriate register to the audience is vital in maintaining the writer–reader relationship.

As with media articles, the best way to start when considering this genre is to research the key features and conventions associated with it.

Extension activity

Choose a non-English-language-related academic topic – perhaps from another A Level you are studying (for example the functions of the brain from biology, or youth culture from sociology).

Using your school/college library, the internet and any other suitable resource, find five examples of texts which discuss or present ideas on your chosen topic. Make a list of the different structural elements that these texts use to convey information or assess understanding.

Audience and form

If you choose to produce an educational text for your coursework, there are two key questions you need to answer:

■ Who are you writing for? (Your audience.)

■ What type of text do you want to write? (Its form.)

Audience

You need to consider factors such as the age of your readership, their educational level and how they will be using the text. A revision guide for GCSE students is going to require a very different approach to a general interest book aimed at adults. Likewise, a resource aimed at speakers of English as a second language will require a different strategy.

In selecting your audience, you need to think about how its expectations, abilities and limitations will affect what you are able to produce.

Your intervention task needs to be aimed at a non-specialist audience, so producing materials aimed at very advanced learners would not be appropriate. Your writing will need to show a transformation of complex ideas into ones accessible by the non-specialist, so a text introducing ideas to students at AS or to a more general adult readership is probably as high as you should go in terms of subject complexity.

On the other hand, your piece needs to make 'an informed contribution to social debates about language'. This means its audience needs to be sophisticated enough to handle reasonably complex ideas and concepts. Consequently, in aiming a text at five-year-olds you would struggle to fulfil the assessment requirements that look for appropriate form, style and content: either the text's style would be too complex for the young audience, or its ideas would be too simple to make an informed contribution.

Form

Educational resources come in a variety of forms that are subtly different in their layout and purpose so you will need to be specific in your choice of piece. Textbooks, general interest books, wall charts, revision materials (such as cue cards), worksheets, webpages, radio programmes and podcasts are all examples of forms that these resources might take. As with media texts, these forms can vary in themselves so it is a good idea to narrow down the type of text you wish to produce by finding a particular type of writing as a model. The textbook and the general interest forms are examined below.

■ Textbooks

In producing a section from a textbook you will need to decide its particular purpose – an introductory piece, an overview of a debate, a summary of key ideas, etc. Fifty years ago, educational texts tended to be fairly formal, straightforward and similar in style. Nowadays, however, these texts vary hugely and employ much more creative language use and structural elements to make them lively and interesting. Even textbooks covering the same topic and aimed at the same audience will differ in terms of style.

A different but connected genre that has gained in popularity in recent years is the general interest book. These types of book aim to combine informative and factual content with an engaging and entertaining style, giving non-specialists a tour of issues, ideas or debates in certain areas. Bill Bryson, the author of Text E, is one of the best known writers of this type of book and has written on a variety of subjects, from the life of Shakespeare to the history of the American nation.

■ Data response exercise 3

Look at the following two extracts, from a textbook and a general interest book, which both focus on the idea of political correctness. Under the following headings, highlight the key similarities and differences in terms of style and technique.

- ■ Structural elements (subsections, **graphology**)
- ■ Address (pronouns, sentence **moods**)
- ■ Complexity and formality (lexis and grammar)
- ■ Tone

Text D

Key terms

Graphology: the visual and layout features of a text – the things you can see that aren't actually linguistic features.

Mood: there are four sentence moods – declarative, exclamatory, imperative and interrogative.

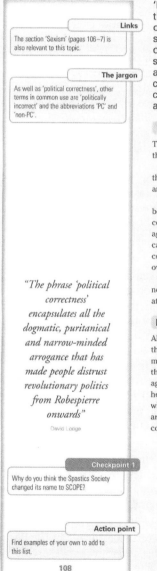

Political correctness

Links

The section 'Sexism' (pages 106–7) is also relevant to this topic.

The jargon

As well as 'political correctness', other terms in common use are 'politically incorrect' and the abbreviations 'PC' and 'non-PC'.

"The phrase 'political correctness' encapsulates all the dogmatic, puritanical and narrow-minded arrogance that has made people distrust revolutionary politics from Robespierre onwards"

David Lodge

Checkpoint 1

Why do you think the Spastics Society changed its name to SCOPE?

Action point

Find examples of your own to add to this list.

108

'Political correctness' is a broad term used to describe the opinions and attitudes of those who are actively opposed to prejudice on such grounds as race, gender, sexual orientation and physical appearance. In terms of language, they also oppose vocabulary that reflects such prejudices. However, many people who hold these attitudes would not describe themselves as politically correct. This is because the term has acquired negative connotations (as explained below) and is now often associated with extremism, aggression and intolerance.

What is political correctness?　○○○

The earliest known use of the term 'political correctness' in print was in the United States in 1970.

The linguist Deborah Cameron, who has researched the history of the term, found that initially it was used ironically by left-wing activists and intellectuals to mock their own attitudes.

During the 1980s, left-wing radicals (especially in the United States) became increasingly concerned with the rights of minority groups and conducted campaigns against discrimination on such grounds as race, age, gender and sexual orientation. Right-wing opponents of these campaigns grouped them together under the disparaging label 'political correctness', and the term came to be associated with extreme, over-zealous attitudes.

It is now often said that it is only the opponents of political correctness who actually use the term. Those who hold 'politically correct' attitudes prefer not to use it because of its negative connotations.

Examples of political correctness　○○○

Although supporters of political correctness distance themselves from the term, it is undoubtedly the case that the radical campaigns and movements of the last 20 years have had a real impact on the language that we use. Words and phrases have been identified as sexist, racist, ageist, ableist (discriminating against those with disabilities) and heightist (discriminating on the basis of height, especially against those who are short). Alternatives have been proposed and in many cases are now in general (if not universal) use. Some examples of politically correct and incorrect usage are shown below.

Incorrect	Eskimo	'Eskimo' is considered offensive because
Correct	Inuit	it is possibly derived from an Indian word meaning 'eaters of raw flesh'.
Incorrect	Spastics Society	The Spastics Society changed its
Correct	SCOPE	name in 1994.
Incorrect	Unemployed	'Unwaged' is sometimes preferred
Correct	Unwaged	because not being in paid employment does not necessarily mean that time is not usefully employed.
Incorrect	Christian name	'Christian name' is considered offensive
Correct	First name	to non-Christians.

A. Gardiner, A Level Study Guide, *2000*

Text E

… apart from the perceived decline of educational standards, almost nothing in recent years has excited more debate or awakened a greater polarity of views than the vaguely all-embracing issue that has come to be known as *political correctness*.

Since 1991, when the term appears to have sprung wholly formed into the language, journals and newspapers have devoted much space to reports that have ranged for the most part from the mildly derisive to the openly antagonistic. Some have treated it as a kind of joke (a typical example: a *Newsweek* report in 1991 that pondered whether restaurant customers could expect soon to be brought a *womenu* by a *waitron* or *waitperson*), while others see it as something much graver. Under leading headlines like 'The New Ayatollahs' (*US News & World Report*), 'Politically Correct Speech: An Oxymoron' (*Editor and Publisher*) and 'The Word Police' (*Library Journal*), many publications have assayed the matter with a mixture of outrage and worry.

Most of the arguments distil down to two beliefs: that the English language is being shanghaied by people of linguistically narrow views, and that their verbal creations are burdening the nation with ludicrously sanitized neologisms that are an embarrassment to civilized discourse.

Two authors, Henry Beard and Christopher Cerf, have made much capital (in every sense of the word) out of these absurdities with their satirical and popular *Official Politically Correct Dictionary and Handbook*, which offers several hundred examples of absurd euphemisms designed to free the language of the slightest taint of bias. Among the examples they cite: *differently hirsute* for bald, *custody suite* for a prison cell, *chemically inconvenienced* for intoxicated, *alternative dentation* for false teeth, and *stolen nonhuman animal carrier* for milkman. What becomes evident only when the reader troubles to scan the notes on sources is that almost all of these excessively cautious terminologies, including those just listed, were made up by the authors themselves.

This might be excused as a bit of harmless, if fundamentally pointless, fun except that these entries have often been picked up by others and transmitted as gospel.

Most of the genuine examples of contrived neologisms that the authors cite are in fact either justifiable on grounds of sensitivity (*developmentally challenged* for mentally retarded), widely accepted (*date rape, pro-choice*), never intended by the creator to be taken seriously (*terminological inexactitude* for lie), the creations of jargon-loving bodies like sociologists or the military (*temporary cessation of hostilities* for peace), drawn from secondary sources of uncertain reliability (*personipulate* for manipulate, taken from another book on political correctness, but not otherwise verified), or become ridiculous only when given a barbed definition (suggesting that *wildlife management* is a common euphemism for 'killing, or permitting the hunting, of animals').

What remain after all this are no more than a few – a very few – scattered examples of genuine ridiculousness by extremist users of English, mostly from the women's movement and mostly involving the removal of 'man' from a variety of common terms – turning manhole into *femhole*, menstruate into *femstruate*, and so on.

I don't deny that there is much that is worthy of ridicule in the PC movement, but it seems to me that this is a matter that deserves rather more in the way of thoughtful debate and less in the way of dismissive harrumphing or feeble jokes about waitrons and womenus.

Bill Bryson, Made in America, *1998*

Further reading

Look at 'Political Correctness – The Rules' on page 72 of Terry Deary's *Wicked Words* (Scholastic, 2011) for a different take on how the idea of political correctness can be addressed in a humorous but educational way.

Topic revision summary

■ Educational texts come in a wide variety of forms and genres.

■ The textbook genre usually adopts an objective standpoint and fulfils the purpose to inform.

■ Other genres may take a particular stance on an issue or debate but this must be considered and fully supported.

■ You need to consider your intended audience and how this will shape your use of language.

Fictional texts

Introduction to fiction texts

One of the most challenging genres to produce for an intervention is a fictional text. Writing this type of text will allow you to use a whole range of creative language techniques and to demonstrate the ability to employ innovative and inventive strategies. But these types of text can be difficult to do well and require much thought and planning.

The main issue with producing this type of text is how to incorporate a contribution to a language debate into an engaging and entertaining piece of fiction. Your piece must deal with language issues in reasonable depth whilst employing aspects of, for example, plotting, characterisation and drama. It would be easy to fall into the trap of either producing an engaging fictional text that fails to debate language in enough depth, or writing a detailed overview of an issue which lacks the dramatic elements expected in this type of writing. You will need to consider carefully how a short story or extract from a longer piece is going to deal with meaningful issues while conforming to the expectations of fiction.

Short stories

The short story is a genre often used to illustrate an issue through an engaging and entertaining narrative. Plot, character, dialogue and description can be used to present a debate explicitly or to implicitly persuade the reader into taking up a certain viewpoint. Take a look at some key elements.

Plot

The short story requires a plot that will engage and interest the reader. Plots can be complex with many dramatic twists and turns or relatively simple focusing on a specific event or situation. With only 1,250 words available to you, choosing something fairly straightforward would be advisable – if you try to overcomplicate your plot you may end up with a story that fails to address a key issue in enough depth because of the need to get everything in. In fact, short stories often leave much unsaid, using subtle techniques to present ideas or implications. Look at the (very) short story below. How does it create drama in just a few words?

 The last man on Earth sat alone in a room. There was a knock on the door …

The 'horror story' by Fredric Brown uses the reader's imagination to 'fill in the blanks' relying on what remains unsaid for its dramatic impact. We are left wondering who or what is on the other side of the door. We imagine what the man might be thinking and place ourselves in his situation imagining how we would feel. This dramatic moment in time points forward to a variety of possible outcomes creating suspense and tension.

Of course, the story does not deal with a language issue, and is far too short for a coursework piece, but it illustrates quite neatly how simplicity and implication can be effective creative tools.

Character

Short stories rely on creating a dramatic relationship between reader and character. For a story to be engaging, the reader must have some emotional involvement with its characters. In the story above, we sympathise with the last man on Earth despite our almost total lack of knowledge of who he is. The relationship doesn't have to be a sympathetic one, though. A writer may encourage us to dislike a particular character in order to make a point about a wider issue. The important thing is that we must react to characters on an emotional level, imagining they are living breathing flesh and blood.

With your limited word count, it is a good idea not to introduce too many characters into your story. Stories focusing on the thoughts, feelings and experiences of one character, or on the relationship between two characters, are effective in creating a well-focused and dramatic narrative.

Narrative

One decision to make is the narrative perspective you are going to take. Narrators can be first person, telling their stories through their own words, or third person relating the story from an external perspective. First-person narrative can be used effectively to create emotional intensity as this type of narrator tends to be more subjective and human. This type of narrator can also be flawed, and weaknesses can be illustrated through the narrative. Some stories employ a first-person narrator whom we are meant to dislike or feel ambivalent towards. They can be used to represent a contradictory standpoint from the one the writer is urging us to adopt. The limited and personal perspective of the first-person narrator is effective in creating intensity and emotional involvement.

Third-person narrative is more useful for presenting an overview of an issue or event. The objective standpoint of this method allows the thoughts and feelings of more than one character to be expressed. Third-person narrators can range across space and time, looking at things from a variety of angles. The relationship the third-person narrative establishes with its characters can be used to create drama. Some adopt a sympathetic position, empathising with character and telling the story from their emotional perspective. Others take a more distant stance, describing events objectively with little emotional attachment. This can be very effective, as illustrated in the story above. The distant and emotional tone of the narrative clashes with the dramatic nature of the situation, the contrast of style and content adding to the atmosphere of suspense.

Another thing to bear in mind is the use of direct speech. Some stories may use no speech, focusing on the description of events or the feelings of characters for their effect. Others may employ direct speech, perhaps to present conversations, debates or conflicts. Representing spoken language convincingly through direct speech, though, is quite a tricky skill to master.

Style and tone

Short stories can vary hugely in their style so, as with the other types of text we have looked at, it is important to be specific about the type of story you are going to write. Specifying an audience for your story, in terms of age for example, is important in thinking about style.

Some writers use extensive metaphor and dense visual description to create drama in their stories. Others use a sparser style, creating impact through the clarity and simplicity of the writing. Writing in the style of a particular writer is a useful way of approaching this consideration. It will give you a blueprint that will help in the planning of your story and will allow you to make comparisons between your piece and the style of the chosen writer, helping you to assess the success of your writing.

Tone is another important consideration. You may decide to use a serious tone to create dramatic impact. Alternatively, you may think that your story would be better using a humorous or playful tone.

Data response exercise 4

Look at the two examples of fictional writing below, both focusing on issues of identity and representation. Text F is taken from a novel about a girl's struggles with her dual identity as a Muslim and teenager living in Australia. In this extract she is considering the effect that her decision to wear the hijab (a veil that covers the head and chest) will have on her relationship with her school friends. Text G focuses on how a young boy deals with his partial blindness.

How do both pieces use language to create dramatic effect? Think about plot, character, narrative, style and tone.

Consider the suitability of each for an intervention submission.

Text F

Does my head look big in this?

I'm ready for the next step, I'm sure of that. But I'm still nervous. Agh! There are a million different voices in my head scaring me off.

But why should I be scared? As I do my all-time best thinking through lists, I think I should set this one out as follows:

1 The Religious/Scriptures/Sacred stuff: I believe in Allah/God's commandments contained in the Koran. God says men and women should act and dress modestly. The way I see it, I'd rather follow God's fashion dictates than some solarium-tanned ugly old fart in Milan who's getting by on a pretty self-serving theory of less is more when it comes to female dress.

2 Okay, cool, I've got modesty covered.

3 Now the next thing, and it's really very simple, is that while I'm not going to abandon my fashion sense – you better believe I'd never give up my Portmans and Sportsgirls shopping sprees – I'm sick of obsessing about my body, what guys are going to think about my cleavage and calves and shoulder to hip ratio, and for the love of everything that is good and holy I am really sick of worrying what people are going to think if I put on a kilo or have a pimple. I mean, home room on Monday morning can be such a stress attack. There's one girl, Tia Tamos, the resident Year Eleven bitch, who has a field day if you have a pimple. You might as well call a funeral parlour because she makes it seem like you'd be better off dead than walk around with a zit. And some of the guys have this disgusting Monday morning habit of talking about the pornos they watched on the weekend loud enough so us girls can hear. They're the biggest bloody stirrers. According to them, fat chicks should be deported, girls should starve and implants should be a civic duty. Then we all get into this massive fight about respecting girls for their minds not their bra sizes. Well that basically has them sharing around an asthma pump because they lose their breath laughing.

4 At this point, I should say that this is no longer a list and that I am well and truly writing an essay.

I can't imagine what my class will say if I walk in with it on. Oh boy does this give the walking-into-class-naked dream another dimension. Except in my case, I'm not walking in naked. I'm walking in fully covered and yet I'm still breaking out into a sweat. They're all going to freak out and I'm going to go through school officially labelled the biggest loser of all time. Come to think of it, though, it's not like I'm not used to being the odd one out. I attended a Catholic primary school because we lived too far away from an Islamic school and my parents didn't have the time to travel the distance twice a day. Plus, all that 'love thy neighbour', 'respect your parents' and 'cleanliness is next to Godliness' stuff was basically what I would have been taught in R.E. in an Islamic school anyway. I went from Prep to Grade Six as the only Muslim kid at St Mary Immaculate where we had to sing the Lord's Prayer and declare salvation through Jesus every morning at assembly. Not that there's anything wrong with that. If you're Catholic, by all means sing as loudly as you want. When I was in primary school, different coloured socks were enough difference to legitimise a good tease. So when you're a non-pork eating, Eid-celebrating Mossie (as in taunting nickname for Muslim, not mosquito) with an unpronounceable surname and a mum who picks you up from school wearing a hijab and Gucci sunnies, and drives a car with an 'Islam means peace' bumper sticker, a quiet existence is impossible.

Hey Amal, why does a sneeze sound like a letter in the Arabic language?

Hey Amal, want a cheese and bacon chip?

Hey Amal, do you have a camel as a pet?

Hey Amal, did you notice the sub teacher called you 'Anal' at rollcall this morning?

Forget sanity if you're the only one with a pass to sit in the back of church during service

Randa Abdel-Fattah, 'Does My Head Look Big In This'

Text G

A Time to Dance

NELSON, WITH a patch over one eye, stood looking idly into Mothercare's window. The sun was bright behind him and made a mirror out of the glass. He looked at his patch with distaste and felt it with his finger. The Elastoplast was rough and dry and he disliked the feel of it. Bracing himself for the pain, he ripped it off and let a yell out of him. A woman looked down at him curiously to see why he had made the noise, but by that time he had the patch in his pocket. He knew without looking that some of his eyebrow would be on it.

He had spent most of the morning in the Gardens avoiding distant uniforms, but now that it was coming up to lunchtime he braved it on to the street. He had kept his patch on longer than usual because his mother had told him the night before that if he didn't wear it he would go 'stark, staring blind'.

Nelson was worried because he knew what it was like to be blind. The doctor at the eye clinic had given him a box of eye patches that would last most of his lifetime. Opticludes. One day Nelson had worn two and tried to get to the end of the street and back. It was a terrible feeling. He had to hold his head back in case it bumped anything and keep waving his hands in front of him backwards and forwards like windscreen wipers. He kept trampling on tin cans and heard them trundle emptily away. Broken glass crackled under his feet and he could not figure out how close to the wall he was. Several times he heard footsteps approaching, slowing down as if they were going to attack him in his helplessness, then walking away. One of the footsteps even laughed. Then he heard a voice he knew only too well.

'Jesus, Nelson, what are you up to this time?' It was his Mother. She led him back to the house with her voice blaring in his ear.

She was always shouting. Last night, for instance, she had started into him for watching T.V. from the side. She had dragged him round to the chair in front of it.

'That's the way the manufacturers make the sets. They put the picture on the front. But oh no, that's not good enough for our Nelson. He has to watch it from the side. Squint, my arse, you'll just go blind – stark, staring blind.'

Nelson had then turned his head and watched it from the front. She had never mentioned the blindness before. Up until now all she had said was, 'If you don't wear them patches that eye of yours will turn in till it's looking at your brains. God knows, not that it'll have much to look at.'

B. MacLaverty, A Time to Dance, *1999*

Fig. 3 *MacLaverty uses different techniques to present ideas about disability*

Topic revision summary

- You need to think carefully about how a language debate can be incorporated into a fictional text.
- When planning your text, you need to make decisions about narrative techniques and genre conventions.
- You need to consider your intended audience and how this will shape your use of language.
- Using a particular writer or text as a model will help you to be clearer about your intended goals.

Coursework preparation

☑

In this section you have explored the features and conventions of a range of texts suitable for an intervention piece. You now need to think about the type of text you want to produce, and the language debate on which it will focus. Before you start this process, this topic will remind you of the requirements of the intervention task and will give you the opportunity to examine some sample work and to assess it against the marking criteria.

▦ AQA's requirements

- ▦ You should write about a language debate in a particular form for a non-specialist audience.

- ▦ The purpose of your piece should be to inform, argue, instruct or persuade.

- ▦ The topic for the intervention should come from the subject matter that you studied for Unit 3.

- ▦ You need to produce one or two texts totalling 1,250 words.

▦ How the work is assessed

The coursework will be assessed using only one AO – AO4.

AO4: Demonstrate expertise and creativity in the use of English in a range of different contexts, informed by linguistic study.

This AO can be broken down into three distinct parts.

- ▦ **Form:** an assessment of how accurately your piece mirrors the structural conventions of a particular type of text.

- ▦ **Style:** an assessment of how the language you employ adopts a register suitable to its form and genre (you will also be rewarded for using a creative, interesting and effective style).

- ▦ **Content:** an assessment of how well your piece presents, considers and evaluates a debate about language.

The intervention piece is marked out of 30 (10 marks for each of the above elements) and represents 10 per cent of your full A Level (20 per cent of the A2 course).

▦ What to do next

Having worked through this section, you should have at least a rough idea of the text you want to produce. In narrowing this down further, consider the following.

Selecting a text

- ▦ Are you going to produce one or two texts?

- ▦ What kind of text/s do you enjoy reading or writing?

- ▦ Is there a form or genre that you particularly do or don't want to write in?

Having decided on the type of text you wish to produce, find examples of the text type and study its conventions in terms of form, genre and style. Try to be precise about the specific text you are looking to produce – in planning an online article for example, choose examples from a particular newspaper on which to base its style. Make sure that you are confident in its characteristic use of structure and features – draw up a checklist of features to help you in planning and drafting your piece (see Table 3).

Table 3

Sub-ed online article checklist	
Style	
No use of first-person singular	☑
Rhetorical questions used to highlight key ideas	☑
Subjective stance	☑
Persuasive language	☑
Forceful and evaluative conclusion	☑
Use of statistics to support views	☑
Use of irony and humour	☑
Structure	
Headline sets out debate	☑
Use of images to present debate	☑
Use of embedded features (e.g. related articles list)	☑
Use of hyperlinks and other interactive devices	☑

Selecting a debate

Is there a language debate from Unit 3 which you are particularly interested in? If so, is this language debate something about which you feel confident in terms of your knowledge and understanding? Once you have decided on the particular debate on which you will focus, go back through your notes and Unit 3 of this book to ensure that you have a firm grasp of the issues and ideas involved. Do some additional research into your chosen debate – ask your teacher where you can find other sources to extend your knowledge and understanding.

A sample response

Have a look at this student response to an intervention task. The text is a feature article, discussing a book on a prescriptivist view of language use. Read through the Printed and online articles topic on pages 182–92 to remind yourself of the conventions of this type of text, and then make an assessment of how effective the intervention is in discussing a language debate in an effective and convincing way.

Exemplar student intervention piece

The weighty problem of language

John Smith reports on the publication of a new book on language use by broadcaster John Humphrys.

Does today's misuse of language, incorrect grammar and the constant incoming of neologisms anger and frustrate you? If so, then you are not alone.

As a strong prescriptivist, someone who believes in conserving language 'rules', broadcaster John Humphrys' frustration with the growing misuse of the English language has motivated him to write a book, released today, sharing his strong opinions and beliefs.

Today, the English language is constantly changing and this change is something that is impossible to ignore; these changes in language provoke strong views and emotions, some, like Humphrys, seeing it as a deterioration while others see it as a progressive process. Some people link these changes in language to what they see as falling standards in society. Others feel that change is inevitable and that we should concentrate on how language is changing, and not make judgements on how good or bad these changes are.

Along with many other prescriptivists such as Lynne Truss, who published her bestseller *Eats, Shoots and Leaves* in 2001, John Humphrys, who presents the *Today* programme on Radio 4, believes we should stick to rules that identify correct language usage and strongly disapproves of uses of language that break these rules.

Prescriptivism is not the only view of language change, though, with language experts such as John Simpson, chief editor of *The Oxford English Dictionary*, taking a more liberal view. 'The *OED* is descriptive rather than prescriptive, and monitors the use of language' Simpson says. He has no objection to entering a word that Humphrys identifies as 'bad', saying 'if it is widely used' then it is worthy of inclusion.

John Humphrys, though, is well known for his strong belief in prescriptivism. In the past he has compared our language to 'obesity' and stated that people are fed on 'junk words'. By using these metaphors, Humphrys demonstrates his belief that the words entering our language are causing a growing problem that should cause major concern.

In his book, Humphrys is particularly scathing about adding prepositions to verbs where they are not necessary, for example 'test out', 'raise up', 'enter in' or 'double up'. To Humphrys, this tautology, the use of redundant language, adds to the 'obesity' problem which he sees facing language.

Humphrys has also shown his disapproval of the euphemism, which he refers to as 'another enemy of good, simple language'. A euphemism is a mild or inoffensive way of describing something unpleasant. Humphrys talks about how the simple word 'problem' is avoided due to its negative connotations. Builders instead use 'build quality issues' or the word becomes changed to 'challenges'.

On his radio programme, Humphrys has shown his view that euphemisms are ridiculous, by sarcastically correcting himself 'Did I say meat? Try protein packs, maybe'. He states that 'butcher will be next to go', and goes on to describe how our grandchildren will be encouraged to think all meat comes naturally wrapped in cellophane.

In the business world, which he sees as a key enemy of efficient language, Humphrys objects to 'down-sizing' or 'cash flow problem' being used. He explains that euphemisms have always been around but what seems new today is the number of new words that add nothing to language.

Prescriptivism is not a new thing: it became firmly established as a view of language in the 18th century with Dr Johnson's famous dictionary and numerous books on grammar usage. Many efforts were made to standardise the language, making it consistent. Numerous rules and definitions of correct and incorrect usage were set out in books of vocabulary and grammar. Humphrys' new book carries on this tradition, though he is not optimistic about his chances. 'Ultimately, no doubt, we shall communicate with a series of grunts,' he says, 'and the evolutionary wheel will have turned full circle.'

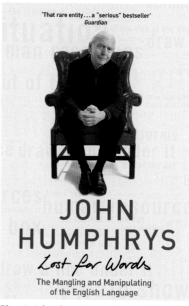

'That rare entity…a "serious" bestseller'
Guardian

JOHN HUMPHRYS
Lost for Words
The Mangling and Manipulating of the English Language

Fig. 4 *A book review can be an effective way of evaluating language issues in an intervention piece*

Humphrys' new book, *Lost for Words: The Mangling and Manipulating of the English Language*, is published today by Hodder & Stoughton, priced £14.99.

Comment

AO4 Demonstrate expertise and creativity in the use of English in a range of different contexts, informed by linguistic study.

This one assessment objective is split into three sections.

Form

The piece uses an effective and convincing form. It employs an introduction and evaluative conclusion, with the intervening paragraphs supplying increasing detail on the issues surrounding the debate. Its structure is cohesive and well shaped and it employs features appropriate for this type of media text such as a headline and quotations from the individuals concerned. Its use of direct address in the first paragraph is suitable for the feature article genre and its objective stance conforms to its informative intent.

Style

The register uses a convincing level of formality, and the vocabulary is sophisticated enough to present complex ideas that are explained and discussed in a manner suited to the non-specialist audience. The writing is fluent and accurate with the numerous quotations neatly embedded into the body of the text. Many of the quotations employed use metaphorical language which makes the piece a lively and interesting read.

Content

In discussing the book, the piece makes an informed response to the debate about prescriptivism in language use. It presents ideas from a number of perspectives and positions and explains their relevance and the historical context of views on correct language use. It incorporates wider discussion of the issues without losing sight of its main focus, the discussion of Humphrys' book.

▍ Beginning your own work

Having worked through the material here, you should now be ready to get started on your own piece. Look back through this section of the book to help you in your selection of a particular form and genre, and go back to Unit 3 to consider what language debate you wish to focus on. Once these decisions have been made, produce a plan listing how each part of your text will contribute to the debate in question – ask yourself what each section or paragraph of writing will deal with and how these sections fit together to give the piece a convincing shape and structure.

▍ Further reading

General

Bryson, B. *Mother Tongue*, Penguin, 1991

Crystal, D. *Making Sense of Grammar*, Pearson Longman, 2004

Crystal, D. *Rediscover Grammar*, Pearson Longman, 2004

Crystal, D. *The Stories of English*, Penguin, 2005

Russell, S. *Grammar, Structure and Style*, Oxford University Press, 2001

Thorne, S. *Mastering Advanced English Language*, Macmillan, 1997

Language intervention

Morkane, S. *Original Writing*, Routledge, 2004

Shuttleworth, J. *Living Language: Editorial Writing*, Hodder & Stoughton, 1999

Thorne, S. *Mastering Advanced English Language*, Macmillan, 1997

▍ Topic revision summary

- ▪ Be clear on the AQA requirements of the intervention coursework.
- ▪ Choose a type of text that you enjoy reading or writing.
- ▪ Choose a language debate from Unit 3 which you are particularly interested in.
- ▪ Plan your piece carefully in terms of its structure and content.

Feedback

This part of the book provides all the feedback for the Coursework activities and Data response exercises in Unit 4, Section B.

Choosing a topic

Coursework activity 1

Some suggestions for these areas are listed below, although you may have come up with ones not listed here. This demonstrates the scope available to you in your selection of topic.

- **Why language changes**
  - Text messaging and English spelling
  - The effect of political correctness on English
  - War, politics and the euphemism
  - Americanisms and their effect on the English language
  - English and the effect of youth culture
  - Technology and its effect on English
  - War, colonialism and their effect on English
  - Globalisation and its effect on English pronunciation
- **Language and social variation**
  - Cockney rhyming slang and other coded varieties
  - The rise of Estuary English
  - Jargon in the medical profession
  - Management speak – attitudes and views
  - Variation and youth culture
  - Changing attitudes towards RP
  - Languages and anti-languages
  - Sociolect and status

Printed and online articles

Data response exercise 1

1 Address

News articles do not explicitly refer to the reader or writer in their address. First-person and second-person pronouns are never used unless they form part of a quotation from a participant in the story. Consequently they tend to utilise third-person address and are written mainly in the declarative mood (e.g. 'Parents can breathe a sigh of relief', 'Mrs August responded').

2 Descriptive/factual language

The headline uses a short introductory exclamatory clause to create dramatic impact and attract the reader's attention before going on to summarise the story's main point. This type of strategy is common in news article headlines, though they also often use wordplay or puns to make their stories seem more intriguing. A short quote from the school trust's deputy chief executive is embedded into the headline, giving one perspective on the linguistic debate that the article is covering.

Description tends to be functional and not elaborate. Detailed description is usually used only when it is important to the story

or within quotations, which are often used to get ideas and opinions from those directly involved.

Further detail about events, issues, places or people is often used to increase the understanding of the non-specialist audience, often through relative clauses and lengthy noun phrases (e.g. 'which has 1,100 students aged from 11 to 18', 'Penistone & Stocksbridge MP Angela Smith'). Ellipsis of relative pronouns (which/that/who) in relative clauses is often used, along with simpler and shorter relative phrases, to reduce word length.

3 Objectivity, bias and tone

News articles tend to be, at least explicitly, unbiased and objective. They attempt to give an overview of a story and often look at it from different perspectives. They can, though, use their structure, use of quotation or description, etc. to give an implicit bias on a story. Their tone is generally serious, although this depends on the topic – an article about research into language and youth culture, for instance, may contain elements of humour or irony. This article stands back from the debate, allowing the quotes from those involved to paint the full picture of the issue being debated. The exclamatory clause in the headline, could suggest a sense of shock on the part of the writer, pointing, perhaps, to an implicit critical stance on the decision of the school to ban slang, although it could just as easily be seen as a tongue in cheek parody of the reaction of the local MP, who disagrees with the decision.

4 Sentence/clause/phrase structure

Sentences tend to use complex clause and phrase structures mainly because of their use of referencing through relative clauses and phrases, as already mentioned. The sentence structure allows the article to build the story in a logical manner, inserting additional detail or information where necessary. In the paragraph below, the essential elements of the sentence are given in bold.

The United Learning Trust which runs the school, which has 1,100 students aged from 11 to 18 and is in a working-class area of the city, **believes slang creates the wrong impression during interviews**.

Kathy August, deputy chief executive of the trust, **said: 'We want to make sure that our youngsters are not just leaving school with the necessary A to Cs in GCSEs but that they also have a whole range of employability skills.'**

The phrases and clauses not in bold are not integral to the meaning of the sentence but add additional information as the article progresses. This is a standard technique in news reporting.

5 Discourse structure

Because of the time and space constraints on the writing of news articles (they are written daily to strict deadlines) and the way that they are read, they have a unique structure. Rather than having a clear introduction, middle and conclusion they tend to repeat the story in each paragraph, though with more detail added in each successive one. This means they can be 'chopped' at the end of any paragraph to match the available space in the newspaper, and this also allows the reader to get a good grasp of the story from just the first few paragraphs. This gives news articles a cumulative feel, with information increasing in detail and complexity as the story progresses. This article uses contrasting quotes from those with opposing views on slang to juxtapose the key issues, each new quote adding additional layers to the contrasting perspectives on the debate.

Data response exercise 2

1 Address

The headline uses antithesis ('ain't'/'cultural diversity') to mimic the two language styles that it is discussing. As with all media texts, the headlines of feature articles often employ wordplay, puns and humour to create an interesting opening to the debate in question.

The piece uses both the first person ('I sigh over essays', 'The other thing that I value') and an implied second person through direct address and inclusive first-person plural pronouns ('provided we know', 'let's add in words'). These plural pronouns, along with the writer's frequent references to herself, set up a more informal register and create a close reader–writer relationship. In responding to issues around language use, the writer refers to her own life ('my divided skirt', 'I live in Gloucestershire') to establish a conversational tone.

The comments, similarly, employ first-person address, emphasising the writers' engagement with the issues being debated.

2 Descriptive language

Informal and emotive words and constructions are used ('kaput', 'going to the dogs') to emphasise that this is a personal opinion piece. The writer presents views as more instinctive and spontaneous than the considered arguments of the editorial or op-ed article.

Other techniques used are metaphor ('she carries on her lonely crusade', 'the crossbred product') to personify ideas, and the mimicking of linguistic styles ('put out the trash, dude', ''Pon my word') to create caricatures of people and ideas which help in presenting the debate in a more arresting way.

3 Objectivity, bias and tone

Like the editorial, the article takes a particular stance on an issue ('I care more that my students think for themselves') but is less explicit in its persuasive intent. The extent to which an article will attempt to persuade will vary, but in this example the writer seems to give an overview of issues before coming to a, perhaps surprising, conclusion.

The tone is light in places, and humour is used to illustrate aspects of the debate. However, the writer does not overdo this, and her use of emotive language to illustrate her views ('I care', 'respect for the interests and feelings of others') implies that the issues at hand are important and not to be trivialised.

The comments present different levels of formality and tone, from the humorous 'Miss Spelt was the Roman Bread Association's face of AD 57' to the formal 'one hopes, endowing coming generations with the ability to understand it'.

4 Sentence/clause/phrase structure

As with the other articles, a variety of sentence structures and types are used for different purposes. Declaratives explain the nature of the issues, and interrogatives are used to pose views and create standpoints. Both the main article and the comments

that follow use quite complex multi-clause structures, the writers perhaps demonstrating that they are sophisticated users of written English – this being the main focus of the debate.

5 Discourse structure

The structure reflects that of a debate, in which the issue of declining standards of English is raised in the first section, arguments criticising them are put forward in the second, and counter-arguments given in the final passages, which present the writer's viewpoint. The comments, because of their varying length and focus, again use a variety of structures, though they often add to one perspective only on the debate so tend to be linear in their format.

6 Mode

The writer includes lexis one would expect to see in the spoken mode ('going to the dogs', 'dude'), though these are often contained in the direct speech that presents different English styles. Although used here satirically, this adds to the informal nature of the opening of the piece, helping to establish the relationship between writer and audience. This contrasts with the more formal approach later on in the article where a more sophisticated lexis and form fits in with more serious tone.

Writers of this type of piece often contrast informal and simple language with more formal complex expressions creating a mixed register that is, at the same time, friendly and sophisticated. This is common in this type of article where the writer attempts to present both educated and streetwise credentials.

■ Educational resources

Data reponse exercise 3

■ Structural elements (subsections, graphology)

Text D uses clearly differentiated structural elements for different purposes. It introduces the topic in a short opening section that outlines key ideas and concepts. The presentation of concepts through detailed examples helps learners to understand complex ideas such as political correctness. Having presented the main ideas, Text D illustrates and develops them through a section that looks at how the debate relates to specific words and phrases. Ideas are further extended through the use of supporting elements.

Text D uses definitions of key terms and a quotation that introduces a specific viewpoint on the debate. By using this quote, the piece avoids taking a subjective stance on the issues and retains its position of objectivity. Text D also employs Checkpoint and Action sections. These have a subtly different purpose from the informative nature of the main text, seeking to raise questions or encourage the reader into further research or extension work.

In terms of structure, Text E does not use subsections, but it does present the key ideas in a logical and systematic way. It begins with a definition of political correctness and a discussion of its origins, moves on to give examples of words and phrases, presents a range of views on the topic, and finishes by stating its own position on the debate.

In terms of graphology, both articles vary their use of fonts or styles. Text D uses different text sizes and fonts to separate different sections – a larger font size for the introduction, and italics for the quotation. The varied styles give the piece a lively and interesting appearance that aims to encourage readers. The different sections are separated by areas of empty space; cramming too much information onto a page, or laying out writing in long continuous prose passages, can be off-putting to the potential reader of this type of text. Text E, though less varied, uses italics to highlight the examples of politically correct terms and to label publications and books from which it quotes.

Address (pronouns, sentence moods)

The two pieces adopt different types of address that reflect their specific purposes and audiences. The main body of Text D does not attempt to directly address the reader, and the writer does not refer to him/herself. This gives the piece a professional and academic feel, which is suitable for the level and type of the ideas discussed. Some of the subsections (e.g. the Action point) do employ second-person address ('find examples of your own') and this fits in with their purpose of pointing the reader towards wider thinking or extension work.

Text E, though largely written in the third person, does use first-person address in places to emphasise the author's stance on the debate ('I don't deny …'). This gives the article a more conversational tone that suits its content, audience and its broader 'educational' purpose.

Both texts use the declarative mood throughout to explain ideas and issues – this is the only sentence mood employed in Text E. Text D, however, uses interrogatives and imperatives in the Checkpoint and Action point sections where the reader is directly addressed. These moods are used to raise questions or to suggest further avenues of research.

Complexity and formality (lexis and grammar)

Both texts use a fairly high level of complexity, both lexically and grammatically. Words such as 'disparaging', 'extremist', and 'over-zealous' (Text D), 'sanitized', 'satirical' and 'polarity' (Text E) are in keeping with the sophisticated reader. Both use some linguistic terms – 'connotations', 'linguist' (Text D)'; 'euphemism' and 'neologism' (Text E) – on the grounds that the reader will be at an advanced educational level and will have some basic knowledge of the kind of technical language terms that fall within the vocabulary of a reader with a good general knowledge. Any terminology considered specialist, however, needs to be explained and illustrated to fit in with the informative and educational purpose of the text and its non-specialist audience.

Grammatically, Text D uses a complex structure. Multi-clause sentences help ideas and concepts to be discussed and developed, though simple sentences are used to make key points clearly and succinctly ('the earliest known use of … 1970').

Text E also employs grammatical complexity, which is needed to build its presentation of the complex debate. Sentences are often quite long especially where listing is used to challenge the examples of 'absurd' terms in the *Official Politically Correct Dictionary and Handbook* ('Most of the genuine … animals'); the length of this sentence, in which each example is considered and rejected, gives a cumulative persuasive effect helping to manoeuvre the reader towards a particular perspective.

Tone

The tone of both texts, through their address and formality, is professional and serious. Again, this is suitable for the more-sophisticated readership. The use of first person in Text E reduces its formality somewhat, but this is used only towards the end, where the writer presents an opinion. Text D takes an objective stance on the debate but does illustrate differing views through quotes and feature sections. The considered but subjective stance of Text E is reflected through the use of modal verbs ('This might be excused …'), emotive noun phrases ('genuine ridiculousness', 'absurd euphemisms', 'barbed definition', 'feeble jokes') and metaphorical verbs ('when the reader troubles …', 'language is being shanghaied …', 'awakened a greater polarity…').

Text D fits all of the criteria for an intervention piece and is a good example of a conventional but effective educational text. Text E illustrates how creativity and originality can be introduced into this form, and how conventions and expectations of educational writing vary with particular genres.

Fictional texts

Data response exercise 4

Both extracts focus on a particular character, their thoughts and their relationships with others. This limited focus allows the reader to gain a good understanding of character, encouraging an emotional response. Text F uses a first-person narrative, whereas Text G employs a third-person narrative, which seems sympathetic to Nelson and his struggles. Both techniques tell us the central characters' stories from their own points of view. They are different, though, in their positioning. Amal, the first-person narrator of Text F, gives us a real sense of the dual nature of her identity, highlighting her independence but also her doubts about her decision to wear the hijab. Text F uses humour, both in the situations described and the language used to do so, but the humour has a serious purpose, attempting to make important points about the nature of identity and the way individuals are represented. In Text G, the narrator is close to the main character. There is no separation and, at times, the narrative becomes a blend of first and third person ('She was always shouting'), exaggerating the proximity of narrator and character.

The 'plot' of Text F involves the narrator telling us of her life as a Muslim in 21st century Australia. Although nothing actually 'happens', the presentation of Amal's teenage years gives us an insight into her character. In glimpsing various aspects of her life, we are able to see her in a number of different situations, which allow us to explore her relationship with her diverse identities of devout Muslim and ordinary teenager.

In Text G, the plot focuses on Nelson's attempts to avoid being caught truanting. The narrator intrudes into his thoughts and feelings which, along with the descriptions of his behaviour, creates a sympathetic bond between character and reader. Text G uses detailed description of Nelson's actions, whereas in Text F we are given more of an overview of Amal's character. Both techniques, though, establish a bond.

Both characters' struggles with their identity are presented through their relationships with others. Text G uses direct speech to illustrate the seeming indifference of Nelson's mother to his situation, her harsh words intensifying our feelings of sympathy for him. Amal's relationships with other teenagers and her family give us an insight into the dilemma that she faces.

Despite their differences, both pieces are successful in illustrating ideas about identity. The humorous approach of Text F gives a positive representation of how Amal deals with her situation, as well as identifying the problems faced by those who are seen as different from 'the norm'. Text G, through its more serious tone, presents a less optimistic picture, but in creating a sympathetic response in the reader, highlights the issues in question.

Text G is a good example of effective fictional writing. It uses skilful descriptive and narrative techniques and would score highly on the form and style elements of assessment. But, in its present form, it would not be suitable for an intervention piece as, despite dealing with aspects of disability, it does not address these issues from a language perspective and would fail to score highly on the content aspect of the assessment criteria.

Text F is also an effective piece of fictional writing. It is lively and interesting, has a convincing form, and uses language in creative and interesting ways to communicate its message. It begins to present ideas about language and identity in a

way that would be accessible to a non-specialist audience, especially towards the end where Amal discusses the insults she receives from her fellow students. However, because it only touches on these and does not consider linguistic theories around representation, such as pejoration or reclamation, it would also struggle to score highly on the content aspect of the marking criteria. With some reworking, for example the narrator considering the insults she receives in more linguistic detail, the extract could easily be made into a successful intervention piece.

Both examples illustrate the difficulties of writing a fictional text that is dramatic and engaging, but at the same time deals with issues of representation in a technical and analytical fashion. Blending these two things together, without producing a submission that feels contrived, is the key to success in this type of writing.

Answers to Topic revision exercises

Unit 3, Section A Language change and variation

Note: These answers are offered as possibilities only. Others may be equally valid, if you can justify them.

How does language change?

1 The six main areas described are historical events, generational transfer, geographical and world language issues, social factors, technological advancements, education and politics. Use the notes on page 3 to check the details you wrote about your chosen three factors.

2 The inflection system made widespread use of altered word endings to change the functions and meanings of words.

3 A form of the French language was used by the rulers of England during this time and it was used in areas of government, the Church, the law and the military, among others. The French language drew heavily from Latinate words (words from Latin) and these became a major part of the language used in the areas mentioned – even to the present day.

Early Modern English

1 The printing press meant that written English could be mass-produced and many people would see the same version of the language. This created a more definite written standard. The King James Bible in particular added

to this effect by being an authorised and official printed form of English that was read aloud to a large proportion of the population.

2 The prescriptivist approach to language involves applying rules and defining what is 'correct' and 'incorrect' usage. The Grammarians mostly took a strongly prescriptivist approach. They set grammatical rules for correct English usage (often based on ideas from Latin) and were critical of other ways of using the language. A side effect of prescriptivism is that varieties deemed 'incorrect' often become of a lower status.

3 Because standardisation was only just starting to take hold during this period, there were many examples of non-standard spelling. The more common patterns included:

- interchangeable letters, e.g. u/v, i/y
- additional final 'e's
- doubling up consonants, especially 'll'.

Modern English

1 Education underwent considerable reform. During the period, the majority of children began to have some sort of schooling, and compulsory attendance until the age of 12 came about in the late-19th century. Printing meant that many school books were produced, giving children access to the written word and to educational resources. Literacy rates improved, meaning that children began to be able to read and write in Standard English – which reinforced the process of the standardisation of the language.

2 The *OED* gathered words and their uses by looking through a wide range of written texts at the language used. Although it would present spellings and definitions, these were more descriptive because they reflected actual ways that the word had been used, rather than imposing a rule for 'how they should' be used. Previous dictionaries (e.g. Samuel Johnson's), although they also gave some sources for words, tended to be more subjective or random in what they included in the dictionary, and often applied rules to words quite arbitrarily.

3 *The Times* and other national newspapers made the printed word cheaply available to a wide audience, and the BBC brought the spoken word to a mass audience for the first time. Their influence was similar to that of the printing press in the late-15th century.

Contemporary language change

1 Large industries like Hollywood and the rock and pop music industries have had a global influence. The main effect of this has been to spread American English features through films and popular music. In the more recent decades, other varieties have had a significant influence, for example that of the Indian Bollywood industry.

2 'txtspk' includes a range of non-standard features, including the use of smileys and emoticons to represent ideas. Other features include highly contracted spellings, often with vowels omitted, and the use of non-alphabetic characters to represent sounds, like 8 for 'ate'.

3 Internet-based texts like webpages make use of hyperlinks to link between different parts of the text and even different texts, by the click of a mouse, or even automatically. Other types of text like blogs, forums and wikis have other new features. A wiki can be authored and edited by many different people, which can be done at any time, so the written text is constantly evolving. Forums also allow many contributors, and are structured by interactions between different writers.

Attitudes towards language change

1 Prescriptivists seek to impose rules upon language, and make judgements about the relative merits of different varieties. Descriptivists seek to understand the way that different varieties use language, and describe the features that they display, rather than interfere with them.

2 PC was initially strongly linked to issues of sexism and patriarchy in the language. Over time, it became attached to any area of inequality in the language used to represent different people, and particularly on grounds of race, disability and employment.

3 'The crumbling castle' sees the language as a precious artefact that needs to be preserved and restored to its former glory. 'The damp spoon' metaphor presents the belief held by some prescriptivists that non-standard language use enters into the language owing to the laziness of users. 'The infectious disease' symbolises the view that non-standard language features are substandard in some way and are 'caught' by contact with people who speak that way.

Language change theory

1 Linguistic determinism suggests that language shapes people's thoughts and therefore can 'determine' the way that they think. Linguistic reflectionism takes the opposite stance, suggesting that language is just a reflection of how people think, and that these attitudes will always 'come through' in language, even if you change it.

2 Functional theory stresses the fact that language is simply a tool that is changed and modified by the people who use it. In this theory, it is the needs of users that cause language changes to take place.

3 The S-curve theory suggests that, at first, a change to the language is slowly taken up by people at large. Then it is rapidly taken up, before the pace slows again to settle at the rate at which any remaining users then adopt it.

What is language variation?

1 The main areas of variation with examples of a language variety influenced by each one.

- **Age:** colloquial youth language
- **Sexuality:** Polari
- **Gender:** Deborah Tannen's theories of male 'report' and female 'rapport' language
- **Social class:** RP
- **Ethnicity:** London Jamaican
- **Deviance:** Thieves' Cant
- **Occupation:** legal language
- **Region:** Scouse
- **Hobbies:** Leet

2 Non-standard language is language that differs in some way from the standard variety which, in the UK, is Standard English and RP. It might differ by pronunciation, the meanings of words, the particular words used, or the grammatical structure and aspects.

3 Labov described prestige as the status that a way of using language is given. He put forward the idea that there are two different ways of understanding this idea of status. Overt prestige involves applying the usual rules and expectations of society, while covert prestige is where status is given to things that oppose these usual values.

Social variation

1 Features that Robin Lakoff defined as 'women's language' are:

- affective adjectives: adjectives that describe feelings or emotional responses
- emphatic stress: explicit, exaggerated pitch or volume stress on particular words
- hedges: phrases such as 'you know' or 'sort of'
- hypercorrect grammar: a tendency to stick more closely to Standard English forms
- precise colour terms: a greater range of hyponyms within a particular colour
- rising intonation: adding a rise in pitch at the end of an utterance
- superpolite forms: the use of euphemisms and a lack of swearing

- tag questions: adding phrases like 'do you?' or 'shall we?' to the end of an utterance
- the intensifier 'so': using the word 'so' to add strength of meaning
- vocabulary of women's work: words about activities typically carried out by women.

2 The researchers tend to present findings that have a similar overall trend. Non-standard language forms are more frequently used by speakers of lower social class, whereas speakers of middle to higher social classes tend to stick more closely to standard forms.

3 MEYD is a term that comes from research by Sue Fox, Paul Kerswill and others. It describes forms of language, used by young people across the UK, that are a blend of regional urban, slang and immigrant language forms, and seem to share some basic features. The variety of MLE that Fox describes is a kind of MEYD. These MEYD forms borrow phrases from a number of non-English language sources and involve the ability to blend and switch between features of Standard English, ethnic language and local colloquial forms.

Regional variation

1 Watson described the unique nature of the Scouse accent in several ways. He suggested that it was geographically quite isolated from the influence of other northern English accents and has remained quite distinctive from other accents in the north-west of England. The actual phonological patterns of Scouse are highly distinctive, in particular the 'sing-song' prosody of many speakers. Watson noted that Scouse was unique in the way that it seemed to be strengthening and growing as an accent within the Merseyside area, at a time when many regional accents are losing their identity and individual features through dialect levelling.

2 Distinctive pronunciation features of the local Dublin accent.

- Breaking of closed vowel diphthongs into two separate syllables: for example, in 'clean' this would become /klee – un/, with a clear separation in the way the two halves are said.
- Changing /th/ consonant sound to /t/ or /d/: for example, 'thought' becomes similar to /tort/ or /dort/.
- Deletion of /t/ or /d/ sounds that come after /l/ or /n/: for example, 'bend' would become /ben/, or 'melt' becomes /mel/.

3 Non-standard grammatical forms often associated with Estuary English include:

- the contracted word 'ain't' as a verb
- non-standard past tense forms like 'come' for 'came'
- the use of double negative forms
- using the adverb 'never' with primary verbs to express negative constructions.

English as a world language

1 The main differences between American English and British English come in the form of different spelling rules, prosody and the stress patterns in specific words, and alternative words in the lexicon.

2 Jamaican Creole has a simpler distinction between singular and plural forms, across the first-, second- and third-person forms. In terms of singular/plural pronouns, the first person has just mi/wi, second person yu/unu, and third person im/dem.

3 The range of east-Asian languages that have come into contact with English and formed pidgins have very different pronunciation systems to English. This means it is difficult to reproduce some of the sounds used in English words. Strange phrases can come about when east-Asian languages are 'translated' into English because of similar differences between their semantic and grammatical systems.

Attitudes towards language variation

1 Pidgin forms of English are often regarded as a lower status form, and even established creoles are considered 'incorrect' in the ways that they differ from standard Englishes. As they gain a history, however, they seem to rise in status and in some countries are used in occupations like government and teaching.

2 RP was described by Giles's respondents as being more reliable, and was said to give an air of confidence and good education to the speaker. Regional forms were thought to sound more sincere, friendly and persuasive.

Language variation theory

1 Aspects of anti-language set out by Halliday.

- It is the language of an anti-society that exists within society as an alternative to it.
- Word lists often form the main evidence of anti-languages.
- Anti-languages are mostly formed by relexicalising existing vocabulary items.
- Anti-languages have a different lexicon but use the same grammar as the main society.
- Anti-language users communicate meanings that are inaccessible to a non-user.
- Subcultures with an anti-language view it as a fundamental part of their identity.
- Conversation is the main form of communication used to uphold the anti-language.
- Anti-language is a vehicle of resocialisation.
- There is continuity and exchange between language and anti-language.

2 Estuary English is often put forward as an example of a dialect form that is rapidly growing in the number of speakers that use it. What is more significant is that it is spreading far outside of the region of the Thames Estuary in which it originated. This is the main link to dialect levelling. Dialect levelling is where the distinctive differences between regional dialects are reduced as they become more similar to each other. Estuary English, through its popularity in the media, for example, is seen as a dialect that is influencing the way people speak right across the UK and causes them to pick up its features in place of those of their local regional variety.

3 Code-switching was a concept described by Sebba, particularly in his work with speakers of 'London Jamaican'. He noticed that there were now children growing up in families that had come to Britain several generations ago, who were exposed to several varieties of language in their lives. For example, the family home might be dominated by a form from the country from which the family emigrated; the language used on the television and at school would be a standard form of English; and the local forms that these children would use with friends that they made would be a vernacular, more colloquial variety. Code-switching is used by speakers in these kinds of situation, where they become able to communicate in several varieties, and switch between them, particularly when with other speakers who can understand two or more varieties also.

Exam preparation

1 The exam paper advises you to take about 75 minutes preparing for and writing the answer to the question that you choose. The actual number of words that you write will vary but, going on the number that good essays have needed to produce in past exams, aiming for approximately 1,000 words would be a good guide to your revision and practice.

2 The Section A question you choose will determine the skills you use to a certain degree. However, both questions involve analysing the distinctive features of the text or data that you are provided with, making comparisons between the two pieces of data, and evaluating them by bringing in some of your wider study into language variation and change.

▇ Unit 3, Section B Language discourses

Studying language variation and change

1 **Synchronic language** study focuses on studying the context of an instance of language use at one particular time. This is much more like the way that variation researchers have tried to describe and understand different varieties of English that they have come across.

Diachronic language study looks at language across time. It can be used to compare English of different time periods, where a historical aspect is emphasised. It can also be used to chart language change and development over time in individuals and groups, for example, investigating the milestones of child language acquisition in a child at different ages.

2 **Etymology** is the study of the origins and history of words. It is particularly interested in the source language(s) that a word has come from, the way that its use might have altered over time, and the context of its usages.

3 **Psycholinguistics** refers to the things that go on 'inside' your brain. Many of them are often subconscious, such as the way that a person pronounces words, or the word choices made. These influence language use in a different way – a person might pronounce a word differently not because other people do, but because they have not learned its pronunciation fully or they find it easier to say that way.

Sociolinguistics refers to the wide range of ways that society and a person's role in society influence his or her language use. These can be understood as 'external' forces because they are outside of the person. For example, the social class a person belongs to may well shape the way that he or she speaks, because of the influence of the large group of other speakers in that class, and the way that people outside of that class may interact with that person.

Exam preparation

1 The four major areas of language variation and change are:
- ▇ international, regional and social accents and dialects
- ▇ language change
- ▇ gender and interaction
- ▇ political correctness.

2 AO2: Demonstrate critical understanding of a range of concepts and issues related to the construction and analysis of meanings in spoken and written language, using knowledge of linguistic approaches is worth the most marks (20).

3 The Section B question takes the form of a pair of texts for each area of debate (discourse), and an essay question to evaluate the sociolinguistic topic they cover.

Glossary

abbreviation: a word shortened by removing a letter or clusters of letters.

abstract noun: a subcategory of nouns – the name of an abstract idea, concept, emotion or belief.

accent: the specific way words are pronounced according to geographical region.

accommodation: the process of adapting one's speech to make it more or less similar to that of other participants in a conversation.

acrolect: the form of speech in a region or a country that is regarded as the standard and prestige version of the language.

acronym: a new word created by using the initial letters of a particular phrase. An acronym can be pronounced as a word, rather than said as a series of letters.

active voice: a name given to grammatical constructions which relate to the roles of subject and object in a clause. In an active sentence, the subject acts as the agent of the verb, e.g. the dog chewed the bone.

address: the relationship a text establishes between writer and reader.

adjective: a modifier used to add detail, usually to a noun.

adverb: a word that modifies a verb, or an adjective, or a whole clause.

adverbial: a word or phrase acting like an adverb.

adverb type: adverbs can be divided into groups relating to: *manner* – how something is done; *time* – when or how often something is done; *frequency* – how often something is done; *place* – where or in what direction something is done; *degree* – to what intensity/how much something is done; *comment* – adding an opinion to a clause or phrase; *linking* – used as connectives.

affixation: modifying an existing word by adding a morpheme to the beginning or end of it.

agent: the person (or thing) carrying out the action of the verb.

agent noun: a noun describing a person who 'does' something, usually derived from the verb describing the action involved, for example an 'adviser' being the agent noun for someone who 'advises'.

aims: a statement or set of statements detailing what the investigation is attempting to find out.

alliteration: a sequence of words beginning with the same sound.

amelioration: a change in the meaning of a word that causes it to gain status. For example, positive, colloquial adjectives like 'sweet' and 'cool'.

analysis: in this book, the main section of the investigation where the data is explored and commented upon.

anaphoric: a word or phrase that refers 'backwards' in a text to something mentioned earlier.

anomaly: an unexpected result in a data set, or a result that goes against the general patterns of the study.

anti-language: a variety of language intended to prevent non-users understanding it.

antithesis: a contrast or opposition between two things.

antonym: a term indicating a word with the opposite meaning.

appendices: (singular appendix) a collection of supplementary material at the end of the submission.

archaic: no longer in common modern use.

argot: the particular jargon or slang-based language variety used by a social group.

articulation: the creation of different speech sounds by the modification of air flow in the vocal organs.

aspect: a verb form relating to the duration of an event.

aspirated: pronouncing a word with the 'h' sound added to it, to create a 'breathy' sound.

assimilation: the way that language (most commonly individual words) becomes altered to 'fit in' with another language.

assonance: the repetition of vowel sounds for effect.

asterisk: the word for this typographical sign (*) comes from the Greek for 'little star'. It is used in CMC to mark a word or phrase as a correction, or add emotional or physical commentary to a text, in a similar way to an emoticon.

asynchronous communication: a communication in which participants do not need to be present simultaneously.

attributive adjective: an adjective used to premodify a noun.

audience positioning: the concept of how the writer/author or speaker seems to be imagining the audience.

auxiliary: a verb that supports or 'helps' another verb.

backchannel behaviour: also known as support or feedback to the speaker, it describes a range of ways in which a listener encourages the speaker to continue.

backronym: an acronym that fits an existing word or abbreviated form, usually brought into use for comic effect.

backslang: the creation of a new word by spelling and pronouncing an existing word backwards.

balanced structure: (usually) a sentence where the two halves balance each other.

basilect: the variety of language with the lowest status in a speech community.

bibliography: a record of all the secondary sources used.

blended mode: also known as *mixed mode*, a term that primarily expresses the mode of new electronic forms of communication.

blending: joining morphemes or syllables from existing words to form a new word. For example, 'internaut' from 'internet' and 'astronaut'.

blog: (also weblog) a kind of online journal.

bound morpheme: a morpheme that can only have meaning when attached to a free morpheme.

borrowing: a word or phrase taken from another language and brought into English usage.

broadening: extending the range of meanings for a word by adding a new meaning and/or use to an existing word. For example, 'to boy' gaining a meaning as a verb meaning to humiliate someone.

C

capitalisation: using an upper case letter form (for example, 'G' for 'g'), whether in standard or non-standard places.

cataphoric: a reference that links a word or phrase to a word or phrase that is further 'forwards' in the text and yet to come, e.g. the way the pronoun 'It' links to the noun phrase 'my new bicycle' in the sentence 'It was the best ever, my new bicycle.'

clause: a unit of grammar used to form sentences, traditionally seen as being based around a lexical verb, although verbless clauses are possible.

cliché: an overused phrase or saying.

clipping: the shortening of an existing word to leave a single part. For example, 'retro' from 'retrograde'.

closed class: prepositions, determiners, conjunctions and pronouns are said to be closed class words as they are very rarely altered or added to over time.

closed question: a question that can be answered with a 'yes/no', a specific piece of information, or a selection from multiple choices.

closed vowel: a vowel sound that has consonants 'either side' of it, as in the /a/ sound in 'cat', which has a /c/ and /t/ sound enclosing it.

code-switching: a term for the way speakers with several strong linguistic influences will form a variety that mixes features of pronunciation, grammar and vocabulary from them, and will then 'switch' between these forms as they speak.

coherence: a measure of how a text makes sense.

cohesion: a measure of how well a text fits together as a whole, its internal logic and construction.

collective noun: the name for a number of things as one unit.

collocation: a set of words, often a pair or a phrase, which has become strongly associated.

collocational clash: a play on words where one item in a collocation is replaced by another word, usually which sounds like the original in some way.

colloquialism: a word or phrase from everyday spoken language.

colloquial language: language used in informal, ordinary conversation.

common noun: the name of an object, type of animal, person or idea.

comparative: adjectives inflected with -*er* or combined with 'more' are in the comparative form.

complement: an element which adds information to a subject or an object.

complex sentence: a sentence containing a main clause with one or more subordinate or dependant clauses, often connected with a subordinating conjunction.

compound-complex sentence: a sentence containing at least two main clauses and at least one subordinate clause.

compound sentence: a sentence containing two or more main clauses, connected by coordinating conjunctions, or sometimes just separated by punctuation (semi-colon).

compounding: joining two or more words together to create a new word.

computer-mediated communication (CMC): communication achieved by means of computer technology.

concord: the correct grammatical agreement of word classes and syntax, e.g. the use of the correct singular pronoun in 'I am feeling better.'

concrete noun: a subcategory of common nouns – the name of a tangible, physical object.

conjunction: a function word that connects elements and clauses together.

connotation: an associated, symbolic meaning relying on culturally shared conventions.

consonance: the repetition of consonant sounds for effect.

consonant: a basic sound of speech that involves stopping the breath while you say it. Letters of this kind are also known as consonants, e.g. b, c, d, etc.

consonant cluster: a group of consonants pronounced together.

context: the temporal and spatial situations in which a text is produced or received, e.g. where the producer of the text is, what he or she is doing, who he or she is talking to, what has occurred previously.

continuum: a way of representing differences by placing texts along a line showing degrees of various features.

contraction: a word shortened in speech or spelling.

convention: a set of agreed, stipulated or generally accepted rules of layout and language use for a particular form or genre.

convergence: when a person's speech patterns become more like those of the other person in a conversation.

conversion: creating a new meaning for a word by using it to fulfil a different word class function, e.g. using a noun as a verb.

coordinate clause: a clause that is also a main clause, in a sentence containing more than one main clause.

coordinating conjunction: a conjunction that connects main clauses together to form compound sentences.

copula verb: a verb used to join or 'couple' a subject to a complement.

corpus: a body of language, e.g. a collection of political speeches.

corpus analysis: a systematic investigation of the language of a collection of texts.

covert prestige: a form of status shared by minority groups in society, usually with alternative or opposing values to mainstream society.

creole: a language variety created by previous language contact and then developed over successive generations of users.

creolisation: the creation of a new language variety by language contact and new speakers growing up using it.

cryptolect: a secret language devised for use by a particular group of people.

D

data: literally 'facts and statistics used for reference or analysis' (*Concise OED*); in this book it often refers to the texts you are asked to analyse.

declarative: a sentence function used to make statements.

definite article: the determiner 'the' used to show a noun is referring to a particular thing.

deictic reference: a reference to something not in the text; a word that changes meaning according to context.

deletion: the non-pronunciation of a sound from the normal, standard pronunciation pattern.

demand characteristics: a problem in research, where participants in a study behave, act or answer questions in the way that they think the researcher wants them to.

demonstrative pronoun: a pronoun used to differentiate between possibilities: this; these; that; those.

denotational meaning: the meaning of a word as you would expect to find it in the dictionary.

derivational morphology: ways of developing new words by adding prefixes and suffixes to existing words.

descriptivism: an approach to language that seeks to understand the varieties of a language and not to interfere with them.

determiner: a function word or phrase used before nouns to determine their number and specificity.

determinism: the theory that language determines or shapes our thoughts.

dialect: the language variety of a geographical region or social background.

dialectics: conflict, opposition or contradiction.

dialect levelling: a phenomenon in which dialect forms lose their distinct differences and begin to share common language forms.

diphthong: a vowel sound with 'two parts' to it, e.g. the sound in 'bear', 'care' or 'air' where the sound is 'eh-uh', if you exaggerate the way you say it a bit!

discourse: a continuous stretch of language (especially spoken) which is longer than a sentence; also a formal discussion of a topic in speech or writing; a written or spoken communication or debate.

discourse marker: a word or phrase that indicates a change in topic, or a return to a previous topic.

discourse structure: the structure of a text, in terms of how its component parts fit together to give cohesion and form a whole.

divergence: when a person's speech patterns become more individualised and less like those of the other person in a conversation.

downwards: when applied to convergence/divergence, movement away from Standard English.

dysphemism a word or phrase used to present something with a harsh, more extreme or offensive tone. They can appear in tabloid newspaper headlines, swearing, taboo or politically incorrect language, and insults.

E

Early Modern English: the origin of the modern form of English we recognise today. It can be understood to extend from the emergence of the first printed English texts through to the expansion of the British Empire.

elicitation task: a data collection method that sets respondents pre-planned tasks (e.g. reading out a list of words) designed to give them the opportunity to produce particular standard or non-standard features of language.

elision: the missing out of sounds or parts of words.

ellipsis: the missing out of a word or words in a sentence.

elongated: used to describe a long vowel sound.

emoticon and smiley: both words refer to the use of combinations of alphabetic characters to create a pictorial representation of an emotion or thing.

ethical issues: issues relating to the collection and presentation of data that may affect the rights of the participants. These can include confidentiality and whether permission is gained from participants to collect or publish data.

ethnographic study: researching the way language is part of a particular community and culture.

etymology: the study of the history of words, and what the origins were for any particular word, in terms of a source language or particular context of use.

euphemism: a word or phrase used in place of something considered taboo in a particular context, to soften or disguise its meaning.

evaluation: the discussion of the significance, value, or quality of something, based on careful study of its good and bad features.

evaluative adjective: an adjective that implies a judgement about what it's describing.

exophoric: a reference that links to something 'outside' of a text and not described or explained within it, e.g. the way that the noun phrase 'that article' is used in the sentence 'I have never read anything as biased as that article.'

eye-dialect: an unusual and non-standard way of spelling used to represent patterns of speech.

F

facsimile: an exact copy of a text, as if it has been colour photocopied, showing all graphological and orthographical elements in their original form.

factive verb: a verb used to express a truth, or a conviction that what follows the verb is true.

false start: when a speaker stops what they're saying and begins again, changing tack somehow.

feature article: a non-news article in a newspaper or magazine, written partly to entertain or amuse as well as to inform.

final e: a remnant from Middle English, where the written final e reflected that vowel being pronounced at the end of the word.

figurative language: language used in a non-literal way (*see* imagery).

first-person narrative: a story or account written from the 'I' position.

folk etymology: a 'made-up' origin of a word, applied to it after it has been used for some time. Although folk etymologies are not the actual source of the word, they can sometimes reflect something about the way the word is used, and appear to 'make sense' linguistically.

form: the outward appearance or structure of a text, e.g. a novel, play, newspaper article.

formal/informal lexis: *see* lexical register.

forum: an online message board, representing messages as linked to each other in threads.

framework: *see* linguistic framework.

framework depth: the extent to which a particular level or feature is explored.

framework range: the number of language levels or features within a level to be investigated.

free morpheme: a morpheme that can stand independently and act as a meaningful unit on its own.

fricative: a sound that is created by the slow and controlled release of air through the mouth, creating friction.

functional word: also known as a *grammatical word*, it is a word which has a grammatical function but doesn't carry as much meaning as the lexical words.

future tense: English has no future tense as such (refer to the Grammatical framework for more detail).

G

genderlect: a term to describe distinctive language differences attached to gender, as described and reported by some linguists.

gender-marked: a word or phrase that has been modified to show the specific gender it refers to.

General American: Like British Standard English and Received Pronunciation forms, General American (GA) is the standard form of English in North America and surrounding regions. It is similar to a generalised form of Midwestern accent, and is the form most commonly used in the American media and film industry.

generic masculine: the practice of using masculine forms of English to refer to all people.

genre: the category or type of text within a form, such as romance or thriller (novel); comedy or tragedy (play); review or editorial (newspaper article).

glottal stop: a sound produced by stopping the flow of air in the throat, often used in place of the consonant /t/.

grammar: used in this book to refer primarily to word class and morphology.

Grammarian: this term has come to refer to the writers of the Early Modern English period who published texts that set out prescriptive rules for the language.

grammatical cohesion: grammatical cohesion is often achieved by ellipsis or pronouns being used to avoid repetition.

grammatical word: *see* functional word.

grapheme: the smallest functional unit in a writing system.

grapheme–phoneme correspondence: the relationship between letters and sounds in words and, consequently, the way we write them and say them.

graphological cohesion: a graphologically cohesive text uses an appropriate layout and set of graphological features.

graphology: the visual and layout features of a text – the things you can see that aren't actually linguistic features.

Great Vowel Shift: a general change to the pronunciation of a range of vowel sounds in English that took place between the 13th and 16th centuries. The vowels involved were generally more fronted or raised in the way they were pronounced, to become the vowels that we are using today.

H

half-rhymes: words that almost or nearly rhyme, or look like they should rhyme but don't.

hashtag: the use of the number sign character (#), now more widely known as 'hash', to mark a particular word or phrase to show that it refers to another text. Rather than just a label, these are increasingly used in writing as a part of sentencing – even to the extent that 'nonce formation' versions are coined for humour (#NoReallyItIsTrue).

headline: a heading that may summarise the story to follow or offer a pun which makes complete sense often only after the story has been read.

hedge: a word or phrase used to pad out or soften what's being said.

high rising intonation (HRI): or high rising terminal, referring to the use of higher pitch at the end of an utterance to indicate it is being delivered as a form of interrogative.

homonym: a word that looks like another word, but is in fact different. It may sound the same, or be pronounced differently.

homonymic pun: wordplay based on words which look the same but are not. *See also* pun.

homophone: a word which sounds the same as another word or words.

homophonic pun: wordplay based on words which sound the same but are different. *See also* pun.

hyperbole: a figure of speech involving exaggeration.

hypercorrection: a phonological change involving the adoption of an incorrect emphasis or pattern of pronunciation because the person saying it thinks it is the high prestige form, e.g. saying /expresso/ for 'espresso'.

hyperlink: a connection from a textual element, like a word, phrase or image, to another text.

hypernym: a category into which other words fit.

hypertextuality: the phenomenon of a text that does not possess a single sequence that it is intended to be read in, and makes use of linkages to combine it with other texts, images or sounds.

hyponym: a word that is more specific than a word with a related but more general meaning: e.g. 'azure' is a hyponym of 'blue'.

hypothesis: a prediction of what the investigation will find out.

I

icon: a small graphical image used to represent or symbolise something. For example, computers use icons for files, buttons and programs, and they are used in websites to 'tag' content and represent particular categories such as the range of services a supermarket offers.

idiolect: an individual style of speaking, made up of choices in all frameworks.

idiom: metaphorical or non-literal sayings common in their cultural context.

imagery: language used in a non-literal way (*see also* figurative language).

imperative: a sentence function that gives directives, commonly known as commands.

implicature: expressing meaning indirectly.

inference: drawing out meanings from others' speech.

infinitive: the 'base form' of the verb preceded by the preposition 'to', used to express its action without linking it to a specific subject.

inflection: a word is said to be inflected when it has a suffix attached to change the meaning.

inflectional morphology: the study of how morphemes are used to create different grammatical functions.

initial: referring to the start of a word.

initialism: the abbreviation of a phrase using the initial letters of the words within it.

inkhorning: bringing a new word into use by taking it from one of the classical languages of Latin, Greek, or Hebrew. This term is usually only specifically used to describe this practice in writers of the Early Modern English period.

intensifier: a word used to strengthen the meaning of another word or phrase.

interjection: a spoken word or phrase used to express emotion.

International Phonetic Alphabet (IPA): a detailed system containing over 160 symbols to represent the sounds of spoken language (including things like lisping and teeth grinding!).

interrogative: a sentence that functions as a question.

interrogative pronoun: a pronoun used to ask questions and to stand in for unknown nouns.

interruption: beginning a turn while someone else is talking, in a competitive way.

intertextuality: a way of expressing the relationship between different texts and the way that texts can affect the meanings of other texts.

intervention: an attempt to take part, or engage, in a debate.

intonation: the way the pitch of our voices goes up and down as we speak.

irregular: a word that doesn't follow the standard patterns of inflection for change of meaning or function, e.g. a verb that does not use the -*ed* suffix to create the past tense, or an adjective that does not use the -*er* suffix to create the comparative form.

J

jargon: technical language in any field.

K

koineisation: the creation of a new standard language form by combining two existing dialect forms by language contact.

L

language contact: the instance of speakers of different languages interacting, often resulting in some form of exchange or blending of the languages.

Latinate: describing a word or other aspect of language derived from the Latin language.

leading question: a question that suggests the answer or contains the information the research is looking for.

lexical cohesion: a text can be lexically cohesive by repeating key words and/or by maintaining an appropriate register.

lexical field: a collection of words that are related by a link to the subject they refer to.

lexical register: a coverall term relating to the general level of formality of a passage, based on the formality and complexity of vocabulary (or lexis) used.

lexical word: a word that carries meaning.

lexicon: all of the words in a particular language. 8

lexifier: the language that provides the majority of words and structural elements in a dialect created by combining two or more language varieties.

lexis: the total stock of words in a language; synonymous with 'vocabulary'.

ligature: a feature of printed text that uses a line to join particular common combinations of letters together, especially clusters of consonants like 'st' or 'ct'.

linguistic framework: a list of the particular language features that will be explored in the investigation with commentary on reasons for their use.

linguistic purism: the view that one particular language, or language form, is the most authentic and must be promoted over other, inferior varieties.

linguistic variable: a specific language feature that linguists test or observe in use to see how it varies between different people or contexts.

liveblog: an online text authored over a period of time, usually to cover a particular event. It is more fragmented than standard published blogs, bringing in multi-author content from outside sources, lots of hyperlinks to other texts, and frequent multimedia material in the form of icons, images, videos and audio clips.

long s: an archaic way of writing the modern letter 's', which looks a bit like an 'f'. Its usage began in Old English and can be found right through the Early Modern English period, including as part of a ligature between two letters.

l-vocalisation: substituting the /l/ phoneme with a vowel or semi-vowel.

M

main clause: a clause that can stand independently and make sense on its own.

main verb: a verb that expresses an action, event or state.

manner of articulation: the way in which a sound is produced.

marked term: a term in which the gender of a person is (often unnecessarily) foregrounded through a gendered premodifier or suffix.

medial: referring to the middle section of a word.

meiosis: a figure of speech involving understatement, the opposite of hyperbole.

meta-analysis: a research method that involves combining the

findings of many different studies in order to identify patterns or anomalies within a large results set.

metaphor: a figure of speech or figurative usage where an object is described as being or as though it were something else.

methodology: the design of a particular experiment.

metonymy: when a part of a larger object or institution stands metaphorically for the whole.

micropause: a period of silence of less than half a second.

Middle English: the English language after the Norman invasion, often seen as lasting until the printing of English texts began to appear.

minimal response: a single word, very short phrase or non-verbal filler used in response.

minor sentence: a grammatically incomplete sentence.

mirroring: when a speaker uses words, phrases or other features previously used by another speaker.

mixed mode: *see* blended mode.

mocking the opposition: this is commonly used in political speeches and allows the speaker to set up the opposition as ridiculous or unreasonable before stating their own position.

mock-PC: satirised examples of politically correct terms designed to make fun of and discredit more genuine forms of PC.

modal: a verb used to express possibility, probability, certainty, necessity or obligation, e.g. will, would, can, could, shall, should, may, might, must.

modality: the degree of certainty or doubt conveyed by a text.

mode: the medium of communication, e.g. speech or writing.

modifier: a word, usually an adjective or a noun used attributively, that qualifies the sense of a noun. Adverbs of comment also act as modifiers, e.g. obviously.

mood: there are four sentence moods – declarative, exclamatory, imperative and interrogative.

morpheme: the smallest unit of grammatical meaning. Morphemes can be words in their own right or combine with other morphemes to form lexical units.

morphology: the study of word structure, especially in terms of morphemes.

multi-authorship: texts with more than one contributor or author, often occurring simultaneously in social media formats.

multimedia: texts with a combination of written language, audio and video material, and graphological elements such as photography, animation and other images.

multiple negatives: the use of more than one form of negation in a phrase.

N

narrowing: the loss of the range of meaning for a word by a particular use becoming archaic or obsolete. For example, 'skyline' coming to be used only for a horizon with tall buildings.

nasal: a sound produced by resonance in the nasal cavity.

naturalisation: a process in which certain ideas can gradually appear to become normal or natural.

nominalisation: the process of turning an event or action normally expressed as a verb into a noun which can then be used at the head of a noun phrase.

nonce formation: a word created as a 'one-off' for that use and occasion only.

non-fluency features: features of spoken language that are due to spontaneity and the speed of normal speech.

non-standard: used to describe any word, phrasing or feature of language that does not adhere to the rules of Standard English.

non-standard English: words, phrases or constructions not usually found in formal contexts.

noun phrase: a phrase with a noun as its main word.

O

objective case: this describes nouns or pronouns when used as the object of a verb or preposition in a clause. Some English pronouns have particular forms for the objective case, for example, 'me', 'him' and 'her'.

observer's paradox: this states that the results of an experiment can be affected by the presence of the observer, or the unnatural context of an experiment.

obsolete: used to describe a word or part of the language that has disappeared from use entirely.

Old English: the earliest form of the English language, formed during Germanic invasions of Britain and lasting until the Norman invasion.

onomatopoeia: a term which describes words that create the sound they are describing.

open class: the four word classes (adjectives, adverbs, nouns and verbs) within which the words constantly change as new ones are created and old ones fall out of use.

open question: a question to which there are no specified choices of response.

orthography: the way in which letter shapes are formed on a page and the characters used.

over extend: to stretch the meaning of a word.

overgeneralisation: the over-application of a grammatical rule; a form of virtuous error.

overt prestige: a form of status valued and shared by mainstream society and culture.

P

participle: a tense indicator ending in *-ed*, *-en* or *-ing*. They can be used as modifiers as well as part of a verb element.

particle: a word used in a verb phrase to provide meaning, e.g. an adverb or preposition in a phrasal verb.

passive voice: a name given to grammatical constructions which relate to the roles of subject and object in a clause. In a passive sentence, the subject of the clause has the action of the verb carried out upon it, e.g. the bone was chewed by the dog.

past participle: a past tense verb form used with an auxiliary to express something that has happened ('had broken'), or as a modifier in describing a noun ('the broken vase').

past perfect tense: a verb form used to describe an action that completed before a particular time, e.g. 'the man had stopped laughing'.

patriarchal: this term describes ways of thinking or doing that are male-centred or male-dominated.

pause: a gap in the flow of speech, or a period of silence.

pejoration: a process whereby words 'slide down' the scale of acceptability and pick up negative connotations over time.

periphrase/periphrastic: the use of several words to create a grammatical phrase, e.g. a verb phrase using an auxiliary verb in conjunction with a main verb.

person: verbs inflect to show the person or the subject – i.e. who is carrying out the action of the verb: I, you, he, she, we, you, they.

personal pronoun: a pronoun used in place of a person.

personification: a figure of speech where an animal or inanimate object is described as having human characteristics.

phatic: (speech) used to fulfil social purposes such as greetings, and small talk and humour.

phoneme: the smallest unit of sound in a language.

phonemic alphabet: a system containing 44 symbols to represent a range of vowel and consonant sounds in English pronunciation.

phonetic spelling: using letters to spell out exactly how a word is pronounced, rather than using its standard spelling.

phonology: the study of the way speech sounds are used in language.

phrasal verb: a verb that is made from a lexical verb like 'put' and a smaller word like 'out' (making 'to put out').

phrase: a group of words functioning as a single unit.

pidgin: a simplified language form created as a result of language contact, usually to support some sort of activity like trade.

pitch: high or low sounds.

plosive: a sound that is created by a sudden release of air (like an explosion) from the mouth.

plural: the marking of a noun to indicate how many are being talked about.

political correctness (PC): the name given to the movement which began in the 1970s campaigning for the removal of offensive language from everyday vocabulary.

possession: the marking of a word to indicate that it is possessed or belongs to someone or something.

possessive pronoun: a pronoun that demonstrates ownership: mine, yours, hers, his, its, ours and theirs.

postmodification: the placing of modifiers such as adjectives and adverbs after a noun.

pragmatics: a broad term often used to relate to the gap between what words used actually mean and what the intended meaning is.

predicative adjective: an adjective used as a complement, following a stative verb.

prefix: a beginning that adapts the original word in some way.

prefixation: creating a new word by adding a prefix to the start of it.

premodification: the placing of modifiers such as adjectives and adverbs in front of a noun.

preposition: a function word that expresses a relationship between words, phrases or clauses. Prepositions usually relate to space or time.

preposition stranding: using a preposition that is unattached to an object, e.g. 'The angry man was difficult to talk to' as a re-ordering of '[it] was difficult to talk to the angry man.'

prescriptivism: an approach to language that seeks to impose particular rules for language use in order to maintain a specific standard form, and, in some cases, to restrict or prevent the use of non-standard forms of the language.

present continuous tense: a verb form used to express an action that is still happening.

prestige: the concept of status applied to a particular language variety or the person who uses it.

primary language data: examples of original spoken language collected by the researcher.

primary verb: a small group of verbs that can be main or auxiliary verbs: be; have; do.

progressive aspect: a grammatical construction of a verb used to express an action that is in progress.

promises and threats: a common rhetorical technique.

pronoun: a function word which stands in place of a noun.

proper noun: the name of a specific person, animal, place, work of art, day, etc. Proper nouns begin with a capital letter.

prop-word: the use of the word 'one' in place of a noun.

prosody: the elements of pitch, pace and volume that can be altered in the intonation of a human voice.

psycholinguistics: the study of the way 'internal' factors like thought and speech production affect language use.

pun: a play on words. *See also* homonymic pun and homophonic pun.

Q

qualitative: an approach to language study that involves analysing examples of language use in detail and context.

qualitative data: data concerned with describing meanings and effects, rather than with making statistical analyses.

quantitative: an approach to language study that makes use of statistical analysis of data that has been gathered.

quantitative data: data measured in numbers. This kind of data can be analysed using statistical methods, and results can be displayed using tables or charts.

question: a key question that the investigation sets out to answer.

R

rebus: a way of representing a word or phrase by using letters, other characters and images in non-standard and imaginative ways.

Received Pronunciation (RP): the prestige form of English pronunciation, sometimes considered as the 'accent' of Standard English.

reduplicative: the repetition of a word, phrase or sound pattern for effect or to create a new term.

reflectionism: the theory that language reflects our thoughts.

reflexive pronoun: a pronoun used to refer the action back to the subject, often emphatically.

register: the general language 'level' of a text, based on the formality and complexity of vocabulary (or lexis) used.

regular/irregular: verbs' behaviour can be described as regular (i.e. following the usual pattern) or irregular (i.e. unusual).

relative clause: a subordinate clause that is used to add more information about another clause element. It acts like an adjective.

relative pronoun: a word such as 'which' or 'who' when it is used to introduce a relative clause and give more information about another phrase in the sentence.

repetition: frequently used in rhetorical speech to help an audience retain the key points.

retraction: used to express the movement of the place in which a particular speech sound is produced towards the back of the mouth. Also referred to as 'backing'.

rhetoric: related to the art of public speaking, or oratory.

rhetorical cohesion: in rhetoric, cohesion may be achieved through syntactic parallelism, repetitions and phonological patterns.

rhetorical device: rhetorical devices tend to be used for persuasion or to make a speech memorable.

rhetorical question: a question which is not intended to be answered, or which the speaker/writer answers him/herself.

rhoticity: the extent of the use of the /r/ sound in speech.

rhymes: words that end in the same sound.

S

secondary data: data previously collected by others and used by the researcher.

secondary semantic field: a semantic field which is not directly related to the subject matter of the text.

secondary source: work done by others, e.g. surveys, other people's research, books, websites and articles.

semantic cohesion: texts can cohere semantically by using a semantic field as an extended metaphor or using semantic fields related to the topic.

semantic field: words that are similar in range of meaning and properties, i.e. a collection of words all related because of a link between the things they relate to.

semantic reclamation: a process whereby the victims of a particular word's offensive usage adopt the word themselves.

semantics: the study of how meaning is constructed in language.

sentence type: refers to the structure of the sentence – i.e. minor, simple, compound, complex or compound-complex.

simile: a figure of speech comparing two things in a more explicit way than a metaphor, usually using 'like' or 'as'.

simple sentence: a sentence consisting of a single main clause.

slang: informal vocabulary associated with a particular social group, more usual in spoken than written language.

smiley: *see* emoticon.

sociolect: the language variety used by people with a shared social background.

sociolinguistics: the study of the way 'external' factors like culture and social status affect language use.

split infinitive: placing an adverbial in between the preposition and verb in an infinitive verb form.

Standard English (SE): a universally accepted dialect of English that carries a degree of prestige.

stative verb: a verb that describes a state of affairs rather than an action, e.g. know.

stereotype: an often widely held view in society about the nature or behaviour of a particular group or type of person. The word is derived from an 18th-century word from the development of printing: a kind of plate used to make duplicate copies of text.

subject: the main focus of a sentence.

subject position: the perspective from which events or issues are perceived and recounted.

subordinate clause: a clause that is dependent on another to complete the full meaning of a sentence.

subordinating conjunction: a conjunction that connects a subordinate clause to a main clause.

substitution: swapping a letter, cluster of letters, or sound with another in its place.

suffix: an ending that adapts the original word in some way.

suffixation: creating a new word by adding a suffix to the end of it.

superlative: adjectives inflected with -est or combined with 'most' are in the superlative form.

suspended sentence: a sentence that uses a complex style, with multiple complex clauses, and which usually withholds the main meaning of the sentence until near to its end.

synonym: a term indicating a word with a very similar meaning.

syntactic parallelism: the repetition of sentence structure.

syntax: the linguistic framework dealing with word order and sentence structure.

T

taboo language: words that cannot or should not be said in their context. Historically, taboo words tend to relate to body parts, urination and excretion, religion, sex and death. Currently some of the most taboo words are racist terms.

tag question: a brief ending tagged on to a statement which turns it into a question.

tail: a word or phrase added on to the end of a sentence.

target population: the population group that the researcher wishes to draw conclusions about. The target population will be dictated by the people in the data sample.

tenor: relating to the relationship between the participants in a conversation or between a writer and audience.

tense: relating to when an event took place. In English, verbs can be in either the present tense or the past tense.

t-glottalling: replacing the /t/ phoneme with a sound made by a glottal stop.

th-fronting: moving the pronunciation of the /th/ phonemes forward in the mouth so they become /f/ and /v/, as in /fink/ for 'think' and /bovver/ for 'bother'.

transactional: (speech) used to facilitate some kind of exchange, for example of goods, services or information.

transcript: an accurate written record of a conversation or monologue, including hesitations and pauses.

trend: a pattern or definite tendency suggested in the data and results of research.

triad: a pattern of three words or phrases.

U

unvoiced: a speech sound produced without sound from the vocal cords.

upwards: when applied to convergence/divergence, movement towards Standard English.

utterance: the spoken language equivalent of a phrase or sentence.

V

validity: a measure of how the design of the methodology allows the conclusions of an investigation to carry weight. Internal validity refers to whether the conclusions drawn from data used in a specific investigation can be justified within the context of that investigation. External validity refers to whether these conclusions can be applied in a wider context.

velar nasal: a type of consonant sound produced by stopping the flow of air with the back part of the tongue pressed against a part of the roof of the mouth.

verb: a 'doing word'. Verbs may be dynamic and describe action or process, or they may be stative and describe states.

verb phrase: a phrase with a main verb as its main word.

vernacular: the language form naturally spoken by the people of a particular region or country.

voice: this refers to the verb as active or passive.

voiced: a speech sound produced using the vocal cords.

vowel: a speech sound created through an 'open mouth' without stopping the flow of air. The letters used to represent these sounds are: a; e; i; o; u.

vowel fronting: moving the place in which a vowel sound is generated towards the front of the mouth.

W

webpage: an electronic page that can interlink text, images and multimedia.

wiki: a collaboratively produced webpage; users switch between reading the material and editing/writing it.

word class: words that have the same formal properties, e.g. nouns, adjectives, verbs.

Y

yod-coalescence: merging the /y/ phoneme with consonant phonemes adjacent to it.

Index

Key terms and their page numbers are in **bold**.